Sociological Theory

*An Introduction to Concepts,
Issues, and Research*

SECOND EDITION

Mark Abrahamson
University of Connecticut

D0075331

PRENTICE HALL
Englewood Cliffs, New Jersey 07632

Library of Congress Cataloging-in-Publication Data

Abrahamson, Mark.
  Sociological theory: an introduction to concepts, issues, and
research/Mark Abrahamson.—2nd ed.
  Includes bibliographies and index.
  ISBN 0–13–816067–8:
  1. Sociology. 2. Social psychology. 3. Social problems.
I. Title.
HM51.A248 1989   89–3985
301—dc20   CIP

Editorial/production supervision: Fred Dahl
Cover design: 20/20 Services, Inc.
Manufacturing buyer: Carol Bystrom

©1990, 1981 by Prentice-Hall, Inc.
A Division of Simon & Schuster
Englewood Cliffs, New Jersey 07632

Printed in the United States of America

10 9 8 7 6 5 4 3 2 1

ISBN   0-13-816067-8

Prentice-Hall International (UK) Limited, *London*
Prentice-Hall of Australia Pty. Limited, *Sydney*
Prentice-Hall Canada Inc., *Toronto*
Prentice-Hall Hispanoamericana, S.A., *Mexico*
Prentice-Hall of India Private Limited, *New Delhi*
Prentice-Hall of Japan, Inc., *Tokyo*
Simon & Schuster Asia Pte. Ltd., *Singapore*
Editora Prentice-Hall do Brasil, Ltda., *Rio de Janeiro*

To my pal, Jonathan

Contents

v

3
Social and Personality Systems, 35

TALCOTT PARSONS

4
Social Organization and Estrangement, 50

MARX AND DURKHEIM

II
SOCIAL STRUCTURE, PROCESS, AND CHANGE, 69

5
Human Ecology, 71

PARK, BURGESS, HAWLEY

9
Behavioral Exchange, 140

HOMANS AND OTHERS

10
Deviance and Change, 156

DURKHEIM, MERTON, ERIKSON

11
Values and Change, 171

WEBER, MARX, OGBURN

Preface
to Second Edition

People who read the first edition of this book will find much that is familiar in this edition. The text provides some more detailed explanations of several of the theories. I endeavored to keep it a compact text, however, so that instructors who were so inclined could continue to assign supplementary readings around this core text. Suggestions for additional readings have been updated and are now placed at the close of each chapter. This format replaces the bibliography formerly included at the end of the book.

The major thrusts of the book remain as before, namely to:

- clarify the kinds of concrete, contemporary questions the major theories can be used to answer; and
- to forge a link in students' minds between theory and research by examining pithy examples of research that the theories have inspired.

Although the pedagogical value of these studies in illuminating theoretical concepts is not dependent upon their recency, many of those included in the first edition nevertheless seemed not to age well. Approximately one-half of the studies now included are new to this edition.

The subject matter examined by the newer studies is as diverse as the theories it helps to clarify. However, in the decade between editions of this book, there was an impressive burgeoning of studies focusing upon women's work and family roles. Many of the newly included studies reflect this trend, as studies of women's roles are utilized to elaborate upon the applicability of the theories.

While the surveyed research is very contemporary, the theories remain of classical vintage. Marx, Durkheim, and Weber—each of whose theories is discussed in three chapters—continue to provide the core. This edition does, however, give slightly more attention to a later generation of sociologists whose writings made more recent contributions to theory. Included here are Merton, in particular, along with Gouldner, Coser, Hawley, and others.

I

THE INDIVIDUAL IN SOCIETY

INTRODUCTION TO PART ONE

In many major sociological theories, individuals are not, strictly speaking, the primary subject matter. As conventionally defined, the discipline's focal concerns are with an aggregate analysis of the organization of society, its institutions and organizations, roles and norms. At some point, however, individuals usually enter the picture because it is the actions of individuals that ultimately provide substance to these sociological abstractions.

The degree of attention that is devoted explicitly to individuals corresponds with micro and macro approaches in sociology. These two approaches differ from each other in terms of the units of analysis that they emphasize, at least initially. Macro approaches—in sociology, as in biology, economics, and a variety of other disciplines—entail aggregate analysis while micro approaches dissect aggregates into components and then focus upon the components. In a macro approach, individuals' motives, aspirations, needs, or the like are more easily disregarded because individuals are so far removed from the primary units of analysis. By contrast, the relevance of such individual-level qualities is enhanced when an analysis focuses upon interaction or other micro-level issues. As would therefore be expected, the greatest overlap occurs between psychology and micro sociology.

Because of the macro–micro overlap, the boundary which separates them is typically ambiguous. Stressing the distinction could lead to the omission of the fact that theorists beginning from either position tend to work toward the other. Most large scale macro theories of social organization include an interest in how social organization is maintained or changed via (micro) patterns of social interaction. Similarly, most theories of social interaction regard patterns of interaction as shaped by the (macro) institutional contexts in which they occur. In recent years, a number of sociological theories have explicitly attempted to integrate these two levels as an important part of their contribution.*

In the first section of this book, we will examine a number of micro sociological theories. In many instances, these theories have explicitly borrowed, or built upon, perspectives that were developed in psychology. For example, Parsons' reliance upon Freud will be apparent in Chapter Three. Utilizations of this type raise the question of whether sociology, and micro sociology in particular, can stand alone; that is, free from psychological presuppositions. This issue will be briefly considered in a number of chapters and extensively discussed in Part Three.

Sociology's concern with its independence from psychology is mirrored in psychology's concern over its independence from biology. This specifically entails the question of whether psychological processes are autonomous, or whether they rest upon a biological basis. By extension, the degree to which social processes are independent of biological forces can also be brought into question. Great impetus was given to this question by the formulation of theories of evolution during the last half of the nineteenth century.

Initially developed in biology, the same principles of evolution were applied to psychological and to sociological phenomena. The impact of these ideas was great, both within the scientific community and beyond. Particularly for sociological theorists who were writing during and shortly after the turn of the twentieth century, biological theories of the evolution of behavior and social organization provided an important backdrop.

Several of the theorists to be considered in this first section reflect the continuing concern over the autonomy of social processes. George H. Mead, Margaret Mead, and W. I. Thomas—discussed in Chapters One and Two—should be viewed, in part, as trying to differentiate between social and biological factors; and in most instances, as attempting to demonstrate the autonomy of the former. These were not attempts to reject the existence of genetic endowments. Rather, they were directed at extricating the social from the biological.

One of the most enduring questions in sociological theory concerns the nature of the relationship between individuals and society. For example, does society restrain or support individual development? Nurture or repress it? Part of the fascination with the question stems from the fact that it simultaneously confronts the core of both macro and micro conceptions. Opposing views on some aspects of this complex issue are presented in Chapter Four's discussion of Marx and Durkheim.

---

*The perceived importance of their linkage to sociology is reflected by the theme of the 1989 American Sociological Association meetings: "Macro–Micro Inter-relationships."

1

The Social Self
G.H. Mead and Others

In 1949, Aaron and Bella Stern emigrated to America. They had married in Warsaw, and he was a survivor of German concentration camps. They settled initially in Brooklyn, and in 1952 they had a daughter whom they named Edith. When she was born, Aaron Stern called a press conference and two reporters showed up. They listened incredulously as he announced: "I shall make her into the perfect human being."[1]

As soon as Edith was brought home from the hospital her father began his project. Only classical music was permitted in the house. No baby talk was allowed. Her father made flash cards and slowly passed them in front of the infant's eyes. He was determined she would be a genius; that was "the perfect human being." By the time Edith was five years old, she had read the entire *Encyclopedia Britannica*. At twelve and one-half, she entered college. By age fifteen, she was teaching college mathematics and working on a Ph.D. After completing her degree, Edith went to work as a scientist at IBM. Her IQ is so high it cannot really be accurately measured, but it is apparently something over 200. However, in her own view she is clumsy and overweight. "I don't care for my body," she has been quoted as saying. "I'd be happy to leave it at home . . . ," and according to Bella Stern, Edith's mother, "She's a nasty little thing."

Aaron Stern is convinced his project was a success. He has offered to duplicate it as an experiment by raising Tasaday infants. (The Tasaday are an isolated tribe in the Philippine jungle.) They, too, can be geniuses, he insists, if subjected to "total immersion."

Has this "nasty little thing" who expresses disdain for her nonintellectual self—that is, her body—missed out on anything? She thinks not, indicating she

[1]This discussion of Edith Stern, and all quotations, are taken from Richard Cohen, "Genius Goal Brings Failure," *Washington Post*, April 9, 1977.

would raise her own children in the same manner. One reporter familiar with her history disagrees and believes that smartness is not enough. There is more to childhood, he claims, such as: "Running through fields . . . and spending hours pretending you are both the horse and the rider."

Personally, as a product of a time when cowboys dominated the mass media, I can relate to pretending to be both the horse and the rider. I remember doing it, though it was in empty lots in between houses, rather than in open fields. (If you had any imagination, however, it was as good as any vast expanse of prairies.) Times change, of course, and so do the things youngsters pretend to be. Perhaps you can remember pretending to be both the doctor and the patient; the rock singer and the audience; or two friends who were discussing you.

Pretending to be someone else, the essence of childrens' play, is typically an important part of childhood. It may even be a critical part of the process by which homo sapiens come to be "people," as we know them. Moreover, it was an important part of the very influential theory of George Herbert Mead.

MEAD AND HIS PERSPECTIVE

Most of Mead's career was spent at the University of Chicago where he was a professor of social psychology and social philosophy. His major, direct impact upon sociology was by means of an advanced social psychology course he taught which was taken by a large number of the graduate students in sociology. Mead's impact has also continued through his writings. Although he wrote numerous articles for journals, he never authored a book. After Mead's death, however, his major ideas were brought together in a book entitled *Mind, Self and Society*. It was compiled largely from the lecture notes of former students.

The editor of Mead's posthumous book quotes him as saying in one of his lectures: "the philosophy of a period is always an attempt to interpret its most secure knowledge."[2] The most "secure" knowledge, at the turn of the twentieth century, was Darwin's theory of evolution. It stressed the continuity between humans and other animals. The differences between humans and nonhumans were seen as quantitative—matters of degree—rather than qualitative—differences in kind. Mead saw his own work within this context as an attempt to explain the emergence of human beings as the most rational and self-conscious of animals.

Mead accepted Darwin's view that biological impulses provided the motivation for peoples' behavior. He insisted that these impulses were also social, however, because hunger, sex, and so on, usually required social relationships in order to be satisfied. Perhaps most important was Mead's modification of Darwin's view of communication. The latter regarded communication as expressing emotions. Indeed it does, Mead agreed; but to tie the gestures and symbols of communication only to

[2]George H. Mead, *Mind, Self and Society*, edited by Charles Morris (Chicago: University of Chicago Press, 1943), p. ix.

inner emotions is to leave too much unexplained. Mead proceeded to dissect the process of communication into various components and to relate them to the larger social structure. What ultimately emerged is probably the most coherent explanation for why someone might be regarded as a "nasty little thing" or wish that she could leave her body at home.

Any act made by a person in relation to another—a movement of the hands, a verbal request—is termed a gesture (by Mead). These gestures, whether verbal or not, tend to be symbols; that is, they are acts which stand for something else. A shrug of the shoulders, for example, typically indicates confusion or lack of understanding, especially if it is accompanied by "huh?" The shrug of the shoulders ordinarily conveys other meanings as well, such as do not expect me to do something because I do not understand. Thus, gestures typically communicate both immediate messages (for example, "what?") and more abstract ones (for example, "I cannot comply").

To be more precise, the above messages are probably the ones that were *intended* by the shoulder-shrugging person. Will the other person understand, though? Will the other person recognize the intent? If not, these two parties may be in for a difficult time. Suppose the other person responds to the shrug by saying, "fine," and then walks away. Now what is the first person going to do?

Let us back up for a moment. How does anyone ever know whether another person understands them? That is, how does one tell if the intended symbolic meaning has been communicated to another? An interesting question, no? Mead's answer was: By the response of the other. If the other person says, "fine," and walks away, the first party will probably conclude that the intended meaning was not received. On the other hand, if the other were to nod in response and proceed to say, "Look, all you have to do is . . . ," then the first party could figure that the other did understand what the shrug meant.

This discussion of the shrug and the response is an attempt to clarify one of Mead's most important distinctions, namely, between a gesture and a significant symbol. The former is merely an act. The latter, a significant symbol, involves an act whose intended meanings correspond closely with the meanings responded to by the other. For a gesture to be a significant symbol, Mead argued that it must arouse in the sender the same tendency to respond that it elicits in the receiver. Both are inclined to respond, at least inwardly, to the sender's gesture. Mead clarified this point by comparing people to animals and because the idea of a significant symbol is important to grasp if Mead's perspective is to be understood, let us examine his argument.

The gestures of animals, like the whine of a dog or an extended paw, can approximate significant symbols. The ways in which they fail to do so, however, further illuminate Mead's distinction. Two dogs, for example, may square off to fight. As one crouches, it is a signal to the other to make an adjustment. Each moves in response to the other; but each does so instinctively. Because it is instinctive, neither's acts arouse within themselves the same tendencies to respond that are aroused in the other. In other words, neither is taking the point of view of the other.

What is lacking, by comparison to humans, is a self-conscious awareness of one's self.

Human interaction also varies in the degree to which it possesses a self-conscious quality. At one extreme might be two people who are boxing or fencing. In this situation they might respond to each other's actions with conditioned reflexes. They might not think about their actions any more than the fighting dogs. At an opposite extreme might be a rehearsing actor or a writing poet. A writing poet may respond to his or her own words while carefully listening to the reading of a line. The rehearsing actor may study responses to expressions in the mirror. In order to assess the likely effect of some expression, each deliberately responds to their own gestures and utterances.

Most human interaction occurs somewhere between those two extremes. In every-day conversations, "we are not frightened," Mead noted, "by a tone which we may use to frighten somebody else."[3] We are thereby different from the rehearsing actor. However, unlike animals, we do have the capacity to respond to ourselves in a self-conscious manner, even if it is not fully employed all of the time.

This capacity, Mead continued, requires thought; more specifically, it requires reflective thought. The individual must be able, subjectively, to "structure" his or her environment. Such structuring requires that impulsive acts be inhibited while appropriate gestures are being considered. To return to our earlier example, if the first party is shrugging his shoulders and simultaneously asking if the other had some specific meaning in mind, then "interference" may be created by the two actions. The other party does not know whether to respond to the shrug or to the question, and both cannot be responded to simultaneously. If the other party tries to respond, the other's multiple responses are likely to become multiple stimuli for the first party. Spiralling confusion for both parties is likely to ensue. It is like meeting someone face-to-face in the middle of a sidewalk. You and the other each start to move first to your left and then to your right almost simultaneously. In effect, you feign left, but before the other can respond, you feign right while the other is keeping you off balance in the same way. Before either of you can inhibit the responses that confuse the other, there is a period of time in which it almost looks as if the two of you are dancing—which is neither party's intention.

Thus, effective communication—in which intended meanings are conveyed—initially requires that potentially confusing gestures be inhibited. Then the person must decide what actions will convey the intended meaning; that is, will produce the desired reaction from the other. *To communicate intended meaning is to elicit the desired reaction.* According to Mead, to isolate the gesture that will work is the essence of thought, and it requires that people respond, subjectively, to their own actions.

Our emphasis thus far has been on the sender rather than the recipient. This emphasis is initially helpful because it simplifies the process of communication, but it does lead to distortion. Communication, from Mead's perspective, is an on-going

[3]Ibid., p. 149.

process in which people continuously exchange roles as senders and receivers. Which one of the parties is considered to be the sender (or receiver) is arbitrary and depends entirely upon what sequence in the larger process is being examined. The shrug of the shoulders, for example, was earlier viewed as the first act. In fact, however, it was almost certainly a response to a previous gesture of the other party. Therefore, each party is subjectively responding to his or her own acts with some degree of deliberate self-consciousness. In order to illustrate this process, Mead used to ask students to imagine themselves giving instructions for completing a task to another person. The other is slow to respond though, so you reach over and complete it yourself. Your actions indicate, he concluded, that, "your request stirred up in you that same response which you stirred up in the other individual."[4]

Mead's realization that significant symbols involve a deliberate self-consciousness opens up the important question of what is self-consciousness. For Mead it was the person's recognition of a "me"—a self that is an object to others. The process by which an awareness of self emerges begins in infancy. At first babies do not even recognize their bodies as unitary things. From others' stimulation, a partial self-perception arises, a "me" that is equated with hands or feet. Eventually, of course, most children will develop a unitary conception of their bodies, of their physical selves. They accomplish this initially by relating others' actions to their own sensations. A parent's outstretched arms or soothing tones, for example, become associated with the experience of comfort.

Later, children become able to call out these same responses in themselves, by talking with themselves, even by constructing imaginary companions. These imagined others function as the counterpart of adult thought.[5] In order to imagine the response an act will elicit the child must think—isolate these connections—and the child must be reflective—that is, self-conscious. The essence of self-consciousness, the "me" in Mead's theory, is a recognition of one's self as seen by others.

PLAY AND GAMES

Mead saw self-consciousness, or the view of one's self as an object, as emerging first in children's play. As he viewed it, play was largely a solitary activity, even if other youngsters were around, and it was characterized by a great reliance upon relatively unbridled imagination. Thus, an important part of children's early play is pretending to be others: a parent, a teacher, a mountain climber, and so on. When fully immersed in play, young children may at times believe that they are the other. Typically, however, they will simultaneously bring (the role of) themselves into the pretended situation as well. Thus, Bob may pretend he is the nursery school teacher who is praising Bob for putting away all the toys. "The child says something in one character and responds in another character, and then his responding in another

[4]Ibid., p. 70.

[5]George H. Mead, "The Mechanisms of Social Consciousness," *Journal of Philosophy*, 9 (1912), pp. 402-405.

character is a stimulus to himself in the first character, and so the conversation goes on."[6] By bringing themselves into the imagined dialogue, while playing the part of the other, children clearly heighten their awareness of themselves as external objects.

As children grow older, play declines in frequency and games increase. Play and games, from Mead's perspective, differ in a number of regards. Play is relatively unstructured, which means that at play the child is rather free to go from role to role according to momentary whims. Games, however, tend to be organized, involving roles which are relatively fixed, compared to play. (Examples of such roles include center fielder, holder of a jump rope, and the like.)

In organized games the child must be able to take the attitudes of many others, all of whom stand in formalized relationships to each other. The participating child must, therefore, know what others will do under a variety of conditions. Perhaps even more importantly, the child must know what they expect of him or her. To illustrate, consider what Nancy must do in order to play shortstop in a baseball game. In different situations, she must know what the other infielders will do, what the pitcher and catcher will do, and what the team expects her to do in these situations. In play, only Nancy's wishes mattered; but in a game, Nancy must take the perspective of others—see herself as an object—in order to carry out her part of the game.

In a sense, life can be regarded as a series of games. There is the game of school, the game of love, of work, and so on. There are parts to play in each game, and rules that govern how they are to be played. One of the more difficult aspects of growing up is learning the roles and the rules in each of life's games. Within these games, people see themselves from the position of different others: parents, teachers, friends, roommates, and so on. From these diverse experiences, an individual develops a *universe of discourse* (the field within which significant symbols operate).[7] It is comprised of the collectivity of individuals whose common social experiences lead them to assign the same meaning (i.e., make the same response) to symbols. These commonalities identify the symbolic/behavioristic boundaries of a group, a community, or a nation.

Associated with a universe of discourse is a *generalized other*. It is my amalgam of many others' attitudes toward me, crystallized into a single standpoint. The generalized other is associated with a "unity of self" and it is presupposed, by Mead, for games (as opposed to play) and for rational, abstract thought.

In order to appreciate the role of the generalized other, consider mature thought, from Mead's standpoint. It involves an "internal" conversation, such as one between Mary and herself, for example. When this conversation occurs between Mary and the generalized other conception of self it is removed from any concrete other person. More universal and impersonal thought is then possible. The result is that more abstract terms are stated in a form that will be significant to anyone else within the individual's universe of discourse.

[6]Mead, *Mind, Self and Society*, p. 151.
[7]Ibid., p. 89.

Prior to the development of the generalized other, Mary may be able to anticipate her own mother's responses by carrying on an internal conversation between her mother and herself, as viewed by her mother. However, this line of thought would probably not be very effective if Mary wanted to communicate with a friend across the street, or her teacher, for example. Thus, more universal communication becomes possible with an abstract and impersonal generalized other.

Preliminary Summary

Before building further upon Mead's theories it may be helpful to briefly summarize the preceding discussion. Thus far, our attention has primarily been directed toward understanding the terms in Mead's famous book, *Mind, Self and Society.* We have defined each of the terms in the title as follows:

1) Mind, or thought, involves the subjective structuring of a situation to permit purposive behavior; namely, to call forth desired reactions. For such purposive behavior to occur, the person must be able to take the point of view of the other which requires self-consciousness.

2) Self, or self-consciousness, entails a capacity to regard one's self as an object. The emergence of a self, or conception of "me," results from a reflective interpretation of others' reactions.

3) Society involves on-going, patterned activities. It is the series of "games" out of which the child's experience of diversity leads to a conception of a generalized other and the capacity to employ symbols that are significant throughout a society. With this capacity, the child can think and plan in a deliberate, self-conscious manner.

CHILDRENS' DEVELOPMENT

It is clear that, in Mead's formulation, mind, self, and society are highly inter-dependent processes. In other words, each requires the other. From an evolutionary perspective, it is tempting to ask which might have come first. As Mead's perspective is applied in contemporary sociology, it is largely an irrelevant question. Children are born into an already existing society, for example. However, an interesting developmental view of the connection between self-consciousness and reflective thought is presented by the Swiss psychologist, Jean Piaget. It is presented here because it helps to clarify aspects of Mead's perspective.

Thought and Self-Consciousness (Piaget)

In order to examine the social origins of children's intelligence Piaget has posed thought problems to Swiss children of various ages. In one study he asked school children to respond to absurd (that is, self-contradictory) statements.[8] For example: "A poor cyclist had his head smashed and died on the spot; he was taken

[8]Jean Piaget, *Judgement and Reasoning in the Child* (Paterson, N.J.: Littlefield, Adams, 1959).

to the hospital and it is feared he will not recover." In order to resolve the absurdity, children must accept the premises as given, then reason deductively.

Prior to the age of about seven or eight, Piaget found that most Swiss children do not detect the absurdity of such statements.[9] They do not detect the internal contradictions because of their own egocentrism. They view themselves as the center of the universe. For example, they may believe that they are personally being followed by the sun and the moon; that members of their families have no lives when they leave for school; and so on. Egocentric children are too self-oriented to be able to reason from another's given premise.

After about age nine, many of the children can reason through the absurd statements, but they still have difficulty resolving contradictions that explicitly involve adapting another's point of view. For example, "Someone said, if I ever kill myself from despair I won't choose a Friday, because Friday is a bad day and would bring me ill luck." Most of the nine to twelve year olds could not deduce the absurdity in such statements because they responded according to their personal sense of reality with replies such as, "Friday is not unlucky."

A still more difficult problem is posed for children (or adults!) when they must not only take another's point of view, but must also see themselves from the other's standpoint. The following statement is illustrative: "I have three brothers: Paul, Ernest, and myself." Youngsters typically respond by arguing that there are only two brothers. For example, "You, you're not a brother." To judge from their statements, they do not yet differentiate between relationship and membership. Until they can assume the role of another, and see themselves as an object, they do not recognize that brother (or sister, or friend) denotes a reciprocal relationship.

Piaget concludes that the requirement for reasoning is an ability to work from others' premises; to make logical deductions in a "world of the possible," rather than in one's private world. This detachment from one's own point of view must be sustained; that is, one must reason from another's premise without subtly returning to a private point of view. From Mead's perspective, Piaget may be interpreted as pointing out the consequences of the generalized other. The younger, more egocentric Swiss children cannot think in the universal and impersonal terms associated with the generalized other.

Like Mead, Piaget viewed children's games as an important part of the process by which thought and self-consciousness develop in an interwoven fashion. Also like Mead, he viewed games as microscopic reflections of society. To fully understand the rules of games, a child must apparently go through a series of stages from a private insistence on rules' intrinsic morality to a recognition of the relationship between rules and the members of a group. What is not as clear in Piaget's writing as it is in Mead's is whether social organization, as represented in games and rules, is absolutely essential for the development of thought and self-consciousness. Would an "isolated" child go through the same developmental stages?

[9]There are disagreements concerning the ages at which Swiss and American children are capable of making certain types of distinctions. They need not concern us here, however, because we are interested solely in the sequence of development.

The Isolated Child

Given the lack of self-sufficiency characteristic of the human infant, no truly isolated infant could survive. One of the closest approximations is provided by the case of a girl given the fictitious name of Isabelle. She was "discovered" in 1938 when she was about six and one-half years old.[10]

Isabelle was the illegitimate child of a deaf-mute mother who, because of the stigma of her birth, kept Isabelle secluded in a darkened room. They did not speak, and Isabelle did not have contact with other persons who could. So unused were her senses that, at first, there was serious question about whether she too was deaf. Her body was also misshapen as the result of inadequate diet and sunshine.

The speech therapist and psychologist who initially worked with Isabelle found her utterly lacking in the qualities of a normal six-and-one-half-year-old child. She did not speak or understand the speaking of others. Her IQ measured near the zero point of a scale. Strangers, and men in particular, terrified her, and she was described as responding like "a wild animal."

It seems apparent that the qualities that would be considered normal in a child—speaking, playing, an ability to interact with others—were utterly absent in Isabelle. They did not become manifest as the result of a simple (innate) maturation process. Over the next few years, however, she made dramatic progress. By the time she was a teenager, for example, Isabelle almost caught up to her peers in school. The key to her rapid progress appears to have been her language development. With extensive training she began to verbalize. From Mead's perspective, she became able to respond to her own utterances; that is, to take her self into account. Within about two years, her measured IQ tripled.

Thus far, we have examined the interdependence of society, thought, and self, without paying any attention to the content of self; that is, who and what do people think they are? Why, for example, did Edith Stern think of herself as clumsy? Answers to these questions have, however, been implicit in the preceding discussion. Specifically, through interaction, people develop a view of themselves; a *self-concept,* or an identity.

RESEARCH ON CONTENT OF SELVES

Mead's own view of the self, as previously noted, emphasized a process of communication that occurred within a person. A man's self might be considered developed to the degree he was able to see himself as an object and converse with that object. However, we might still wonder what qualities he attributes to that object, and whether or not it pleases him. To address issues of this type, many of Mead's followers have tried to focus more explicitly upon the content of the self, quite apart from the processes by which it arises.

[10]Kingsley Davis, "Final Note on a Case of Extreme Isolation," *American Journal of Sociology,* 52 (1947).

The most obvious aspects of identity tend to consist of noun-like labels, such as "student" or "mother" or "roommate". Labels, or roles, of this type are an important part of most people's self-conception. Words associated with these labels tend to be adjectives, such as "clever" or "attractive" or "helpful," which describe the way the person sees himself in the role. Finally, there are self-evaluations associated with both the nouns and adjectives. The person may think it is good to be a "student", better to be a "clever student", and so on.[11]

In order to complete this view of the content of selves, we must also recognize that it tends to be characterized by a hierarchy of prominence. Put differently, we are saying that all identities and qualities are not of equal importance, or salience, to people. Even if two people each saw themselves as good "teachers," and both were pleased by that view, their self-concepts would still be different if being a teacher was a very prominent role to one person, but not to the other.

One of the most favored techniques for measuring the content of self-concepts is a twenty statements test in which people are asked to respond to the question, "Who Am I?" They are specifically instructed to write the best statements as if they were answering the question for themselves. Interpreting the responses to indicate the content of a person's identity is sometimes difficult because of *situational variability*. Characteristics of the test situation, such as who else is simultaneously taking it, can apparently alter the saliency of some attributes, raising or lowering the likelihood that they will be noted. For example, a woman may be more likely to note gender as a component of her self-concept if she is the only woman taking the test in a room full of men. To some theorists, situational variability is to be expected because they view identity, itself, as situated; that is, the identities one attributes to oneself depend upon specific contexts in which interaction occurs.[12]

Most people's responses to the "Who Am I" question also exhibit a marked degree of consistency, however. For many people, an important part of the answer involves pointing to work, family, and church roles. Thus, they identify themselves as engineers, parents, members of a Catholic church, and so on. It is assumed that these identifications both reflect and reinforce their membership in groups and organizations. Thus, as Mead described, social interaction enjoins selves with organized activities in a society.

Changes in Selves

In order to clarify the inter-connections Mead was stressing, let us consider the effects of a loss of a spouse for elderly people who have been married for a long period of time. Because identity is dependent upon interaction, the death of a spouse can create an identity crisis. Thus, a man may think: "If I am no longer Mary's

[11]This view of the content of selves is based upon Morris Rosenberg, *Conceiving the Self* (New York: Basic Books, 1979); and Jerold Heiss, *The Social Psychology of Interaction* (Englewood Cliffs, NJ: Prentice-Hall, 1981).

[12]For further discussion of the situational perspective, see Gregory P. Stone, "Appearance and the Self," in Stone and Harvey A. Faberman (eds.), *Social Psychology Through Symbolic Interaction* (New York: Wiley, 1981).

husband, who am I?" In addition to the direct loss of an important interaction partner, the loss of a spouse may affect the survivor's relationship to family and friends. After many years of marriage, people often have a "coupled identity" to other couples with whom they interact. The death of one spouse changes that, of course, and other couples may now avoid the surviving spouse, leading to further isolation.

As part of a large study of bereavement, Lund and three associates obtained information from nearly 200 widows and widowers in the Salt Lake City area. From obituaries in the newspaper, they identified surviving spouses and initially contacted them between three and four weeks after the death of their husband or wife. The investigators re-interviewed the survivors several more times over the next two years. For comparison purposes, the investigators also selected a sample of married people over age fifty, whose spouses did not die.[13]

The findings showed that loss of a spouse immediately reduced *social anchorage* replies to the "Who Are You" question. By social anchorage the researchers meant statements about the self that signified important social relationships and group memberships. Examples include: grandmother, citizen, church member, neighbor. The decline in statements of this type was the same for widows and widowers and it continued, unabated, for the entire (two year) duration of the study. Thus, loss of a spouse appeared to result in an enduring change in the identities of widows and widowers.

We can, of course, turn the process around. Getting married would probably add social anchorage, for example, by linking each spouse to another family and set of friends. Routine transitions in most people's lives—graduating from school, taking a job, changing jobs, having a child, and so on—are all associated with changes in people's identities.

In addition to life-course changes, there may well be more macroscopic changes in the contents of identities within a society. For example, Zurcher has analyzed trends in people's replies to the twenty statement test over several decades. He reports that in the 1950s there was an emphasis upon institutionalized roles— occupational and familial, in particular. The social and cultural upheavals of the 1960s seems to have changed that, though. While institutional roles remain important parts of most people's self-concepts, they are less stressed, and ways of acting and feeling have become more emphasized. Specifically, beginning in the 1970s, Zurcher notes more people identifying themselves in terms such as: happy, religious, worried, and so on.[14]

COOLEY'S "LOOKING-GLASS SELF"

Another influential early description of the effect of interaction with others upon a person's self-concept was provided by Charles Horton Cooley. He summarized his

[13]Dale A. Lund, Michael S. Caserta, Margaret F. Diamond and Robert M. Gray, "Impact of Bereavement on the Self-Conceptions of Older Surviving Spouses," *Symbolic Interaction*, 9 (1986).

[14]Louis A. Zurcher, Jr. *Social Roles*, (Beverly Hills, CA: Sage Publications, 1983).

analysis with the term, *looking-glass self.*[15] In his view, other people act like mirrors to a person's imagination. More specifically, Cooley proposed that there were three elements, or steps: an imagination of how we appear to another, an imagination of how the other judges that appearance, then some emotional reaction to the other's judgment. Cooley employed the looking-glass metaphor because it captured the reflected aspect of self-concept formation. However, he also recognized several obvious deficiencies in the metaphor. A looking glass, or mirror, connotes an actual and nonjudgmental image. By contrast, Cooley describes an image that is imputed and evaluative.

Cooley, like Mead, had a special interest in the way self-concepts developed in children. From a number of observations of infants he concluded that they were, from an early age, very concerned with their effects upon others. They were, Cooley inferred, trying to exert control over people around them, parents in particular. Correspondingly, they developed ways of crying or tugging on parents' clothes which would produce the desired effect. (In Mead's terminology, they were thinking; that is, isolating the connections between their acts and others' responses.)

With increasing maturity, children typically become more sophisticated. Cooley observed that they try harder to hide their desires for approval or affection and seek such gratifications in more subtle ways. They also become more sensitive to differences among others. Throwing a tantrum may work with one parent while pleading is effective with another. In effect, their characters change according to whom they are with at the time. They change, in other words, according to the other in whose mind they see themselves. "We always imagine," Cooley noted, "and in imagining share the judgments of the other mind." For example, a person may boast of things to one that would be too embarrassing to discuss with another. Thus, both Mead and Cooley regarded personal quantities as being more situational than fixed.

Despite a number of apparent similarities in their perspectives, Mead was quite critical of aspects of Cooley's writings. The fundamental disagreement was between their theoretical orientations. Mead regarded himself as a behaviorist which entailed focusing upon people's overt behavior and not their motives; thus his emphasis was upon the *reactions of others.* From this position, he considered Cooley to be too concerned with people's inner wishes, and he expressed disdain for Cooley's introspective emphasis. This basic difference lay behind several of Mead's specific criticisms. For example, he claimed that Cooley failed to distinguish sufficiently between actors as subjects and as objects, a distinction that was critical to Mead.[16]

According to Cooley, the most important self-feelings were pride and shame. People's anticipation of feeling these emotions in response to anothers' reaction to their behavior was considered, by Cooley, to be the core of people's selfmonitoring. In particular, it was the desire to avoid shame (in the reflection of themselves) that he viewed as shaping people's behavior.

[15]Charles Horton Cooley, *Human Nature and the Social Order* (New York: Scribner's, 1902).

[16]See George H. Mead, "Cooley's Contributions to American Social Thought," *American Journal of Sociology*, 36 (1930).

Following Cooley, Thomas Scheff has argued that shame is ubiquitous, but that adults are embarrassed to display it. They may even be uncomfortable at recognizing that they feel it. Scheff summarizes the results of several studies as indicating that when shame occurs (because a person feels the self is being negatively evaluated by self or others), it tends to be followed by *hiding behavior*. This entails an attempt to disguise the shame experience by calling it something else: feeling foolish, acting stupidly, looking ridiculous, feeling exposed, and so on. In addition, hiding behavior entails disruptions of interaction as people who feel shame: stammer, blush, avert their eyes, and so on.[17]

Scheff also notes that overt sanctions for deviance in everyday life are infrequent; so are explicit rewards for conformity. Because social life goes on, however, he reasons that informal sanctions (or the threat of informal sanctions) must be very effective. Conformity, perhaps even rigid conformity, he concludes, results from people's continuous and nearly invisible monitoring of selves to avoid the possibility of negative evaluations of the self, by one's self or by another.

GOFFMAN'S STAGE METAPHOR

Throughout the preceding discussion of symbolic interaction theory it has been clear that people evaluate each other, and that a reflected sense of an evaluated self is conveyed to each party. What we have not yet considered is the role people play in *presenting* selves for evaluation. At one extreme, individuals are regarded as manipulative; self-consciously and deliberately concealing certain bits of information about themselves while conspicuously displaying other bits. At the opposite pole, people are regarded less cynically. For example, their interactions with others may be assumed to be governed more by habit than by calculation.

None of the perspectives sees people playing an essentially passive role; rather, people are thought to actively convey a sense of self to others as a first step in the symbolic interaction process. Thus, in everyday life people resemble professional actors who, in a more systematic and deliberate manner, work to acquire the gestures and mannerisms associated with their roles. The rehearsals of nonactors are less formalized, but remember, Mead viewed all purposive behavior as entailing a rehearsal-like quality. People think through how to elicit the reactions they desire; how to be humorous by making others laugh, how to be sad by making others cry.

In order to understand the different motives people possess, it may be helpful to focus for a moment upon how the same act can be interpreted differently. When people quietly consider how to elicit the response they desire, Mead, in a noncynical way, viewed them as *thinking*. The gestures they used toward this end were noncynically labeled *significant symbols*. From the more cynical dramaturgical perspective, however, presenting cues to elicit the desired response is called, *impression management!*

[17]Thomas J. Scheff, "Shame and Conformity." *American Sociological Review*, 53 (1988).

It is Erving Goffman who has most developed the dramaturgical model in which there are abundant analogies between everyday interaction and a theatrical performance.[18] For example, he identifies a frontstage and backstage that correspond both with actual places and with social norms. People prepare for their parts, like actors, in backstage regions. This is where teenagers dress for a prom, where salespeople escape from the floor, and so on. Like the backstage of a theater, access to these areas in everyday life is also carefully guarded. It is a place where people can retreat or rehearse in private; where others with whom they interact frontstage are not free to follow; "employees only" or "Craig's room" may be posted on the door, for example.

Like actors on a stage, people also make extensive use of props in their performances. This includes portable props that people take with them, such as clothing or accents; and more permanent props, such as the arrangement of furniture in their home. The emphasis, according to Goffman, is upon impression management, that is, presenting cues to elicit the desired response.

The similarities between routine interaction and staged performances also extend to the role of others—the supporting cast. People typically help each other, Goffman notes, to make "unblemished" performances. Thus, they honor the privacy of backstage areas, pretend not to notice unzipped clothing or an untimely belch.

Going to a dentist, for example, is in some respects like going to a play. Some areas of the office are off-limits to patients. They are the backstage areas where the dentist and other members of the performing "company" rehearse presentations of self, drain tensions by making fun of complaining patients, and so on. Nurse, receptionist, and dentist all have parts to play vis-à-vis each other in order to convey an image to the audience (that is, patients) and each other. Uniforms, utensils, furnishings, and other props are as indispensable to their performance as make-up and costumes are to a theatrical performance.

Goffman's first publications were penetrating essays that explored how people presented selves in everyday life. Those essays were combined into the book we have summarized in the preceding pages. Several of Goffman's subsequent essays and books were attempts to further understand how selves are maintained by examining the conditions which lead to their destruction. For example, he devised the concept *total institutions* in order to generalize about the similarities among: the armed services, mental hospitals, monasteries and prisons.[19] In each of these settings, there are powerful similarities among recruits, inmates, and patients. All are stripped of the props which are normally used to maintain personal identities. Clothing, rooms, food, and the like are all standardized. In place of individualized treatment, the staff responds to inmates solely in their roles as inmates, by number or rank, rather than by name. Goffman concludes that the entire process leads to the mortification of former selves. This makes total institutions of interest in their own right and also of comparative value because they highlight the processes by which identities are preserved in ordinary establishments.

[18]Erving Goffman, *The Presentation of Self in Everyday Life* (New York: Doubleday, 1959).
[19]Erving Goffman, *Asylums* (New York: Doubleday, 1961).

Goffman also examined conditions which "compromise" selves. Here he analyzed and generalized about people who: have prison records, are blind, deaf, or crippled, and so on. In each instance the person has a stigma.[20] Each of their social identities is dominated by one single facet: their record, their handicap, or the like. All of their other attributes (such as their sense of humor, height, or painting ability) tend to be ignored when they interact with others who are "normal." As a result, persons with a stigma tend to prefer to associate with others who are like themselves. However, while this permits more aspects of their selves to be validated, the self-identification that results from exclusive interaction with other similarly stigmatized people can also be a source of discomfort.

Goffman's observations have extended and clarified Mead's pioneering writing, and they have added new insights, as well. They are important to note for these reasons. In addition, Goffman's work is a fine example of a methodological style advocated by many of Mead's followers. Specifically, according to Blumer (who was a key figure in the development of symbolic interaction within sociology), only qualitative methodologies are appropriate.[21] The objective of symbolic interaction, he insists, is to understand the meaning of situations for participants. Correspondingly, an investigator must spend a lot of time with participants, doing case studies, in order to understand them and their circumstances. For these purposes, in his opinion, the statistical manipulation of typical questionnaire data would likely be meaningless.

Blumer's methodological position is not the only, and perhaps not even the majority, view among current symbolic interactionists, however. For many, following in the theoretical tradition of Mead, Cooley, and others imposes no methodological restrictions upon their research. Conventional quantitative approaches seem appropriate. Thus, they utilize techniques like the "Who Am I?" test, statistically analyze people's responses, and offer generalizations.

CONCLUSION

In summation, Mead's perspective regards the self as formed by the responses of others. Identity is, therefore, an intensely social phenomenon which possesses both situational and enduring features. A degree of stability, or continuity, is characteristic because of the cumulative effects of prior validations of self, especially from significant others. Situational variation is also expected, however, because of the importance attributed to the role of the immediate other. The differential responses of the other (in Mead) and the characteristics imputed by the others (in Cooley) are crucial in shaping the momentary identities of an individual. Thus, others both nurture and reflect the identities people project, thereby providing the person with a social identity.

---

[20]Erving Goffman, *Stigma* (Englewood Cliffs, NJ: Prentice-Hall, 1963).
[21]Herbert Blumer, *Symbolic Interactionism* (Englewood Cliffs, NJ: Prentice-Hall, 1969).

From a developmental perspective, the formation of social selves was viewed by Mead as an intimate part of the processes in which both individual thought and society emerge. According to Mead, a basic characteristic of the human species is a high degree of impulsiveness. Self-consciousness and reflective thought were regarded as the "mechanisms" which inhibited impulsive action and permitted (or facilitated) purposive behavior. Despite these mechanisms, Mead still saw a tendency for people to act first, impulsively, with reflection and self-consciousness occurring only after the act has begun (if they occur at all). Thus, there is a lag between behavior and reflection, and identity formation can be thought of as akin to a delayed videotape replay occurring within the actor's mind in which the actor is portrayed both as subject and object.

The identities which emerge are a product of the content of these instant replays. Based upon what qualities others respond to, the content of people's identities could emphasize intelligence or stupidity, importance or worthlessness, or so on. The possible *content* of selves is virtually limitless. The great insight of Mead's theory is its clarification of the *process* by which varied contents develop.

Now let us apply symbolic interaction to the questions about Edith Stern with which this chapter began. If in the course of socialization, significant others rarely responded to an infant's body, it would not be surprising if physical aspects of the self had little salience to the person. As previously described, Edith Stern's father apparently focused all of his energies upon her intellectual development. Therefore, it would not be surprising if, as an adult, she would just as soon "leave her body at home."

A preoccupation with intellectual development can also lead to a relative disregard of unrelated personal and social characteristics. If gregariousness, humor, and so on are not responded to, they are likely not to become salient aspects of one's self-concept. If such traits can not be called out in a situation where they are deemed appropriate by another, then the other is likely to regard the person as one-dimensional, as a clod.

To apply symbolic interaction, or any other, perspective to a single person is fraught with peril. Sometimes it will not fit. Furthermore, we really know much too little about Edith Stern to know whether the above observations are as fitting as they appear to be. Our speculations are intended merely to help to illustrate some important features of the symbolic interactionist perspective.

SUGGESTIONS FOR ADDITIONAL READING

JOHN D. BALDWIN, *George Herbert Mead*. Beverly Hills, CA: Sage, 1986.

GARY ALAN FINE, *With the Boys: Little League Baseball and Preadolescent Culture*. Chicago: University of Chicago Press, 1987.

ELAINE HATFIELD AND SUSAN SPRECHER, *Mirror, Mirror ... The Importance of Looks in Everyday Life*. Albany: SUNY Press, 1986.

2

Culture, Society, and Sex Roles
Margaret Mead and W.I. Thomas

During the 1970s, there was a very popular commercial for a brand of little cigars called Tiparillo's. (They are still sold in stores, but they are rarely advertised anymore.) Their most popular advertisement, set to a catchy tune, posed the question: Should a gentleman offer a Tiparillo to a lady? At first glance the question seems to raise the simple question of whether smoking any kind of cigar is appropriate for a female. It is an intriguing question though, because it simultaneously raises several issues. First is the question of whether the little cigar should be offered at all, by any male to any female. Note, however, that the question asks about a gentleman. Perhaps some men would make the offer, but a gentleman would not. Does being a gentleman signify anything with respect to appropriate sex-role behavior, or is there a single set of standards for all males in this regard?

The question of how she ought to respond logically follows. She could accept, politely refuse, or act offended and refuse. How should any woman respond? Note again, however, that the question more specifically involves what a lady should do. Perhaps some women would accept, but not one who saw herself as a lady. Does being a lady signify anything distinctive with respect to appropriate sex-role behavior?

There are also a number of other questions that are less directly implied. Assuming the couple has just met, how will her response to his offer affect their future relationship? If she refuses and acts offended, no relationship is likely to develop. On the other hand, would her acceptance, in and of itself, lead to further intimacy? This is a difficult question to answer because the context of the offer is unclear. Is it offered in public—at a party, for example—or in private? The public-private dimension interacts with the gentleman-lady distinction and raises additional possibilities. For example, perhaps a lady could accept in private, not public, and would accept (in private) only if she thought him a gentleman and wished to pursue the relationship. (We are, of course, ignoring the obvious consideration of whether she smokes cigars.)

Years ago, when the advertisement that raised the question about the little cigar first appeared, it merely posed the question as a provocative way to make people think about the product. No answer was suggested, probably because there were no safe answers; that is, no way to reconcile the issues without offering sex-role definitions that would have offended large numbers of potential purchasers. In the following years more "liberal" sex-role definitions, especially among younger people, permitted the advertiser to answer all the questions in a brief jingle that concluded, "Well, baby it's alright." However, it should also be noted that some vestiges of tradition were maintained by having the gentleman offer the Tiparillo. This avoids the question of whether a lady should (be so bold as to) ask for a cigar or purchase it herself.

As changes in the sponsor's willingness to answer the question suggest, recent decades have involved rapid changes in sex roles. Such changes could not, of course, occur without controversy. One of the fundamental issues that has been raised concerns "human nature"; that is, do the changes that have been occurring violate a "natural state" in which women are passive and submissive; and happiest when they are working in (rather than outside of) their homes? Perhaps the best way to respond to the human nature question is to examine sex roles in different societies. If a great deal of diversity in sex roles is observed, it presents a strong argument against the view that innate capacities determine the differences in men's and women's roles.

Long before anyone was wondering whether a gentleman should offer a Tiparillo to a lady, Margaret Mead was in New Guinea studying three different cultures. The observations and conclusions she offered will be our first topics of discussion in this chapter.

MEAD IN NEW GUINEA

In 1931, Mead left the Anthropology department of the American Museum of Natural History and, with her husband and fellow anthropologist, Reo Fortune, spent the next two years studying three primitive societies in New Guinea: the Arapesh, Mundugumor, and Tchambuli. Her basic assumption was that different personal characteristics, or temperaments, were valued in different societies. Each society, through its oral or written histories, its institutions, its art, and so on, shapes individuals in the images that are valued. However, deviants result since all individuals are not successfully molded by their cultures. Further, everyone in a society is not shaped according to an identical mold. The children of high-status parents, for example, may be socialized very differently from most youngsters.

The sex of a child also tends to provide a basis for differential molding. In many societies, gender is believed to be associated with innate differences in temperament. In our own society, for example, males have traditionally been regarded as predisposed to act more aggressively while females have been regarded as predisposed to be more sensitive to others. The social roles of men and women,

Mead argues, are patterned about these assumed differences in temperament. Thus, based upon these American assumptions, women were considered best suited to raise children while men were considered ideally fit for the business world.

Youngsters are molded, at every stage, into the sex roles deemed appropriate in their society for someone of their gender. So pervasive and detailed is this process that Mead refers to it as "a plot," though it is not a deliberately planned conspiracy. All of us have, of course, been the targets of such a plot. Because we only experience one such plot, however, we tend to equate it with human nature. In other words, it is difficult for us to see beyond the plot and recognize that it is simply one of many cultural alternatives. The three different societies described by Mead are particularly instructive in this regard.[1]

The Mountain Arapesh

Among the Arapesh, who lived in the mountains and ravines of Northern New Guinea, there were a few conspicuous sex differences. The most pronounced differences were in work roles: Men hunted, gathered herbs and built houses while women collected fire wood, cooked and gardened. Arapesh culture also called forth some differences in temperament; for example, little boys were expected to imitate their fathers by stamping their feet to show overt anger, but little girls were expected to inhibit such overt displays.

Despite the preceding differences, Mead emphasized the numerous uniform ways of acting that were expected of all Arapesh, regardless of sex. Examples include cooperativeness, an absence of interpersonal aggression, and tender care of children; and these shared traits were especially characteristic of the Mountain Arapesh.

Judged by our standards, the conception, birth, and raising of a child were conspicuously without sex-role distinctions. They recognized no differences in the difficulties faced by either a man or a woman. Thus, the Arapesh verb, "to bear a child," was applied equally to both. To illustrate further, immediately after the birth of an infant, a man joined his wife in bed to wash and protect the infant. At such times the father was said to be, "in bed having a baby." The later feeding, cleaning, and general indulgence of Arapesh children were also shared equally by both parents and considered to be major tasks in life for both. The degree to which fathers shared in the burdens of raising children was illustrated by Mead's recounting of a typical reaction to the observed handsomeness of a middle-aged man. He is handsome, a listener might agree, "but you should have seen him before he bore all those children."[2]

The Mundugumor

About 100 miles south of the Arapesh, living on both sides of the Yuat River, were the Mundugumor. These cannibals and head hunters were as aggressive as

---

[1]The following descriptions are based upon Margaret Mead, *Sex and Temperament* (New York: Morrow, 1963. (Originally published in 1935.)

[2]Ibid., p. 39.

the Arapesh were gentle. In fact, her Arapesh friends warned Mead before she left to beware of those "fierce people."

Given the structure of Mundugumor social organization, prevalent rivalries based on sex were virtually assured. The household situation most valued by the males was one in which each man had many wives to serve as sexual partners and to work his garden. However, there was not an unlimited supply of potential wives which was a source of conflict.

In order to obtain a wife an interfamily exchange had to be arranged. A man would have to trade either his sister or daughter to the family from which he wanted to obtain a wife. Thus, it was an interfamily exchange of daughter for daughter, sister for sister, or daughter for sister. There was the rub, for it created conflict between fathers and sons over trading rights to the same woman, the father's daughter and the son's sister. For which of them would she be traded to obtain a wife? In addition to father-son conflict, this arrangement also generated mother-daughter conflict because a daughter was a potential threat to her mother. A husband might use the girl to secure a more desirable wife for himself.

Pregnancy was generally an unwelcome event among the Mundugumor, in marked contrast to the Arapesh's delight. First, because of Mundugumor taboos, there was the man's annoyance that he would be denied a sex partner during the woman's pregnancy. He also feared the birth of a son as a potential rival to his use of daughters in exchanges. The pregnant woman feared that her husband would now seek other wives, lowering her status in the household. She also dreaded sexual abstinence during pregnancy and feared the threats that would be created by the birth of a daughter.

When an infant was eventually born, there were arguments over whether or not to permit it to survive. Family members of the opposite sex usually "voted" for it while same-sex family members were often opposed. The child that was allowed to live encountered a hostile world and received little affection or indulgence from family members. Distrust, rivalry, and a readiness to resort to violence were the personality traits that dominated as a result of this socialization experience, and it almost equally characterized both males and females. While there were some sex differences in temperament, Mundugumor males and females were more alike than different. With respect to dominant personality types overwhelming sex-role differences, they resembled the Arapesh; but the content of the Mundugumor's shared temperaments were dramatically different, entailing violence and distrust, rather than gentleness and cooperation.

The Tchambuli

The fishing villages of the Tchambuli provided Mead's third stop in New Guinea. Here she encountered the most pronounced sex-role differences. The principal activities of everyday life for the men were dancing, playing the flute, painting, and other artistic endeavors. The dominant activities for women were fishing and making baskets. Youngsters of each sex learned the gender-appropriate tasks from family members of the same sex.

Trap fishing was the Tchambuli's most important source of livelihood. It provided a major source of food and a major item to be used in extravillage trading for other commodities. It was virtually the exclusive domain of women whose working days were strenuous. Their major respites were the ceremonies and other artistic presentations which the men prepared.

Relationships between Tchambuli men and women were perhaps best indicated by Mead's description of the men's shopping trips. They periodically went off to market to sell the women's products and to purchase other items, including their ornamental supplies. Dressed in the finest feathers, the men spent enjoyable days bargaining, trading, changing their minds, and starting over. All of these exchanges were transacted with money and other items that belonged to their wives. Therefore, they had to obtain their wives' approval before concluding their transactions. They sought this approval with, "languishing looks and soft words" which the wives generally accepted with "kindly tolerance."[3]

Mead's Conclusions

Mead's observations and descriptions indicate the awesome power of culture, its capacity to shape individuals according to a predetermined mold. Thus, the individual Mundugumor was generally suspicious and aggressive; the individual Arapesh was typically sensitive and gentle. The molding capacities of culture are not unlimited, though. In every society there are some deviants, people who do not fit their culture's mold. In this regard, Mead described the existence of some Arapesh individuals who were aggressive and some Mundugumor individuals who were gentle.

According to Mead, most individuals are highly malleable. They are born with a wide range of predispositions, including some that are polar opposites to each other. Temperamentally, the same person often has the capacity to be both aggressive or gentle. Which way this person will usually behave depends in large measure upon which of the traits is called forth by the culture and is consistently reinforced. For some people, however, the discrepancy between their innate dispositions and their culture's ideals is too great to be breached. Their subsequent failure to adjust is not simply an individual defect, as is often assumed, but rather is due to the poor fit between the individual and his or her society. Thus, an aggressive Arapesh will be considered deviant, but this same person would not be viewed as deviant among the Mundugumor.

While the power of culture to shape individuals is awesome, it is not necessarily coercive. To be coercive implies that power is mobilized to overcome resistance, in this context, the unwillingness of individuals to be shaped according to a fixed mold. However, for every individual whose innate temperament is

[3]Ibid., pp. 254-255.

discrepant, there is another individual whose predispositions provide an excellent fit. Moreover, there is the majority of individuals who are highly malleable. Thus, all cultures possess an enormous potential for coerciveness, but most individuals will not necessarily experience the molding powers of their culture as coercive.

The potentially constraining force of culture has been emphasized in numerous definitions of the concept itself. Thus, by definition, culture is learned, shared, transmitted across generation—and coercive. Many writers have elegantly captured this coercive quality in their definitions of culture. A few of the more illuminating statements are presented below.

LABARRE: "Culture is . . . the immortality of dead men, a way in which their judgments and choices . . . coerce the living."[4]

CLIFTON: "Culture . . . acts with a deterministic force so as to mould the content and set the limits of . . . behavior."[5]

HALL: "Man as a cultural being is bound by hidden rules and is not master of his fate"[6]

LEARNING THE RULES

The notion of "hidden rules," noted in the last of these definitions, is often regarded as an important aspect of culture's molding capacity. Precisely because the rules of a culture typically pass unnoticed, or else are equated with human nature, people are conditioned to respond without even realizing that they are acquiring an arbitrary set of responses.

The covert qualities of culture are very cleverly illustrated in Miner's study of the Nacirema. Miner identified them only as a contemporary North American people living in between various Canadian and Mexican groups.[7] Their most fundamental belief, according to Miner, is that the human body is both ugly and prone to disease. In order to counteract this natural state of the body, as they regard it, the Nacirema have developed extensive rituals within their household "shrines." A chest built into the wall in each shrine contains various "magical potions" without which no native believes it would be possible to live. If not for these rituals, the Nacirema believe they would face catastrophes: They would become ill, their friends would desert them, their gums would bleed, and their teeth would fall out, and so forth. The ceremonies believed to prevent these harmful consequences are performed in private and are discussed only with children during their initiation period.

[4]Western LaBarre, *The Human Animal* (Chicago: University of Chicago Press, 1960), p. 221.

[5]James A. Clifton, *Introduction to Cultural Anthropology* (New York: Houghton-Mifflin, 1968).

[6]Edward T. Hall, *The Silent Language* (New York: Doubleday, 1959), p. 111.

[7]Horace Miner, "Body Ritual Among the Nacirema," *American Anthropologist*, 58 (1956).

Miner also describes a number of specialists who have emerged in Nacirema society to help the natives. Included are a "holy-mouth-man" who every year, or more, gouges natives' teeth; a "listener" who, like witch doctors, is believed able to exorcise "demons" from the heads of natives who have been bewitched; and "medicine men" who write curative potions for the natives in a secret, ancient language and who must be given substantial gifts in return.

Do the Nacirema sound familiar to you? If you have not yet figured out Miner's parody, spell Nacirema backwards. Of course, it is us, as we might look to an observer who was looking at us from "far and above." The household shrines are our bathrooms, and the daily rituals involve the use of mouthwash, deodorant, and the like, without which (we believe) we would become ill and our friends and lovers would desert us. The "holy-mouth-man" who gouges native's teeth is better known as a dentist; the "listener" who exorcises devils is a psychiatrist; the "medicine man" with his secret language is the prescription-writing doctor.

Looking at this society from "far and above," it does seem as though the "natives" must believe that the human body is naturally ugly and prone to disease. Why else would there be all the daily rituals and various specialists? However, before Miner calls these attributes to our attention, most of us do not think much about the daily rituals—like brushing teeth, rinsing with mouthwash, applying deodorant—by which we make ourselves fit for society. For example, I do not think I ever heard anyone complain about having to use deodorant or mouthwash. They are among the hidden rules which everyone knows, at one level, but no one is very aware of, at another level. They represent examples of cultural conditioning that are typically easier for outsiders to see. Thus, we recognize quickly and easily how the Arapesh have been molded by their culture, but it is more difficult to see how our own hidden rules operate.

In order to appreciate fully the view of culture as a coercive force it must be seen, at least partially, as a response to earlier theories which emphasized the determinism of biological-genetic factors. Innate endowments could not be regarded as determining personality and behavior if the same deterministic potential was attributed to culture. One of the strengths of Mead's theory was its appreciation of the interplay between the cultural and the biological, and this also characterized Thomas' theory which will be examined shortly.

Mead noted that in societies like the Arapesh and the Mundugumor, a single social personality was considered ideal. With respect to deviance, sex is irrelevant in such societies. Excessive kindness is equally likely to characterize a Mundugumor male or female, and such deviance is unaffected by the gender of the deviant. In other societies, such as the Tchambuli or our own, where the social personalities of males and females are differentiated, a poor fit between an individual's temperament and the expectations associated with that person's sex role becomes an additional source of deviation. For example, the Tchambuli man's emotional dependence and "commercial" irresponsibility correspond with historical views of American women, while the hard-working, disciplined Tchambuli woman corresponds with the American male. Thus, sex-role social types that are considered ideal in one society may be highly deviant in another society.

When her field work among these three New Guinea cultures was completed, Mead returned to New York. In subsequent years she made repeated trips to Pacific islands to extend her observational base and made increasing efforts to view American society from this comparative perspective. Most of her observations were full of implications for American society, but American society also presented complexities that were not encountered in studying primitive societies in New Guinea. One apparent difference is diversity. While primitive societies tend to be relatively homogeneous, different ethnic groups, social classes, and the like, make American society very heterogeneous. Social and sex-role ideals vary within distinctive subcultures. A second difference between the United States and primitive societies is in the rate with which patterns change. Traditions remained unaltered in New Guinea for many generations, but in modern societies they can change quickly. Thus, in less than a decade it becomes possible to say whether a gentleman should offer a Tiparillo to a lady.

Despite the diversity, Mead argued that it was still possible to infer some general, overarching cultural patterns in American because the same ideals were continuously intruding into traditionally different ways of life. As an example, she described the modern crib (in 1949), pictured in a two-story white house with green shutters.[8] In lonely shacks on the Western plains or the Southern mountains, the crib, the house, and the way of life they symbolize may be totally foreign in some regards. However, the image is here. Even if the people do not own a modern crib, they have seen it in a mail order catalogue, on a calendar, in a movie. The image of the (standard) "American way" slowly breaks down tradition. Mothers may still wear long calico skirts like their grandmothers, but their daughters are wearing "cheap but authentic" versions of Fifth Avenue and Hollywood Boulevard styles.

Little did Mead realize, in 1949, that grandmother's long dresses would again be in style. However, the important point is not the dress, the crib, or the suburban house, but the values and ways of behaving that are associated with each. In other words, the new images and material possessions signal the diffusion of a new way of life throughout the society.

Gender in the Workplace

In the years which followed Mead's description of grandmother's long dresses, there were consistent increases in the proportion of women who found salaried employment outside of their homes. The organizations in which they work

---

[8]Margaret Mead, *Male and Female* (New York: Mentor, 1955). (Originally published in 1949.) See especially Chapter 12.

remain highly segregated by sex, though. In some instances, segregation is by design; that is, due to men's conscious efforts to keep women out of some male bastions, or due to women's desires to work in jobs that have historically been occupied by women. In many instances, however, occupational sex segregation is maintained by cultural beliefs about men and women which hover in the background, implicitly affecting decisions and operating like hidden rules.

Rosabeth Kanter has observed that within many corporations, women have been excluded from managerial positions by a "masculine" connotation of management.[9] To be specific, it has been assumed that managers ought to have a single-minded concern with efficiency and be completely rational. Women have typically been considered too emotional, too irrational and too preoccupied with family matters to be dedicated and effective managers. As a result, they were bypassed for promotions.

The cultural stereotype of women helped to produce a situation in which the managerial ranks were almost exclusively filled by men. However, past practices have continued to affect organizational actions in a variety of ways. For example, Kanter notes, women were (and are) concentrated in secretarial and clerical positions. This has often meant working in all female groups (e.g., typing pools) with males as their superiors. One result of this work organization has been to limit women's aspirations; and limited aspirations have been realistic because their opportunities for mobility into managerial positions from secretarial-clerical positions have been almost non-existent. The limited aspirations of women then came to be perceived by male managers as proof that the women were not really committed, or loyal, to the organization.

Kanter claims that managers enjoy interacting with others who "fit," and they control access to the managerial ranks accordingly. Women have seemed not to fit. They seemed, for example, to be less loyal. In general, the managers felt they could trust only their "own kind" of person—their own kind almost always turned out to be another man.

There are, of course, other explanations for why so few women have historically been managers. Some more psychologically oriented theories have emphasized women's early socialization experiences. The ways in which females were raised in our society are viewed as making them generally less assertive and less committed to success in the business world. Kanter's position tends to reverse this causal sequence, regarding women's characteristics (e.g., limited aspirations) as the result of their subordinated positions rather than vice versa. Further, even when it may be unclear which came first, it is clear, in Kanter's view, that subordinated positions have reinforced women's work orientations.[10]

---

[9]Rosabeth Moss Kanter, *Men and Women of the Corporation* (New York: Basic Books, 1977).

[10]For a comparison of different approaches to sexual segregation in organizations, see Linda Blum and Vicki Smith, "Women's Mobility in the Corporation," *Signs: Journal of Women in Culture and Society*, 13 (1988).

THOMAS ON MOTIVATION AND CHANGE

When the rate of change is rapid, social disorganization often results. Individuals are caught between conflicting "worlds," with cultural ideals that call forth very different responses. The last decade has provided an interesting case in point, but it is not unique in this regard. There were many rapid changes, especially in American cities, during the first decades of the twentieth century, and they were the basis for the fascinating and timeless analyses of W. I. Thomas.

The theories of Thomas and Mead are alike in many respects. One important similarity is their shared emphasis upon an interaction between biological and social forces. Thomas's doctoral dissertation, for example, was an examination of how biological factors account for different propensities toward criminal behavior in men and women. Thomas is also remembered for his motivational theory of four wishes, an attempt to systematically classify human motives. Specifically, he proposed four universal wishes entailing desires for: new experiences, security, response and recognition. He thought that there was a general correspondence between these motives and the human nervous system and also argued that they were related to the "fundamental instincts."[11]

However, like Mead, Thomas also stressed the interplay between biological endowments and social forces. He viewed social organization, including culture, as shaping both the intensity of the wishes and their form of expression. The first wish noted by Thomas, for example, was the desire for "new experience." It involves a craving for excitement, and Thomas regarded it as a "carry over" from the species' earliest experiences as hunters. In contemporary societies, the craving for excitement can be an impetus to participation in sports contests, gambling, delinquency, even scientific research. The strength of each wish has a biological basis that influences the degree to which an individual's life will be dominated by a desire for excitement or a desire for cautious security. A person's life experiences can temper the drive, but only within certain limits. Its form of expression is completely socially determined, though; that is, social conditions determine whether excitement will be sought at a roulette table or in a research laboratory.

Thomas described hedonistic delinquents, and others, as people who were under the control of the desire for exciting new experiences. Their impulses could be constructively converted into other (that is, nondelinquent) realms, but the force behind the drive could not be totally altered. Thus, it is unlikely that they could be completely remolded into timid and cautious people. Most people, however, are motivated by a variety of drives, and they also have a wish for recognition and approval that helps to keep all the other drives in check. This wish provides society with its most effective means of social control because in order to obtain approval, the individual must express the drives in socially acceptable ways.

---

[11]W. I. Thomas, *The Unadjusted Girl* (New York: Harper and Row, Pub. 1967). (Originally published in 1923.) See Chapter One.

In sum, neither Thomas nor Mead viewed the human infant as an "empty slate." What Mead described as varying temperaments and what Thomas described as the biological basis of the strength of different motives were seen to differentiate among people at birth. However, both viewed most people as malleable and saw society (or culture) as having a vested interest in channeling their development along with coercive powers—when needed—to mold them. Finally, both regarded deviants as being produced by a poor fit between individual predispositions and social expectations.

Because of differences in who they were studying, and when, Thomas and Mead differed in their attention to processes of change. The primitive societies observed by Mead, as already noted, were relatively unchanging. By contrast, Thomas did his graduate training at the University of Chicago (Ph.D. in 1896) and then spent almost 25 years on the faculty there. This was a time when large numbers of immigrants were settling in Chicago and fitfully accommodating to urban and industrial ways of life. Changes between generations of immigrants were pronounced. So, too, were sex-role changes. Correspondingly, Thomas's first major study was an examination of Polish peasants, both in Europe and the United States. While the family had once been the primary group in which these peasants had participated, new political and community groups were becoming increasingly important. The old social hierarchy, based upon family status and tied to a rural way of life, was also declining in significance. All of these changes required individual adjustments that could not be made in accordance with traditional norms because these norms were tied to a rural peasant life that was dying.[12] It was difficult for these people to respond to the new industrial-urban context because it was difficult for them to drop old ways, and new ways had not yet crystallized.

Several years later, Thomas viewed the same kind of problems of transition as creating strains for young girls, many of whom were the offspring of immigrants. He studied their dilemmas by examining numerous personal documents, such as family correspondence, diaries, and letters to the editors of various publications. His books on the unadjusted girl and the Polish peasants are replete with extended quotations from these personal documents that are fascinating in their own right. His skillful utilization of these documents also made an important methodological contribution because it encouraged ensuing sociologists to utilize a wider variety of data sources in empirical studies.

Juxtaposed to the traditional standards of feminine propriety, Thomas observed, were more fashionable images of the "modern girl." They were presented in store windows and newspaper advertisements, and they bombarded women with new dress codes, work opportunities, and so on. The way in which the female sex role ought to be played has become vague, he concluded, because "there are rival definitions of the situation, and none of them is binding."[13]

---

[12]W. I. Thomas and Florian Znaniecki, *The Polish Peasant in Europe and America* (New York: Dover, 1958). (Originally published in 1918.) See especially pp. 87-302.

[13]Thomas, *The Unadjusted Girl*, p. 82.

Definitions of the Situation

This conception of definitions of a situation probably became Thomas's most enduring contribution to sociological theory. He introduced this concept by noting the unique capacities of human beings to inhibit previously learned responses; that is, to change the way they behave in familiar, recurring situations. This internal capacity which permits people to unlearn makes self-determined behavior possible because it enables examination and deliberation to occur before action. This preliminary thought produces a definition of the situation with which the individual decides what behavior is appropriate. Thus, what a person thinks and does is a function of such situational definitions. It was this view that made Thomas's utilization of personal documents so appropriate because understanding a person's definition of a situation often requires extensive understanding of the person as well as the situation. His single most famous remark in this regard was, "If men define situations as real, they are real in their consequences."[14] For example, if you interpreted the creaking of the walls in your house as indicating the roof was going to collapse, you would probably run outside. What you defined as real would be real in its consequences for your behavior.

However, Thomas did not regard definitions of situations as typically being idiosyncratic. The child is always born, he noted, into a group of people who have already defined most situations, including the behavior that is correspondingly appropriate. The socialization process may, therefore, be viewed as entailing the substitution of "moral codes" for spontaneous definitions of the situation. However, the codes of conduct that are considered proper by some segments of the society may be the personification of evil to other segments.

In contemporary societies, diverse definitions of the situation are virtually assured by differences among social classes. Because of vast differences in the resources at people's disposal, the same situations are perceived differently, and different solutions to the same problem are indicated. Consider, for example, the problem of eating, or of obtaining food. An increase in the price of caviar does not affect the frame of reference of poor people. It creates an adjustment problem only for rich people who are accustomed to eating it. By contrast, the difficulties faced by poor people may lead them to define cans of cat food as edible, an alternative that is far outside the frame of reference of the wealthy.

Delinquent Subcultures

Any circumstance that produces a problem can be resolved, according to Cohen, in either of two ways: by changes in actors' frames of reference or by changes in the actual situation.[15] However, it must be recognized that situational definitions, which "create" solutions, do in fact change the situation for the parties involved. Many people, for example, feel apprehensive when they are near a cemetery. Some people

---

[14]W.I. Thomas and Dorothy S. Thomas, *The Child in America* (New York: Knopf, 1928).

[15]Albert K. Cohen, *Delinquent Boys* (New York: Free Press, 1955).

respond by going miles out of their way to avoid seeing one. Upon encountering a cemetery, other people will whistle, hold their breath, clutch a button, or the like. The objective situation—dead people buried in the cemetery—remains unaltered; but the solutions that are believed to be efficacious by people do change the situation, for them. They whistle as though they were unafraid of a cemetery, and they do not feel apprehensive. They define cat food as edible, and they do not go hungry.

Most people acquire the "solutions" of their immediate social milieu. Through interaction, people validate each other's frame of reference. To maintain the respect and acceptance of others, people must ordinarily continue to accept these shared standards. For most people, Cohen notes, it is too isolating to "go it alone."

Some standards permeate an entire society, but many are specific to particular groups. In most instances, the status evaluations of particular groups are based upon the attributes believed to be characteristic of members and the perception of a discrepancy between the way they value these attributes and their apparent value in the larger society. A religious cult, for example, may be based upon a distinctive assessment of personal goodness, a disdain for material possessions, or any other perception that is relatively unique to the group. The more unique these perceptions and the more tightly integrated the group, the more the standards of external groups are rejected, and the more members are dependent upon the group.

Cohen applies this general perspective to delinquent gangs and it seems to provide an explanation for their otherwise unintelligible behavior. If a lower-class youth accepts the standards of the middle class, a low self-evaluation follows. Given the resource differential, a lower-class youth is also less likely to be successful if he or she accepts middle-class emphases upon striving to attain success: Perform well in school, go to college, and the like. However, groups tend to value the attributes their members appear to possess. What qualities can adolescents possess that are unrelated to the class structure? They can be tough, mean, and loyal; and they can enjoy sex, drugs, and excitement of the moment at no class disadvantage. These are precisely the characteristics that Cohen notes are associated with delinquent gangs. Thus, the delinquent does not feel worthless or unsuccessful because the frame of reference of the gang runs counter to adult, or middle-class, norms. The objective class situation, and its attendant problems, have not been altered. However, the distinctive frame of reference developed by the lower-class gang provides as complete a solution to the problems its members confront as would a change in objective circumstances.

Cuzzort likens Cohen's analysis to Aesop's fable of the sour grapes. In the fable the fox could not reach the grapes so he tried to convince himself they were sour, anyway. The reader is pretty convinced that the fox is really disappointed in this story. His attempt to fool himself does not seem very successful. Suppose, however, Cuzzort writes, that a gang of foxes he was friendly with told him that the farmer had poisoned the grapes. The fox's "sour-grapes" attitude would now seem factually justified, at least to the fox and his friends.[16] By analogy, depreciating

---

[16]R. P. Cuzzort, *Humanity and Modern Sociological Thought* (New York: Holt, Rinehart and Winston, 1969).

middle-class values of ambition, self-control, respect for property, and the like provides a thorough solution to the problems of lower-class delinquents.

DIVERSITY AND DEMORALIZATION

The nuclear family, the extended family, and the community have historically been the defining and controlling agents. (To define is to control, in a most effective manner.) The community, in particular, was especially extensive as a controlling agent. Thomas described its extensiveness by quoting a Polish peasant who stated that, "It reaches as far as a man is talked about."[17] Given the nature of European peasant communities, this was very far, indeed. As illustrative, Thomas quotes from a 20-year-old Jewish woman who was born in America, but whose parents were immigrants from Hungary. She was raised in a traditional manner but fell in love with a gentile man whom she met in school and married. This violated her community's fundamental definitions of appropriate behavior. It carried consequences she later regretted and so she sought a legal termination to the marriage.

> I merely ask his aid in somehow obtaining a divorce, so that I may return to my people ... I cannot stand the loneliness and do not want to be hated, denounced and spurned by all.[18]

Today, (that is, circa 1920), Thomas noted, the family and the community have lost most of their capacities to make their definitions of situations stick. Young people travel further from home and even when they are not separated, family member—including young girls—leave home every day to go to work. The mass media present new images and stimulate new cravings. New inventions also change the environment so rapidly that they lead to new and deviant definitions of situations. As examples, Thomas notes that the invention of the bank check led to forgery; the match, to arson; the automobile, to higher rates of seduction.[19] The rate of change, in and of itself, has a disorganizing effect because definitions of each situation abound, and none of them is binding. In other words, what is appropriate increasingly becomes a matter of individual conscience.

This increase in freedom, the ability to define situations according to personal preference, has some obviously desirable features for individuals, but only to a limited degree. Beyond a certain point, the disorganization that is generated by the lack of shared definitions becomes demoralizing to these same individuals. Thomas felt that young women were particularly prone to the demoralizing effects of social disorganization and described numerous examples of women who became prostitutes, alcoholics, "lady bums," and the like. They were forced to develop novel definitions of situations because their actions brought them into unique situations. One of them wrote about her strategy for coping as follows:

[17]Thomas, *The Unadjusted Girl*, p. 44.
[18]Ibid., p. 51.
[19]Ibid., p. 71.

You will argue that a woman with an empty stomach and a fur coat ought to sell the coat for a shabby one and spend the money for food. That is because you have never been a lady bum. A fur coat gets her places that a full stomach never would. It is her entree into hotel washrooms when she is dirty from job hunting. And in the last stages, it gets her help from a certain class of people who would be glad to help her if she lost her purse, but who never would if she never had a purse.[20]

Choices for the 1990s

Since Thomas' death in 1947 there have been dramatic changes in the roles legitimately open to women in our society. Can we conclude from these changes that there has been a crystallization of women's values, resulting in fewer conflicts in their definitions of situations? Are the choices a lot easier for the young women of the 1990s than they were for their mothers?

In order both to document and to clarify the changes, Florentine has analyzed the national surveys conducted yearly, since 1969, among college freshmen. A representative sample of over 200,000 freshmen are surveyed each year at about 350 colleges. The questionnaire results show an unmistakable increase in the importance of occupational attainment goals to young college women. Between 1969 and 1984, it became increasingly important to them to: have administrative responsibility, obtain recognition from colleagues, become an authority in their fields, and so on. In all of the preceding respects they were almost exactly the same as men by 1984.[21]

Male and female college freshmen also became almost identical in the percentage who were planning to go on for advanced professional degrees in medicine, law, and so on. To illustrate: in 1969, freshmen men were more than five times more likely than women to aspire to careers as doctors or dentists. By 1984, they were almost exactly equal.

The importance of raising a family declined for both males and females during the 1970s, then increased again. The values of the sexes also converged on this part of life. Specifically, the percentage of women who considered it very important to raise a family declined from 78 percent in 1969 to under 60 percent in the mid-1970s, then increased to 69 percent in 1984. The comparable figure for men in 1984 was 68 percent. Thus, it is clear that family as well as career plans became increasingly alike for men and women.

It should be noted that a sample of college freshmen tends to exclude young people from poor homes. For the more affluent young people who are represented, however, the preceding figures seem to paint an optimistic picture, especially when examined over time. The sexes have converged, and most women are planning both careers and families. However, it must be stressed that we are examining people's values and life plans and everything may not work out as easily as the freshmen hoped.

Prior to the 1990s, the responsibility for raising a family disproportionately fell to women. When they took time out of work to have and care for children, it

[20]Ibid., p. 33.

[21]Robert Florentine, "Increasingly Similarity in the Value and Life Plans of Male and Female College Students?" *Sex Roles*, 18 (1988).

adversely affected their occupational mobility. Will raising children continue to mean time out of women's careers? If so, will such work disruptions persist in having negative impacts upon mobility? If the answers to the preceding questions are affirmative—in other words, if the patterns of the past continue—then the young women of the 1990s may still face some difficult choices.

CONCLUSION

The theories of Mead and Thomas, as previously noted, are highly compatible. Viewed conjointly, they sensitize us to a number of important issues. First, there need be no pronounced differences in sex roles within a society, or in the temperaments attributed to males and females. The Arapesh and the Mundugumor make that point. Where gender is the basis of differentiation within a society, the roles of men and women can be different from each other in almost any respect. The men can be timid and the women dominant, or vice versa. From infancy on, each person learns what is expected of someone of their gender. These definitions of the situation are pervasive and seem so "natural," they are hardly even noticed. Part of the coercive power of culture is due to the fact that it operates, normally, in a very subtle manner. It is obtrusive, but unnoticed.

The sex roles that are endemic to a society become part of everyone's definition of situations. (Should a gentleman offer a Tiparillo to a lady?) Attributed temperaments and social roles, differentiated by sex, become "engraved in granite," parts of unquestioned moral codes, almost. Almost, because they do change, if ever so slowly. However, such changes either produce social disorganization, or are symptomatic of it, because definitions of situations, differentiated by sex, are an integral part of the social fabric. Rival definitions of situations and ensuing conflicts and uncertainties are inevitable until a new set of expectations (definitions) are in place.

SUGGESTIONS FOR ADDITIONAL READING

PAT CAPLAN (Ed), *The Cultural Construction of Sexuality*. London: Tavistock, 1987.
BETH B. HESS and MYRA MARX FERREE (Eds.), *Analyzing Gender*. Beverly Hills, CA: Sage, 1987.
GARY SCHWARTZ, *Beyond Conformity or Rebellion: Youth and Authority in America*. Chicago: University of Chicago Press, 1987.

3

Social and Personality Systems
Talcott Parsons

In an interesting experiment, Freedman and several associates paid college students to perform some unusual tasks, such as telling lies about tests or knocking stacks of thesis note cards off of a table. Before they served as subjects in this experiment, most of the students had not routinely gone around lying about tests or disrupting thesis research. Even though they were following a researcher's directions, many of them felt guilty about what they had done. Then the students were given an opportunity to serve as unpaid subjects in a subsequent experiment in which they would perform some good deeds. The students who felt guilt after the first experiment were found to be more likely to volunteer for the second. It seemed as though they wanted to make up for their lies and disruptions. Perhaps they thought that a good deed would help to reduce the guilt they felt.[1]

In a simplified way, these students behaved just the way we ordinarily expect people to act. When more consequential acts than telling lies about tests have been involved, vintage literary works have repeatedly explored how guilt can become a driving force. It has been variously portrayed as causing people to experience nightmares, incessantly wash their hands, enter nunneries, commit suicide, join the foreign legion, and so forth. In all of these instances, the attempt to expiate guilt operates as a central and compelling force in peoples' lives.

How people will generally seek to cope with guilt varies historically and across cultures. The conditions under which guilt is aroused similarly varies. If we were stranded somewhere with our dog and became so hungry that we ate our dog, it would weigh heavily upon us. An Eskimo, by contrast, would consider it a prudent and appropriate act and would correspondingly feel no remorse.

---

[1]J. L. Freedman and others, "Compliance Without Pressure," *Journal of Personality and Social Psychology,* 7 (1967).

Even within the same society, the same acts are not equally likely to produce guilt among persons in different social classes, ethnic groups, age categories, and so on. These variations occur because of differences in personal standards. People feel guilt only when they believe they have violated an expectation to which they personally adhere. At the same time, however, most of these standards are shared rather than private; that is, held in common by most members of a community or society. Therefore, they are social as well as personal standards.

The way in which social expectations are internalized by individuals was a central part of the theory presented by Talcott Parsons. His writings will provide our major topic in this chapter. In the final section of this chapter we will consider the possibility that Parsons's theory went too far; that is, robbed people of their private passions by viewing them as mere incorporations of social standards.

PARSONS'S INFLUENCE

From roughly the late 1930s through the first part of the 1960s, Talcott Parsons was probably the single most influential figure in sociology. His domination over sociological theory was especially pronounced in the United States—where he spent most of his career, as a professor at Harvard—but it was by no means confined to this side of the ocean.

Parsons's objective was tremendously ambitious: to present the most inclusive and widely applicable theoretical explanation for the actions of both individuals and collectivities. He began by building upon the work of such earlier social theorists as Weber (whose work he translated and edited), Pareto, and Durkheim. He was also influenced by Freud. Furthermore, he collaborated with major figures in anthropology, experimental psychology, and other social sciences, incorporating perspectives from their disciplines into his theory as well.

Many sociologists have always had great difficulty understanding Parsons's writing. Some of their difficulties can be attributed to the nature of his enterprise. He was attempting to forge a synthesis from among diverse perspectives, some of which—Weber's, for example—were themselves not yet widely understood when he began writing. In addition, Parsons's ambitious goal of developing a broadly inclusive theory resulted in a mode of presentation that was necessarily very abstract.

Apart from the nature of his project, however, would-be readers encountered difficulty as the result of Parsons's writing style, especially in his earlier books. Perhaps because most of his graduate studies were done in Heidelberg, his writing, which was in English, often read like a foreign language. Parsons' fractured syntax produced endless sentences containing clarifications and qualifications that often obliterated the basic points.

After perhaps a quarter of a century in a position of eminence, Parsons's influence declined markedly. During the late 1960s and 1970s, when Parsons was mentioned in sociological writings it was usually with derision. This decline in influence has several possible explanations. One of the most important is a conservative bias that runs through much of Parsons's writing. It contained an implicit commitment to the status quo that ran counter to the desires of many sociologists to enact change, especially during the turbulence of the late 1960s and 1970s. Many sociologists of every political–ideological pursuasion also came to realize that a lot of Parsons's circumlocutory sentences merely inflated some pretty simple notions. Readers were tortured to translate his writing into comprehensible English only to discover that once the ideas were apparent they were already familiar with them. Many readers wearied of the task in light of its paltry return.[2]

While many factors may have contributed to the apparent decline in Parsons' influence, I think that one additional and important reason is that his early writings were so influential that they helped to shape modern conceptions of sociology itself. Then the conceptions and the man were divorced from each other. For example, he certainly was not the first to write about such concepts as social systems and social integration; but his writings contributed to the central roles later occupied by such concepts, and he strongly influenced the way these concepts came to be thought about. To later sociologists, who were thinking in ways Parsons had influenced without recognizing the source of the influence, reading Parsons in the original often seemed to yield few insights.

At about the time of Parsons's death in 1979, there was a resurgence of interest in his writings.[3] Many theorists recognized that for some years Parsons' sociology was unduly equated with the conservative bias in his theory. Seen in a larger context, however, that was only a small part of his legacy. One of the major figures contributing to the reawakened interest in Parsons was Jeffrey Alexander. He proposed to "rebuild" theoretical sociology around the concepts of social action and social order that Parsons had emphasized. While Alexander was also critical of Parsons's biases, in some instances, he helped to recast debate among theorists back to the abstract questions that Parsons had formulated.[4] Our attention turns now to the core of Parsons's actual writings.

THE THREE SYSTEMS

Parsons began by stating that action has four characteristics: a goal, a motivation (involving the expenditure of energy), a situation, and normative regulation. He illustrated each by describing a man driving to a lake to go fishing. Fishing is the

---

[2]For some humorous "translations" of Parsons, see C. Wright Mills, *The Sociological Imagination* (New York: Oxford, 1959).

[3]For an overview, see David Sciulli and Dean R. Gerstein, "Social Theory and Talcott Parsons in the 1980s." In Ralph H. Turner (Ed), *Annual Review of Sociology,* 11. Palo Alto, CA: Annual Review, 1985.

[4]Jeffrey C. Alexander, *Theoretical Logic in Sociology.* Berkeley: University of California Press. Most relevant are volumes 1 (1982) and 4 (1984). For a thorough analysis of Alexander's work, see especially the first half of, Walter L. Wallace, "Review Essay: Alexanderian Sociology." *American Journal of Sociology,* 90 (1984).

goal; driving there takes effort requiring motivation; the car, the road, and so on describe the situation; and the way the man drives down the road reflects normative regulation. Behavior which can be described according to these four characteristics is termed, "action," and action provided the elementary unit in Parsons's theory.[5] However, he went on to state that actions, such as the man's fishing trip, are not usually discrete. They are parts of constellations of actions, termed "systems."

At the most general level, Parsons classified systems of action as organized into two realms: personality systems and social systems. The *personality system* comprises the motivations and goals of individuals; more specifically, it includes both the content and mode of integration of motivations and goals. The *social system* involves interaction between actors and the situational norms which regulate that interaction. Thus, the four characteristics of systems of action are further attributed to the personality system (goals and motivation) and the social system (situations and norms). While these two systems of action are differentiated from each other in this way, Parsons stressed their overlap, or the way in which aspects of one influence the other.

Parsons also described a *cultural system,* comprised of the values, beliefs, and symbols which pervade a society. These values and symbols are organized and integrated vis-à-vis each other. Therefore, they constitute a system. However, they do not, themselves, directly entail action so the cultural system is not a system of action in the same sense as the other two. The cultural system's effect upon behavior is indirect, resulting from its important influence upon both personality and social systems. (Some of Parsons' writing also included the organism as a fourth action system. It was the least developed system in his model and is not presented here for that reason.)

The primary effect of the cultural system upon the social system involves the influence of general value standards over the normative regulation of situations. In other words, while norms vary from situation to situation, they are all likely to be congruent with pervasive cultural values. The derivation of norms (in the social system) from common value orientations (in the cultural system) was termed *institutionalization.* These cultural values also penetrate the personality system in a process called *internalization.* Thus, common values lie at the innermost core and shape both personality and social systems in their image.

Institutionalization and internalization, according to Parsons, create solidarity and integration within a society. Because the social system's rules have a common source, they will ordinarily be congruent with each other. Conflict because of inconsistent rules will occur only in exceptional instances. Because of their derivation from common values, people will also consider the rules to be legitimate, or binding. Further, as a result of internalization, people will personally adhere to the

---

[5]Talcott Parsons, *The Structure of Social Action* (New York: McGraw-Hill, 1937); and Talcott Parsons and Edward A. Shils, eds., *Toward A General Theory of Action* (New York: Harper and Row, 1962). (Originally published in 1951.)

same rules. People will not ordinarily be marching to the tune of different drummers. If there is full institutionalization and internalization in a society, interaction will necessarily have a harmonious and conflictless quality, and the social system will be highly integrated.[6]

Parsons recognized that no actual social system was ever likely to attain perfect integration. Some "slippage" was always to be expected. For example, some individuals may want to comply with particular role expectations, but be unable to do so. At the opposite extreme, however, Parsons considered and rejected the possibility of complete disintegration. Thomas Hobbes's "state of nature," amounting to "war of all against all," could never be realized because some degree of internalization must always occur in the course of youngsters' socialization. Therefore, the personal and social needs of people will lead them to conform with at least some of other peoples' expectations. They will also be sensitive, in general, to the fact that others have expectations. In other words, the socialized human being cannot wantonly disregard others' expectations; furthermore, in Parsons' view, he or she does not want to ignore expectations. Hobbes's question was of great importance to Parsons, however, and the social system he depicted was, in part, an attempt to account for why the state of nature could not characterize human society.

THE PATTERN VARIABLES AND AGIL

In any concrete situation, a person must decide how to act. The personality system of the person is obviously relevant, especially the person's goals and motivational levels of the moment. Is he or she hungry? Feeling the need of social support because of an untimely event? In the final analysis, however, Parsons sees actors as generally being in control; that is, able to decide how to behave in a concrete situation. As the person deliberates about how to act, a series of decisions must be reached. In a discussion that is almost identical to W. I. Thomas's view (see Chapter Two), but includes no reference to Thomas, Parsons describes how an actor must determine "the meaning of a situation . . . for him . . . before he can act with respect to that situation."[7]

There may, of course, be many idiosyncratic elements in any individual's definition of any concrete situation. In general, however, Parsons argued that they could all be classified into one of five dichotomous choices he termed the pattern variables. The five, and their definitions, are as follows:

1) *Affectivity-neutrality*—to seek immediate gratifications or exert restraint.
2) *Self-collectivity*—to pursue private goals or collective interests.
3) *Universalism-particularism*—to treat people (or objects) as elements of a class, or according to their unique qualities.

[6]Parsons and Shils, *Toward a General Theory*, pp. 194 and 203.
[7]Ibid., p. 77.

4) *Ascription-achievement*—to emphasize given attributes of people (or objects), or their performance.

5) *Specificity-diffuseness*—to respond to restricted situational qualities, or to general features.

Definitions of the pattern variables, in general, are necessarily abstract because these five choices between polar opposites have four distinct referents. Specifically, the pattern variables are involved as

A) Individual choices confronted by every actor in every concrete situation.

B) General predispositions in actors' personality systems. A given individual, for example, may consistently have a need to seek immediate gratifications (affectivity) in a wide range of situations.

C) Expectations of role performance in the social system. For example, the president of a bank may be expected to invest some of the bank's funds in low-yield public interest projects (collective interests) rather than in maximum-return ventures (private goals).

D) Value standards in the cultural system. For example, in traditional societies, preferential treatment was generally accorded to persons born into high-status families (ascription), while in modern societies more emphasis is placed upon a person's performance (achievement).

In sum, the same dualities pertain to the personality, social, and cultural systems. Unlike the examples given though, actual decision making typically involves simultaneously taking two or more of the dimensions into account. Thus, when a student comes into my office to "bargain" for a grade at the end of a term and I make a decision how to respond, I will probably take each of the five polarities into account, to varying degrees. For example, I might want to please the student so that he or she will think well of me now (immediate gratification). The student's age, sex, or race might also predispose me to try to help (ascription). However, I also believe that all students should be treated the same (universalism). Therefore, I will have to balance and weigh these opposite considerations. A similar kind of juggling act, involving the same criteria, is occurring in the social and cultural systems.

AGIL

Throughout his career, Parsons was concerned with the *functional imperatives* of action systems. In his later writings, however, he devoted more systematic attention to the issue and a typology of imperatives largely replaced the pattern variables. Specifically, he proposed that there were at least four major functions which every action system had to meet or satisfy:

1) *Adaptation*—every action system must attain resources and/or facilities from its environment and then allocate them, as needed, throughout the system. For different subsystems, resources could entail food, ideas, new business capital, or the like. As situations change, new modes of adaptation must be innovated.

2) *Goal attainment*—each subsystem has a primary objective that it must be successful in attaining to some minimal degree, or the sub-system will not be able to persist

(unchanged). At the overall action system level, goal attainment primarily entails the satisfaction of personality system needs.

3) *Integration*—within any action system there must be coordination among the individuals and collectivities that comprise the unit. In addition, Parsons stressed the need for integration among all the action systems. He viewed this as the primary responsibility of the social system.

4) *Latency, or pattern maintenance*—to remain coherent, systems must maintain symbolic meanings as embodied in moral codes, religious belief systems, and so on. Maintenance of pattern is a need of all systems, but at the overall level, because of its symbolic content, it is the primary responsibility of the cultural system.

STABILITY OF THE SOCIAL SYSTEM

As a sociologist, Parsons' primary interest was in the social system. His attention to cultural and personality systems was based upon the premise that they were so interconnected with the social system that the social system (roughly equated with a society) could not be analyzed in isolation. His analysis of the functional prerequisites of a society further articulated the nature of these interconnections.[8]

By functional prerequisites he meant those processes or conditions which were imperative for a society to persist unaltered from generation to generation. Alternatively, if change occurred, it should be orderly; that is, occur without disrupting social integration.[9] According to Parsons, the major prerequisites involved congruence between the social and the other two systems, and their mutual support. More specifically, the social system must not be incompatible with the biological needs of people. No system could persist if it permanently condemned eating. It must also be consistent with needs that are lodged in personality systems. Thus, there must be opportunities for sexual release, although they are normatively regulated.

Control over the motivations of individuals was especially crucial to Parsons' model. This involved control over both "positive" motivations—those which induced people to participate in and support the social system—and control over "negative" motivations—those which would otherwise lead people to disrupt the system. (Note that these statements are excellent examples of Parsons's conservative bias. The emphasis is upon how to maintain an established system. Efforts to change a system are regarded as deviant or disruptive.)

Given Parsons' emphasis upon the social control of individual motivation, it is not surprising that he paid a good deal of attention to the process of socialization. He viewed it, first, as a learning experience; in particular, learning how to play various social roles (for example, student, mother, boy scout, and the like). In addition, he viewed socialization as entailing the person's acquisition of "equilibrating" processes: internal mechanisms with which individuals cope with their

[8]See Talcott Parsons, *The Social System* (New York: Free Press, 1951), especially pp. 26-36.

[9]The kinds of "progressive" changes Parsons would accept in this context are described by Parsons in two of his later books: *Societies* (Englewood Cliffs: Prentice-Hall, 1966); and the *System of Modern Societies* (Englewood Cliffs: Prentice-Hall, 1971).

personality needs and adjust these needs to current and future (that is, anticipated) role expectations.

Following Freud's conception, Parsons viewed personality as a system comprising components that did not necessarily fit together harmoniously, but would ultimately establish some kind of internal truce. However, Freud described people under the influence of powerful libidinous drives. These unconscious, sexual-in-origin drives were regarded, by Freud, as highly potent. Despite Parsons' acknowledged indebtedness to Freud, his own description of the personality system included relatively weak unconscious drives. In other words, while Freud viewed base, unconscious drives as dictating to people, Parsons viewed them as easy to restrain. A society of people driven by unconscious drives could bring about Hobbes' state of nature, a possibility which Parsons found unimaginable. Correspondingly, he viewed the socialization process as typically resulting in extensive ego development; that is, people who can restrain their impulses while figuring out how to define a situation.[10] In addition, by stressing the internalization of values, Parsons suggests that there will be strong superegos to form coalitions with egos in order to suppress disruptive quests for immediate gratification.

Once a social system is established, Parsons viewed actors as locked into the system via a process termed, *complementarity.* In any integrated social system roles are interlocked such that the rights of one position are the obligations of another. For example, if it is the right of a child to receive support, it is the obligation of parents to provide it. (Rights would otherwise be meaningless.) Complementarity occurs when actors are willing and able to comply with the expectations, or obligations, associated with their roles. As a result of socialization processes, their compliance is congruent with their internalized standards. Therefore, "inner voices" reward them for meeting the expectations of persons in complementary positions. At the same time, the other persons expect and value their compliance and reward it with their own positive responses.

Because of the dual rewards for compliance, and the corresponding control over motivational states, no change or deviance is expected to occur. The social system will persist unaltered. On the other hand, if change does occur, it will be orderly. No additional "special mechanisms" need to be inferred; Parsons stated: "Maintenance of the complimentarity of role-expectations, once established, is *not problematical.*[11]

Shame and Guilt

Role complementarity, in Parsons's view, comprises an individual's overt compliance with another person's expectations; for example, the compliance of a clerk with the expectations of a supervisor. Complementarity also involves more

---

[10]The degree to which this is a cognitive, rather than normative, process is not at all clear in Parsons' theory. For further discussion, see R. Stephen Warner, "Toward A Redefinition of Action Theory," *American Journal of Sociology,* 83 (1978). In the same volume, see the responses by Parsons and by Whitney Pope and Jere Cohen.

[11]Parsons, *The Social System,* p. 205.

than overt compliance, however. This "something more" is made clear by reconsidering the questions about guilt with which this chapter began.

One useful way to clarify the notion of guilt is to contrast it with shame. The latter requires witnesses or the detection of behavior which violates norms. In other words, shame is produced by others' observations. By contrast, guilt is aroused by an inner voice which scolds a person for violating internalized standards. Once moral precepts are internalized even the desire to violate them is sufficient to produce anxiety or a troubled conscience. From the standpoint of social control over an actor's impulses, Parsons viewed internalization (guilt) as more effective than monitoring (shame) precisely because the former does not depend upon external observers.

Following Freud and other psychologists, Parsons viewed internalization as typically based upon *identification*; that is, incorporation into the self of the values of a significant other.[12] It is possible to differentiate between them by viewing internalization as an internal commitment to a standard that is maintained without reference to the values associated with specific others.

EMPIRICAL APPLICATIONS

Aspects of Parsons's theory have been examined in numerous studies, and two of them will be examined in this section. However, Parson's work stimulated relatively few empirical investigations in comparison to its enormous theoretical influence. The abstract nature of the theory is one reason that it encouraged few concrete studies. The form of the theory is an even more important reason. From the preceding discussion of Parsons it should now be apparent to the reader that it was largely definitional in content; that is, presenting definitions of action, institutionalization, and so on. The definitions were intended to provide sociologists with a common frame of reference, and they were successful in this regard. Unlike hypotheses, however, definitions do not ordinarily lead to research. What is there to study?

Hypotheses encourage research by presenting guesses about how variables might be related to each other. When Parsons did not present definitions, he rarely speculated about relationships either. Rather, he emphasized "necessities"; that is, society *must* provide outlets for personality needs; all societies *must* involve institutionalization, and so on. In effect, these statements of necessities were much closer to being definitions than hypotheses.

Despite these shortcomings, Parsons's theory still provided a conceptual framework that has been applied to research questions and has been very widely utilized in interpreting actual results. The two examples to be considered here certainly do not prove that Parsons's theory is "correct." They do suggest its

---

[12]See the analysis by Edward C. Tolman, "A Psychological Model," in Parsons and Shils, *Toward a General Theory.*

usefulness; but most important, they help to clarify further some of Parsons's most basic concepts.

Drug Use

A number of studies have reported that between the ages of about 17 and 27, young people's tendencies to smoke marijuana decline. The decline appears to be associated with people's completion of school and entrance into adult work and marriage roles. The social timetables that people consider relevant to these role transitions seem not to include marijuana use. Among young adults (as opposed to late teens), marijuana use appears to be associated with "anticonforming" values that are incompatible with assuming adult work and family roles.

The timing of these drug use changes may make them very useful as illustrations of the role socialization process that Parsons emphasized. In particular, Yamaguchi and Kandel questioned whether the expectation of an event, such as marriage, exerted an effect upon marijuana use. Would the anticipation of marriage lead to the stoppage of drug use during the year prior to the actual marriage?[13]

The investigators examined the self-reported behavior of 1,325 young adults who were initially interviewed while in high school in New York State in the early 1970s and were then re-interviewed in the early 1980s. During this interim, the respondents reported on their drug taking and life event histories. Three specific family role changes were recorded for each person in the sample:

1) getting married for the first time,
2) getting divorced or separated from a first marriage,
3) having a first child.

Two transitions in marijuana use were also recorded:

1) initiating or resuming use,
2) stopping use.

The findings indicated that in the year prior to marriage and in the year prior to the birth of a first child, both men and women were significantly more likely to stop marijuana use than those who did not marry or have a first child. The incompatibility of marijuana and marriage–parenting was further shown by the fact that married persons who continued to use marijuana were more likely to become separated or divorced.

It is likely that smoking marijuana, in and of itself, is not a very important causal factor leading to the dissolution of marriages. Rather, the use of marijuana is probably indicative of a general lifestyle that entails less commitment to adult family roles. The successful anticipation of these roles correspondingly is apt to involve a host of adaptive changes of which marijuana use is only one indicator.

[13]Kazuo Yamaguchi and Denise Kandel, "On the Resolution of Role Incompatibility." *American Journal of Sociology*, 90 (1985).

This interpretation, it should be noted, is congruent with Parsons' view of a relatively stable social structure whose role expectations/needs are met through pervasive socialization processes.

Value Consensus

Parsons, you may recall, described the cultural system's penetration of the social and personality systems. This means that the values and beliefs that comprise the cultural system shape both situational norms and people's own preferences. So long as there is general agreement about a single set of values, the norms that regulate various situations will be congruent with: 1) each other, and 2) people's desires. Without such consensus, there might be conflicts between situations and/or between people's private selves and their role expectations. Thus, from Parsons's standpoint, value consensus was a very important assumption.

The kind of consensus Parsons regarded as typical was clarified by the results of a crime study reported by Peter Rossi and several associates. They asked a sample of adults in the city of Baltimore to rate the seriousness of 140 crimes. The major issue they wished to address with these ratings concerned the degree of agreement within the population. Specifically, they compared the average ratings of: blacks and whites, men and women, and persons with different levels of education. The correlations between the ratings of each subgroup were around .90 indicating a very substantial degree of agreement.[14]

Almost everyone within the sample considered crimes against persons, such as murder, to be the most serious. Intermediate ratings were accorded to property crimes, such as stealing a car. Least serious were white collar crimes, such as price fixing; and misdemeanors, such as public drunkeness.

It should be noted that the public's perception of the seriousness of crimes tends to correspond closely with the way the criminal justice system treats people who violate the relevant laws. Overall value consensus, from Parsons's perspective, should be reflected in codified norms (i.e., the criminal code), and the way judges, juries and law enforcement agencies carry out their roles.

THE CRITICISMS

Empirical studies, such as the ones reviewed in the preceding pages, have suggested the usefulness of Parsons' theorerical positions. His theories' influence upon other theories has also been extensive. However, Parsons' theory may also be unsurpassed in the number of criticisms it has engendered. Among the main contentions

---

[14]Peter H. Rossi, Emily Waite, Christine E. Boise, and Richard E. Berk, "The Seriousness of Crimes." *American Sociological Review,* 39 (1974). A more recent study, limited to sexual offenses, reports similar consensus. See Judith A. Howard, "A Structural Approach to Sexual Attitudes." *Sociological Perspectives,* 31 (1988).

are that Parsons overemphasized internalization and stability while correspondingly understating individuality and conflict.

Oversocialization

Dennis Wrong began his criticism of Parsons by returning to the Hobbesian question about a state of nature. It was, and is, a critical question, he concedes; but he argues that Parsons (and others) have responded inappropriately. In effect, by overemphasizing the internalization of social norms, Hobbes's question has been *dismissed* rather than answered.

It has been overly assumed, Wrong states, that people will behave in accordance with their internalized standards. Following Freud, and Parsons did, internalization assures only that people will feel guilt when they fail to live up to self-incorporated standards. It does not assure compliance. According to Freud, internalized moral codes are only one of the forces acting within the individual psyche. Superego formation, in and of itself, does not reduce the intensity of emotional drives, fantasies, and other potentially disruptive internal forces.

By ignoring the nonsocialized inner life of people, Wrong concludes, Parsons missed the fact that behavior is a problematic outcome of internal conflicts between impulses and controls. Hobbes's question was thereby dismissed when, for example, Parsons assumed that, once established, the continuation of complementarity is not problematic. In stressing the stability and integration of society, Parsons produced a model of human nature in which people are imagined as a "disembodied, conscience-driven, status-seeking phantom."[15]

Breaching Rules

It is clear that Parsons' model views people as behaving in a manner that is consistent with 1) the rules, and 2) their internalized preferences. In a stable society it is assumed that items 1 and 2 are the same; that is, that the same rules are internalized by everyone. This entails, according to Garfinkel, a view of people as "dopes" in that they are regarded as lacking the commonsense judgement with which to decide how to behave in a situation. Such a model would be all right if not for the fact that people are not dopes. To be more precise, Garfinkel's position is that the norms and roles which Parsons describes as "out there" guiding people's behavior are not what guide people's behavior, at all. Rather, the results of interaction are determined situationally, by the actors themselves as they actively construct and negotiate meanings.

Garfinkel has attempted to show that people confront situations judgmentally and develop a meaningful course of situationally appropriate action—without being totally bound by preexisting standards. Toward this end he has designed little experiments in which people deliberately violate conventional understandings and

---

[15]Dennis H. Wrong, "The Oversocialized Conception of Man in Modern Sociology," *American Sociological Review,* 26 (1961), 193.

then observe how others react. For example, he sent student-experimenters into retail stores with instructions to violate the fixed-price institution and offer the salesperson less than the established price. The student-experimenters initially felt some anxiety when they anticipated violating this shared understanding, but it quickly dissipated. After a couple of tries, discomfort tended to disappear, and most student-experimenters claimed to have enjoyed the task and indicated that they planned to bargain over prices in the future.[16]

It is true, Garfinkel concedes, that anticipatory anxiety often prevents some people from taking the first step and breaking a rule. However, social situations are rarely so standardized that all facets of the situation are governed by agreed-upon rules. Contingencies which require negotiation regularly arise in the course of interaction. Previously established (and internalized) values are seen as sufficient to completely explain social interaction only if people are regarded as dopes. It is more reasonable to expect, he argues, that the value positions people espouse will not perfectly predict how they will behave in a relevant situation.

An interesting example of such a discrepancy between words and deeds is provided by Thorton's long-term study of separation and divorce. Between 1962 and 1980, a Detroit area sample of women were interviewed six times. One part of the interview dealt with their attitudes toward divorce. For example: If there are children, should parents stay together even if they do not get along? As we would expect, attitudes toward divorce generally became more permissive during the study period. The finding that is most surprising from Parsons' perspective is the absence of a significant relationship between women's attitudes and their subsequent experience. Women were equally likely to terminate their marriages between 1962 and 1980, whether they approved or disapproved of divorce in 1962. When women with initially disapproving attitudes experienced difficulties in their marriage, Thorton concluded, they made divorce fit within their existing values or adjusted their attitudes.[17]

Conflict and Exploitation

Every theoretical perspective is ultimately judged on balance by its net contribution. The assets, or strengths, of a theory are the insights it suggests that might otherwise by overlooked. Its weaknesses are the opposite; namely, the observations and generalizations the theory obscures or neglects. Gouldner's critiques focus upon the costs of Parsons' theory, in terms of insights foregone. In particular, Gouldner sees conflict as embedded into both interpersonal relationships and the larger social structure. Despite the actual prevalence of such conflicts, he sees Parsons' theory as consistently leading sociologists to neglect conflict, or understate its prevalence.

Parsons systematically neglected conflict, in part, because he viewed social interaction as typically involving equal reciprocity among participants. Role com-

---

[16]Harold Garfinkel, "The Relevance of Common Understandings," in Irwin Deutscher, *What We Say/What We Do* (Glenview, Ill.: Scott, Foresman, 1973).

[17]Arland Thorton, "Changing Attitudes Toward Separation and Divorce." *American Journal of Sociology,* 90 (1985).

plementarity assumes that people are satisfied with what they are getting out of relationships; that is, enough money, enough respect, enough attention, or the like. For people to be satisfied, and thereby happy voluntarily to comply with others' expectations, does not literally require that they receive precisely as much as they give. At the same time, however, it is difficult to envision stable and continuing complementarity when role obligations are structured such that a preponderance of all the obligations fall to the incumbent of one role while all or most of the rights accrue to the other. Furthermore, role inequalities of this type *can* be viewed as pervasive; for example, as characterizing traditional sex-role relationships, the division of labor (proletarian-bourgeoisie), and so on.[18]

Structured role inequality produces situations in which a class of persons— that is, who occupy a set of roles—are exploited. Parsons's perspective directed attention away from such situations in contrast to Marx, for example, who called attention to them. (See Chapter Six.) Furthermore, regardless of inequalities, Parsons implies that people will continue to be locked into complementary roles and that they *should* be. Their continuing commitment to comply is required by society's need for stability and integration.

In addition to situations in which inequality is built into the role structure, Parsons virtually disregarded other kinds of conflict which could recurrently disrupt complementarity. For example, a person may periodically want to enlarge his or her rights vis-a-vis another's obligations. Alternatively, people may need to threaten or coerce in order to force others to make good on a social debt. According to Gouldner, these commonplace occurrences are virtually ignored by Parsons.

Gouldner also notes that Parsons's very conception of roles and role relationships is presented in a way that prevents sensitivity to conflict. Specifically, Parsons stresses "manifest" roles: those generally considered to be relevant in any social context. In a classroom, for example, manifest roles would include student and instructor. However, "latent" roles are typically involved also: age, sex, race, and the like. Participants would generally consider such latent roles to be inappropriate to consider, but they nevertheless influence expectations.[19]

In any concrete situation, the manifest and latent roles of a person may trigger contradictory expectations: both for the role incumbent and for others. A sixteen-year-old parent provides a relevant example. In many situations this person may be unsure whether to act like a 16 year old or a parent. Others may be similarly unsure of how to respond. Moreover, the expectations, held by self and others, may be contradictory. Role conflicts can be incapacitating to people, thereby preventing their compliance with either set of role expectations. They can also help to generate widespread social conflicts, as evidenced by feminist, black, and other social movements.

---

[18] Alvin W. Gouldner, "The Norm of Reciprocity," *American Sociological Review*, 25 (1960).

[19] Alvin W. Gouldner, "Cosmopolitans and Locals, 1 and 2," *Administrative Science Quarterly*, 2 (1957-58). For further elaboration, see Alvin W. Gouldner, *The Coming Crisis of Western Sociology* (New York: Basic Books, 1970).

CONCLUSION

In sum, Parsons set out to answer Hobbes's question: "Why not a natural state of war in society?" His answer stressed shared values and their intrusion into social and personality systems. The result was social control over individual motivation, and double reinforcement (internal and external) for compliance with expectations. Once stable relationships were attained, their continuance was not problematic. People would keep themselves in line.

The insights of Parsons' theory are notable. Its oversights are too, though. The oversocialized conception removes people's disruptive impulses, manifest roles prevent internal conflicts, and equal reciprocity precludes exploitation. Thus, Parsons' theory so completely answers Hobbes's question that Hobbes appears to be a fool for asking so naive a question in the first place. It is precisely because internalization, complementarity, and institutionalization are considered so unproblematic that Parsons is criticized. A sociological response to Hobbes that did not introduce such conceptions would be equally criticized.

Many of the basic issues involved can be seen in bold relief by reexamining the questions about guilt with which this chapter began. More specifically, what part does guilt play in maintaining social order? According to Parsons, we all internalize many of the same values, and even anticipating noncompliance with them generates guilt feelings that keep us in line. In Parsons' defense, guilt is clearly a powerful and pervasive force. On the other hand, consider the critics' view. Is internalization that pervasive? In other words, is it guilt or fear of getting caught that keeps us in line?

Parsons' assumptions about social order are also a matter of contention. More specifically, is order based upon value consensus, as Parsons assumes, with conflict acting as a sporadic and disruptive influence? Or, is conflict prevalent and does its resolution provide the basis for whatever social order characterizes a society? Answers to these questions typically exert a profound influence over how theorists view the relationship between individuals and society. Parsons's view is close to the one previously articulated by Durkheim, and rather distant from the view associated with Marx. Therefore, the debate continues in the following chapter which focuses upon Marx and Durkheim.

SUGGESTIONS FOR ADDITIONAL READING

JEFFREY C. ALEXANDER, *Twenty Lectures: Sociological Theory Since World War II*. New York: Columbia University Press, 1987.
MICHAEL A. FAIA, *Dynamic Functionalism: Strategy and Tactics*. Cambridge: Cambridge University Press, 1986.
CHARLES CAMIC (Ed), *The Early Essays of Talcott Parsons*. Chicago: University of Chicago Press, 1988.

4

Social Organization and Estrangement
Marx and Durkheim

Around 1970, a long-established singer named Peggy Lee popularized a song entitled, "Is That All There Is?" The lyrics chronicled life's disappointments. From a child's exaggerated expectations of a ride on a merry-go-round through courtship and old age, the song recounts the consistent discrepancy between how much pleasure was anticipated and how much was actually experienced. As the title conveys, the song's writer was always a little disappointed; events in life were never quite as meaningful or exhilarating as expected. Could it be that there is nothing more? The lyrics of the song also question whether the pleasures people can expect to receive are worth the price they have to pay. "If that's all there is, my friend, then why take chances?" went Peggy Lee's refrain.

For the older generation the poignancy of the song was increased by television appearances of Peggy Lee. They remembered her as a young, attractive vocalist in the 1940s. By 1970 she looked old and overweight. It was easy to imagine her singing the song as an autobiography. However, the younger generation also responded, not so much to the singer as to the song. They could also relate to the lyric. Of course, the message of disappointment and despair is not confined to that one song. It has been widely expressed in literature, movies, and plays.

Part of the appeal of the message lies in the universal experience of disappointment. Few events are ever as exhilarating as people's expectations; and with sufficient repetition, almost anything that was once exciting can become boring. However, there is an additional dimension to the message of distress which focuses upon conventional society. It expresses doubt over whether playing by the rules is worth the price one has to pay; whether it is possible to obtain sufficient satisfactions from going the "straight route." Sometimes these songs and movies celebrate detours: the simple pleasures of working a farm and not trying to be successful in a plastic society; hitchhiking across country or dropping into the drug scene rather than trying to compete for overrated rewards. They share in common a feeling of estrangement from conventional society, the belief that people cannot discover or actualize their true potential unless they can escape from the established rules.

Diagnoses of the specific problem vary. Some people personalize the blame, regarding their own socialization as having failed. Others see the fault as lying in the structure of society and perceive those who adjust to conventional society as much worse off than they. In sociology, the historically most important theories of estrangement have focused neither upon individuals nor society, but on the relationship between them. This relationship is emphasized both by Marx and Durkheim, the two social theorists whose writings are discussed in this chapter.

It is obvious that mild feelings of estrangement and meaninglessness are nearly universal experiences which require no profound explanation. They may simply be attributed to life's routine disappointments. It must also be recognized that this "malady" may be extreme in very isolated cases which also need not concern us here. They are problems for the psychiatrist's couch. What we are concerned with here are pervasive outbreaks of feelings of estrangement because their existence suggests that there must be intrinsic flaws in the ties that are supposed to bind individuals to society. Why else would it sometimes attain epidemic proportions?

As already mentioned, we are going to seek answers to these questions in the writings of Marx and Durkheim. The similarities in their treatment of estrangement are surprising in light of the large differences in the main thrust of their theories. Marx generally stressed opposition and conflict while Durkheim tended to emphasize solidarity and consensus. Nevertheless, both regarded widespread estrangement as emanating from the relationship of individuals to the "sustenance structure" of society. Marx described the sustenance structure as the means of production; Durkheim described it as the division to labor. Despite this difference in terminology, both viewed the organized system of production and distribution as the source of estrangement. They did differ profoundly in their proposed remedies though, in line with the more general differences in their theoretical emphases. Before contrasting the two further, let us examine how each described people's relationship to this sustenance structure and the kinds of potentially malevolent consequences each attributed to that relationship.

MARX ON THE MEANS OF PRODUCTION

Marx's perspective begins with the simple recognition that, in order for people to survive, there must be systems of production and distribution. People always need food, clothing, shelter, and so on, and nobody can satisfy all their requirements by themselves. In contemporary society the complex production and distribution of automobiles provides an excellent example. In many modern cities, people's livelihoods are completely dependent upon automobiles. However, their manufacture and their sale each entails a complicated set of arrangements involving thousands of people.

The system of production, according to Marx, is determined largely by the society's degree of technological sophistication. It establishes whether people will work as dirt farmers or in giant factories. It is the economic system of the society, Marx continued, which determines how the produced items will be distributed. Distribution can be accomplished according to peoples' needs (Marx's preference), according to their ability to pay (the capitalistic way), according to kinship obligations (characteristic of pre-industrial societies), or an impersonal marketplace (typical in modern societies). While it is possible analytically to separate systems of production and distribution from each other, they are empirically related. Thus, giant factories (production) are usually associated with impersonal markets (distribution).

Material conditions, such as technology, are only part of the production picture, however. People's labor is also required, and they enter into social relationships about this system of production as factory workers and owners, as serfs and lords, and so on. Characteristic of all such relationships, throughout history, are great differences in power. Those who have only their labor to sell (tenant farmers or factory workers) are in subordinated positions while those who own the means of production (land or capital, such as factories) are in superordinate positions.

Marx claimed that the basic structure of society was contained in these social relationships about the means of production. These relationships were regarded as most fundamental because they were viewed as determining the form of both other institutions and of people's consciousness. Given Marx's emphasis upon power and opposition, it was the legal and political institutions that interested him the most, and he saw them as serving the interests of the powerful; that is, those who owned the means of production. For example, weak centralized authority in the feudal period served lords because it provided no checks upon their control over the serfs who worked their estates. In a similar way, a modern legal system which provides police power to enforce apartment owners' claims, but not those of renters, tends to serve the interests of capitalists, rather than laborers.

However, the most invidious power of the capitalists, in Marx's view, lay in their control over, and distortion of, people's consciousness. A thoughtful awareness of surroundings and conditions was seen by Marx as a basic characteristic of the human species. At first it is a rudimentary awareness; that is, an awareness that entails concrete responses to an immediate environment. Over time, people develop more abstract theories to account for life, "reality," and so on. These abstract ideas supplant more immediate and rudimentary conceptions and provide coherent and pervasive ideologies which people utilize to comprehend their existence. The problem, according to Marx, is that these master representations are divorced from the real structure of society, namely, social relations about the means of production. Hence, they do not sensitize people's consciousness of their actual conditions of existence. They provide a false consciousness which ultimately estranges people from themselves![1]

---

[1]This thesis is presented in Karl Marx and Frederick Engels, *The German Ideology* (New York: International Publishing House, 1960). For further discussion, see Chapter 3 in Henri Lefebvre, *The Sociology of Marx* (New York: Random House, 1968).

What are the perpetrators of this false consciousness? For Marx, there is a long list: science, religion, philosophy, the media, social institutions. All of them present a view of people, their circumstances, and their lives that is divorced from the real underlying structure. Opposition and conflict are the true characteristics of this structure. However, the sources of ideology (religion, philosophy, and so on) determine the "forms in which men become conscious of this conflict and fight it out."[2] For example, American laborers may perceive Japanese or Korean laborers as their competitors, and vice versa. Each may blame the others for their own low wages, high unemployment, or the like. They may correspondingly direct their energies into conflicts with these perceived competitors. Thus, they may urge their unions to lobby their governments to keep foreign-made goods out of their country.

From Marx's perspective they misperceive their enemies. As laborers they all stand in the same *objective* relationship to the means of production. They should, as a result, feel an affinity to each other. Further, they are all being exploited by the same capitalistic forces which they should recognize as their common enemy. Marx's own revolutionary activity was an attempt to get the proletariat of the world—those who had only their own labor to sell—to unite. He hoped they would recognize that their objective conditions (that is, relations to the means of production) were identical. This, Marx argued, would lead them to form cohesive groups in which their actual self-interest would finally be appreciated, and their oppressive enemy would finally be identified. That enemy, of course, was the bourgeoisie—those who owned the means of production.

The discrepancy between objective and subjective conditions was a major issue in Marx's writings. *Objective* refers to people's relations to the means of production. These relations constitute the core of any social structure, but tend not to be recognized as such. *Subjective* refers to what is salient to people; how they experience or interpret events of importance in their lives. Class conflict, Marx insisted, was a fundamental, objective reality. Only when the means of production are collectively owned (i.e., in a communist state), will there be an end to differential class relations to the means of production and objective class conflict. However, this condition could not arise until the proletariat's subjective orientations lined up more congruently with the objective conditions.

EMPIRICAL APPLICATIONS

In the following pages, we examine two studies that amplify aspects of Marx's thesis. The first focuses upon the role of black labor in the American work force and it clarifies how race can inhibit class consciousness among workers. The second study shows how large corporations act together politically in the pursuit of ideological goals that further the interests of the bourgeoisie class.

[2]Karl Marx, *Contribution to the Critique of Political Economy* (Chicago: Kerr, 1904), p. 12.

Blacks in the Labor Force

The unemployment rate among blacks has been about double the rate for whites since the early 1950s. It was not always higher, however. Earlier figures indicate that black unemployment was lower than that of whites prior to about 1940. What happened? Can the current rate of high black unemployment be reduced? Edna Bonacich has carefully examined the history of black-white relations in the American labor force, from the Civil War to the 1970s, and concludes that: "As long as there is 'cheap labor' anywhere in the world, there may not be a solution within capitalism."[3] Let us examine how and why this pessimistic conclusion was reached.

Bonacich begins by considering, and immediately rejecting, one obvious but false explanation; namely, that high black unemployment is due to the technological displacement of unskilled workers. Because blacks are disproportionately in low-skill jobs, they would be most affected by technological advances. The two flaws in this argument are that 1) it views technology as imposing itself impersonally, with no human choice involved, and 2) technological innovations can replace high-skilled as well as low-skilled workers. Therefore, if technology is to be regarded as the immediate cause of black unemployment, a fuller explanation must account for the technological innovations as an instrument of class interests. Toward this end, Bonacich views three groups: white workers, black workers, and capitalists and analyzes the fate of both black and white workers as the by-product of a class struggle.

According to Bonacich, through the 1920s, blacks tended to receive less pay than whites because of racial differences in union activity. Many white unions explicitly excluded blacks from membership. In addition, as a result of their experiences as slaves, blacks were oriented toward personal relationships with employers, unmediated by intervening organizations, such as unions. Thus, capitalists were able to use black labor as a cheap alternative to more expensive white labor, and use black labor to break strikes, and to avoid direct dealings with unions. Black unemployment was relatively low (compared to whites), but black wages were also extremely low (compared to whites). Blacks' relative poverty also contributed to their exploitability because it led them to view low pay and horrible working conditions as more desirable (than the more affluent white workers).

Between about 1917 and 1930 some of this nation's worst race riots occurred in Chicago, Detroit, Harlem, and elsewhere. In many cases, black-white labor conflict or the use of blacks to break (white) union strikes was an immediate cause. The legitimation of unions, by New Deal legislation in the 1930s, largely ended this racially split labor market. Blacks could no longer be used as "strike insurance." In effect, Bonacich concludes, the legislation equalized the price of labor and made race irrelevant to cost-conscious capitalists, though there were loopholes and deliberate evasions.

---

[3]Edna Bonacich, "Advanced Capitalism and Black/White Race Relations in the U.S.," *American Sociological Review*, 41 (1976), p. 51.

One long-term effect of raising the price of labor and eliminating cheap labor was to induce the capitalist class to relocate, both overseas (Taiwan, South America) and in the U.S. from North to South. Both types of moves have disproportionately been at the cost of jobs formerly held by blacks. Thus, black workers are competing with similarly skilled overseas labor and with similarly skilled Southern white labor. However, Northern black labor is more expensive and has therefore lost out wherever capitalists have found cheaper alternatives.

Given the high unemployment and widespread poverty among blacks, Bonacich questions why they do not force down the cost of labor. The answer is welfare. It provides blacks with an alternative to the "sweatshop." It keeps large groups of the population from starvation levels at which they would "demand" to be exploited as cheap labor.

In sum, protective legislation of the 1930s put an end to the large-scale displacement of white workers by black workers. It also raised the cost of labor, encouraging capitalists to seek alternative sources: either relocating to find existing supplies of cheap labor or turning to automation to replace labor, and black labor in particular. The result is high black unemployment and Bonacich's gloomy prediction that it is likely to persist in a capitalistic society.

It is possible to quarrel with some of Bonacich's specific interpretations—such as whether unions have helped or hurt black workers. These are substantively important questions. However, our primary concern here is with examining these studies for their heuristic value in illuminating Marx's perspective. With this in mind we now turn to a study of corporations.

Corporate Politics

The many advantages of the bourgeoisie, in Marx's view, included their ability to control and shape social institutions, in general, and the political and legal institutions, in particular. The contemporary bourgeoisie are clearly represented among the larger owners–controllers of major corporations, such as General Motors, Merrill Lynch and Sears, Roebuck Inc. In the political realm, most of these corporations contribute through *political action committee* (PACs) to congressional and presidential campaigns. The research question posed by Neustadtl and Clausen was, "Do these large corporations act as a solidified interest group?"[4]

From a non-Marxian, pluralistic perspective, it could be argued that large corporations are politically active, but do not speak with a monolithic voice. They might contribute to candidates who appeared likely to favor the region of the country in which they were located, their specific type of industry (e.g., defense contractors), or the like. The money put up by corporations would have little *net* effect if different sectors/interests simply cancelled each other out. From a Marxian perspective, by contrast, overarching class interests of the bourgeoisie would be expected to produce cohesive behavior among these large corporations.

[4]Alan Neustadtl and Dan Clawson, "Corporate Political Groupings." *American Sociological Review*, 53 (1988).

The data for this study came from the reports of the Federal Election Commission, covering the 1980 congressional and presidential elections, and a survey of firms conducted by the investigators after the 1986 congressional elections. Their analysis began by focusing upon the similarities among corporations in the candidates to which they contributed. They were trying to detect *cliques* among corporations, defining cliques as groups of similarly behaving firms.

Their major finding was a very large clique of very conservative firms whose donations went largely to conservative candidates. There were some sub-cliques, based upon specific shared qualities, such as whether firms were defense contractors or dependent upon foreign sales. However, the overall similarities exceeded the differences among these large firms. From their surveys of the firms, the investigators note that nearly half of them communicate at least monthly, with the general Business–Industry PAC. This suggests that the similarities in their corporate behavior are not simply due to commonalities in their perceived self-interest, but to explicit coordination, as well. Thus, the researchers conclude, it is class-conscious activity that is carried out in the interests of the entire class.

CAPITALISM, MONEY AND OVERSPECIALIZATION

The class relations associated with capitalism were, in Marx's view, the primary source of people's estrangement from work, from other people, and ultimately from themselves. He also identified at least two other culprits: money and overspecialization; but both of the latter were seen to have their most deleterious consequences in a capitalistic society.

In some of his early writings, Marx philosophically asked which activity was the most distinctively human. The answer, he said, was work. It is through creative labor that the human species has the greatest possibility of realizing its true potential. It is in the process of work that people can simultaneously find themselves by losing themselves; that is, losing themselves in the intrinsic satisfactions of work. However, the systems of production associated with capitalism estrange workers from the act of production, itself. Assembly line workers, for example, describe the never-ending pace of the line as an external force which prevents them from trying to do their work correctly. Moreover, the size of each person's contribution to the total product is so small that it precludes an individual's identification with the result of his or her labor. For many assembly line workers the work place must simply be endured for about one-half of their working hours. There are no intrinsic satisfactions; only a weekly pay check and occasional breakdowns in the conveyor. Whenever the line breaks down, "the guys yell 'hurrah' . . . you can hear it all over the plant."[5]

Adding a monetary value to the products of labor further estranges the workers from the fruits of their labor. The value of their efforts is externally determined by

---

[5]Charles R. Walker and Robert Guest, *The Man on the Assembly Line* (Cambridge: Harvard University Press, 1952), p. 51.

a price tag. Hence, their products become, in effect, alien things. In addition capitalism attaches a monetary value to the laborers as well as to their products because the bourgeoisie calculate the cost of labor just like the cost of land, tools, borrowing money, or anything else. This process eventually leads the workers to regard themselves as somehow alien. Marx and Engels decried this capitalist separation of workers from their products and labor in a series of pointed questions:[6] If the product of labor is alien to me, confronts me as an alien power, to whom then does it belong? If my own activity does not belong to me, if it is an alien and forced activity, to whom then does it belong?

Marx further observed that, in capitalistic societies, as the productivity of labor increased, the workers themselves became more depreciated. This seeming anomaly is resolved by remembering that labor itself is a production commodity. Therefore, the more commodities it produces, the more its individuality is lost.

The final malevolent force Marx identified was overspecialization. This entailed both overly narrow jobs, as previously described, and overly enduring attachments to particular jobs. Once specialization begins in a capitalistic society, he argued, each person has an exclusive and permanent niche. In order to survive, everyone must become *and remain* a butcher, a baker, or a candlestick maker. In a communist society, by contrast, Marx believed that the fragmentation of activity which estranged workers from the products of their labor would be eliminated. I would be free, he claimed, to hunt in the morning, fish in the afternoon, and write criticism in the evening without ever becoming a hunter, fisherman, or critic.[7]

Marx concluded that work in a capitalistic society was not a stimulating, creative experience. The proof, he claimed, lies in the fact that if people did not absolutely have to work they would avoid it "like the plague."[8] As a result, people feel most human outside of work when they are eating, drinking, and procreating. They feel free and alive in their animal functions, but like animals in their distinctively human function, work!

MARX: SUMMARY AND CONCLUSION

The horrible deprivation the proletariat experience, according to Marx, will enable them finally to develop an ideology that recognizes the true source of their oppression in their relations to the means of production. They will then be able to pursue an enlightened self-interest, wresting the means of production from the bourgeoisie and ending the history of objective class conflict.

Looking at the most capitalistic societies in the world at present, it is hard to imagine any of them having the type of revolution Marx described. They are probably less likely to have one in the 1990s than they were at the time of Marx's

[6]Karl Marx and Frederick Engels, *The Communist Manifesto* (New York: International Publishers Co., 1948), p. 19.

[7]Marx and Engels, *The German Ideology.*

[8]David McLellan, *Karl Marx Selected Writings* (New York: Oxford University Press, 1977), p. 80.

death (in 1883). As a "prophet" it is difficult to honor him; but it is important to distinguish between Marx as a prophet of class warfare and as a social theorist. It is in the latter role that we are studying him.

Especially in retrospect, it is also apparent that Marx was naively romantic in believing that communism could somehow eliminate the evil consequences of money or of overspecialization. However, he certainly identified sources of acute estrangement that have persisted more than 100 years after his death. That estrangement originates in the workplace; in the tedious and meaningless nature of much modern work. According to Marx, the organization of work is not just another institution, though. It is *the* institution in the sense that it largely determines the form of all the other institutions (i.e., political, familial, and so on). To be estranged from work, therefore, is to be estranged entirely. It also means that people are precluded from attaining their true potential as people because that requires an opportunity for creative expression that is denied by work in a capitalistic society. Instead, workers are merely commodities themselves, like the meaningless items they help to produce.

Thus, Marx would not be surprised to hear the dismay that is expressed in a song like, "Is That All There Is?" I think he would agree that it is all there is, but not all it should be, or could be. Don't drop out, I think he would say, because it diverts attention and energy away from the class struggle. So long as the means of production are owned by one group, there is oppression and estrangement. Recognize its true source. Don't blame it on the stars, and don't look to religion or to science for answers. And when you recognize the true source of your estrangement, act!

DURKHEIM ON THE DIVISION OF LABOR

In the closing decades of the nineteenth century, sociological theory was dominated by an evolutionary approach. The major figure was Herbert Spencer who was also an important contributor to evolutionary theories in the biological sciences. It was he who first talked about survival of the fittest, for example. Durkheim was very critical of Spencer's evolutionary perspective, noting how the rate of suicide seemed to increse in modern cities. Is that more civilized, he asked rhetorically; does it indicate progress? Despite such criticisms, Durkheim's writings were nevertheless influenced strongly by Spencer's evolutionary perspective. Thus, we begin our introduction to Durkheim with a brief review of Spencer's once famous principles.

Spencer in the Background

Spencer maintained that an evolutionary progression followed the same form in every realm of life. The same principles would apply, therefore, to mental processes, society, organic or inorganic elements. His first principle maintained that homogeneous forms were unstable and would necessarily change. *Homogeneity*, to Spencer, involved the absence of differentiation. To illustrate: a human group would be homogeneous if all its members were the same. Differentiation is inevitable, however, because the nondifferentiated parts are unevenly exposed to external influences.[9]

As the process of externally induced change begins, the phenomenon goes through a series of stages in which increasing heterogeneity (i.e., *differentiation*) is the dominant feature. Consider a preliterate tribe as an example of an initially undifferentiated unit. Person X's tent may be closest to some hostile neighbors and this external influence may lead the person to work harder at making weapons. X gets better and better at it which does not go unnoticed by person Y. In order to obtain some of X's fine spears, Y offers some fish nets which X accepts. As they become trading partners, differentiation increases because X keeps getting better at making weapons and Y at making fish nets. Now along comes person Z who also wants one of X's spears. X will not trade Z for fish nets. X already has enough of them; so Z offers some animal skins that make good floor mats. In this manner, the amount of specialization within the once homogeneous tribe keeps increasing.

At the end of this process of differentiation, Spencer contended that a principle of segregation applied. Birds of a feather flock together, he claimed. As illustration, Spencer said to look at leaves in a forest in the Fall. In the Spring, all were green. Some, that have not yet turned, are still green and remain fixed to one side of the trees. Yellow ones, that have begun to decay as a result of more exposure to sunlight, are on another side of winds trees. Red leaves are on the ground in a pile as a result of winds that arose when they had decayed. Thus, external influences (like wind and sun) led to differentiation, and differentiation culminated in segregation. In human societies this principle would eventually entail the makers of weapons and fish nets moving to their own (separate) parts of the village.

In viewing the transformation of society as involving a movement from the homogeneous to the heterogeneous, Durkheim's later theory of the division of labor strongly resembled Spencer's view. However, Durkheim did not share Spencer's insistence on the inherent necessity of such transformations. Durkheim also presented an organic biological model that was highly similar to Spencer's. Finally, even though it was poorly developed, Spencer pointed to a relationship between population and social organization that was also to become an important part of Durkheim's theory of the division of labor.

Durkheim, as we previously noted, was critical of Spencer's writings. He argued that Spencer's evolutionary theory denigrated the study of society by maintaining that societal changes occured in accordance with the same principles that accounted for changes in inorganic and psychological phenomena. This contention violated Durkheim's view of society as *sui generis*; that is, a separate entity which could not be reduced to the sum of its parts.

Types of Solidarity

Despite these criticisms, Durkheim's earliest writings were very much a product of the historical period in which he lived. Thus, instead of describing societies as

[9]Herbert Spencer, *First Principles* (New York: Appleton, 1900).

becoming more civilized, he referred to their stages of development. While insisting that society was a "thing apart," he frequently described society in terms of biological metaphors and described societal change in almost the same terms applied by Spencer to other types of evolution. Some of Durkheim's contributions to the study of social change were, therefore, more cosmetic than substantive.[10] However, Durkheim also developed a nonevolutionary, functional theory of social organization which has made a lasting contribution to sociological theory. It contains a view of individuals that stands in marked contrast to Marx's view. We shall focus upon it after briefly considering his evolutionary perspective.[11]

According to Durkheim, the development of a society encompasses a myraid of virtually simultaneous changes occurring in various components of a society. The single most important changes involve a sequence in which the population density increases leading to increased rates of interaction and communication ("moral density") which results in greater specialization in a society's division of labor. Specialization, in this context, has two highly similar referents, depending mostly upon the society's prior stage of development. It entails either differential occupations (in modern societies) or differentiated activities carried out by autonomous groups (in earlier societies). Thus, if hunting ceases to be a widely participated-in activity and becomes instead the exclusive domain of a limited and specially trained group of people, then the division of labor has become more specialized. Similarly, increased specialization occurs with the emergence of priests, merchants, or scientists.

Variations in divisions of labor were utilized by Durkheim as the basis for classifying societies according to their degree of development. However, he tended to employ only two classificatory levels: simple (undifferentiated divisions of labor) and complex (highly differentiated). Societies in between the two extremes were ignored. Associated with each type of division of labor were distinctive types of solidarity. Simple and complex societies, in other words, were regarded as held together in differents ways.

Durkheim's use of the term *solidarity*, in general, refers to the fact that members of solidarity groups or collectives are obligated to conform with shared standards of behavior. However, Hechter points out that it is important to regard solidarity as variable, depending upon two interdependent factors: 1) the extensiveness of the obligations imposed upon people by virtue of membership, and 2) the degree to which members in fact comply with the obligations. Thus, high solidarity would characterize any collectivity to the extent most of its members complied with an extensive set of shared standards.[12]

When there is little differentiation in the division of labor, solidarity is based upon homogeneity, or the fact that people are basically alike. This means that they

---

[10]For further discussion of the distinctive contribution made by Durkheim, see Robert A. Nisbet, *The Sociology of Emile Durkheim* (New York: Oxford University Press, 1974).

[11]The following discussion is based upon, Emile Durkheim, *The Division of Labor in Society* (New York: Macmillan, 1933).

[12]Michael Hechter, *Principles of Group Solidarity* (Berkeley: University of California Press, 1987).

share the same ideas and values. Individual personalities are a microscopic representation of the society. Thus, there is a relative absence of personal qualities that could set an individual apart from the collective entity. Durkheim termed this type of solidarity "mechanical."

As the division of labor becomes more complex, the capacities of a society are enhanced, but the basis of homogeneity is transformed. Solidarity among the now specialized parts is based upon their inter-connectedness and interdependence. He termed this type of solidarity "organic" because of the analogy between the organs of higher animals and the specialized parts of more developed societies. Among animals higher in the phylogenetic scale, hands, mouth, feet, and the like are able to act independently of each other. (A person, for example, could simultaneously walk, chew, and scratch.) The same autonomy characterizes relationships among the specialized parts of a complex society: butchers, bakers, and candlestick makers can all operate independently of each other, but only to a limited degree. The whole, whether a society or an organism, also requires a degree of integration. Solidarity in both instances is based upon the interconnection among the parts.

Durkheim illustrated this transformation by noting the declining prevalence of proverbs. He defined proverbs as expressions of sentiments that were common to a people and noted that a large number of such expressions were commonly found in undifferentiated societies. With functional specialization, however, old adages cease to be widely applicable. They gradually disappear because there are fewer collective ideas for them to express concisely. In sum, as the division of labor becomes more differentiated so too do individual personalities. People retain shared values and ideas, but to a more limited degree, as the amount of individualism increases.

Durkheim very carefully noted that the preceding changes were merely a chronology rather than a causal sequence. In other words, he interpreted the data then available as indicating a tendency for societies to change in this way: changes in the division of labor followed by changes in collective representations, frequency of proverbs, forms of solidarity, and so on. He did not consider this to be a necessary unfolding of society's inherent qualities nor a unilinear movement toward civilization. It was perhaps these caveats, more than anything else, that differentiated Durkheim's evolutionary approach from that which was prevalent in his time.

Regarding this sequence as an empirical regularity, rather than as an intrinsic necessity, sensitized Durkheim to look for discordant cases; that is, societies in which the degree or type of solidarity was out of step with changes in the division of labor. His later analyses of suicide, for example, presented a typology based on incongruities between the amount of specialization and the relative emphasis upon either collective sentiments or individuality. For the most part, such incongruities were viewed as temporary phenomena, because he regarded society as a self-regulating system which would make adjustments until its parts were in accord with each other. Most discrepancies resulted, therefore, from unusual rates of change in some components that had not yet been adjusted to by other components.

While all kinds of discrepancies between divisions of labor and degrees of individualism could logically be deduced, Durkheim most emphasized "pathologies" in complex societies. Even the terms he used convey a view of organic solidarity as being more problematic than mechanical solidarity. Mechanical has an "automatic" connotation of virtual certainty that is absent from the term organic. More specifically, it was the danger of too much individualism, or too little reliance on social norms, that Durkheim most emphasized in his analysis of modern society. He called this problem *anomie* and regarded it as a pathology of a society, rather than of individuals, because it involved disjunction among the components of a society. However, it was individuals who paid the psychic costs of anomie; that is, felt despair, committed suicide, and so on.

ANOMIE

As already noted, Durkheim viewed specialization in the division of labor as "naturally" promoting individualization of ideas and values. Psychic life becomes as variable as social life because it is a response to social life. More spontaneity becomes possible because the collective conscience has shrunk, and what remains of it is less binding; that is, it permits more flexible individual interpretations. However, Durkheim asks, what is the price of this freedom? One type of anomie, that has been termed "bondlessness," is his answer.

This bondlessness comprises a situation in which social norms lose their regulatory capacities. Individuals regard themselves as above the society, hence, not bound by its strictures. In other words, bondlessness involves the disappearance of subjective realizations that peoples' fates are interwoven. What does this leave to regulate peoples' aspirations, Durkheim asks? Biological controls, he notes, are inadequate. For nonhuman animals they control drives, limiting the amount of food, sex, or the like that the animal will crave. Most human needs, by contrast, have no biological basis. Durkheim offers status seeking as an illustration. Therefore, he concludes, peoples' impulses, unlike animals, cannot be controlled by biological mechanisms. He then considers psychological control, but also dismisses this possibility because, in his view, the psychological is a reflection of the social. Thus, the bondless condition exists because of social fragmentation—overspecialization in the division of labor—and the effect cannot "cure" its cause. The only answer to the question of control, Durkheim concludes, is society; that is, only social norms can set the limits, make aspirations reasonable; in short, tell people how much is enough.

When the social norms lose this regulatory capacity, people become un-hinged. Once loosened from the shackles of the social structure, they are off on a never-ending quest for more: more wealth, more new experiences, more kicks, and so on. Because unconstrained desires are, by definition, insatiable, the individual must constantly be driven by the haunting fear that too many of the exciting things in life are passing him or her by. Thus, bondlessness is a one-way ticket to despair.

Winning a Lottery

Durkheim described, at length, the normative regulation of desires in his study of suicide where he noted the surprisingly different effects of proverty and of wealth:[13]

> Poverty . . . is a restraint in itself . . . the less one has the less he is tempted to extend the range of his needs indefinitely . . . Wealth, on the other hand, by the power it bestows, deceives us into believing that we depend on ourselves only.

Durkheim's primary concerns were with anomie in society as a result of a widespread increase in affluence. What happens, he wondered, until a new social scale is put into place? However, without too much modification, his ideas may also be applicable to individuals whose wealth is suddenly and dramatically increased.

The winners of state lotteries provide an interesting group of such people.[14] The study of lottery winners took a sample from the lists of all persons who won any amount of money in the Connecticut state lottery in 1977 or 1978. The amount they won varied from one million dollars to as little as a few thousand dollars. When they were interviewed for this study, the actual date of their winning had occurred between a few months and a few years earlier. This turned out to be important because the study's first finding was described as an *incubation effect*. When people first won, nothing much happened. Their lives continued as before, even though they admitted to spending some time staring at their new bank books.

After about one and one-half years, however, there were some changes of the type Durkheim's theory would lead us to expect. Specifically, the more money people won, the more indulgent their attitudes became with respect to various kinds of gratifications. For example, they expressed less disapproval of smoking marihuana, drinking alcoholic beverages, enjoying leisure time, and so on. The overall results were complicated, and a complete summary of them would take us well beyond our current interests. However, we may note that the findings do illustrate Durkheim's contention that the capacity of social norms to regulate people's aspirations does appear to be reduced when people's income rapidly increases.

MERTON: MEANS AND ENDS

In an extraordinarily influential essay, Merton recast Durkheim's theory of anomie into a set of descriptive categories that had a sizeable impact upon later research. Merton's initial interest in anomie, according to Coser, developed during the Great Depression. The widespread suffering of that time was popularly regarded to be due to moral decay or the decline of old-fashioned virtues. Merton turned to

---

[13]Emile Durkheim, *Suicide* (New York: Free Press, 1951), p. 254.

[14]Mark Abrahamson, "Sudden Wealth, Gratification and Attainment: Durkheim's Anomie of Affluence Reconsidered." *American Sociological Review*, 45 (1980).

Durkheim's writing in order to move the focus from individual qualities to the larger social structure. In addition, Coser notes, Merton did not wish to pursue Durkheim's conservative philosophy about the need to control people's potentially insatiable desires. To the contrary, Merton had been influenced by Marx's emphasis upon class differences in access to everything of value. The result was Merton's theory about the discrepancies between culturally prescribed goals (or ends) and the societal means by which these goals are reached.[15]

Means and ends are both components of the social structure and must be integrated in order to prevent *anomie*. Integration, in this sense, states that means and ends receive approximately equal emphasis. In the American society, however, Merton notes that the goals (fame, fortune, and success) are often stressed much more intensely than the legitimate means (apprenticeship and education) by which they can be attained. Merton epitomizes anomie, or normlessness, with the example of a person cheating at solitaire. (For the uninitiated, solitaire is a card game that is played by a single person. The objective is to utilize all the cards, but players tend to be easily frustrated by a complex set of rules.) When a solitary player cheats at solitaire "the cult of success has truly flowered."[16] The people who evade the institutional rules of the game know they have done so and feel uneasy or find their apparent success to be not very satisfying. However, Merton states, if there is a strong enough emphasis upon success, rules (i.e., means) will be evaded anyway.

A polar opposite situation is presented when conformity with the means (procedures) is stressed while people lose sight of the goals (or objectives). Merton calls this category *ritualism* and illustrates it with the timid bureaucrat in the large organization. This is the person who insists upon a literal application of all the rules, regardless of the consequences. Such employees tend to have very limited personal aspirations, Merton states; they are strictly trying to play it safe.

Drug Dealers and Cheating Scientists

Merton's conception of anomie/normlessness has been widely employed to explain deviant behavior. It has been specifically assumed that plagiarists, corrupt police, drug dealers, and bribed officials were all trying to attain the traditionally valued goals of American society, such as wealth and fame; but that they did not much care about how they attained them, or/and they lacked access to the legitimate means with which to attain them. A couple of very disparate examples help to clarify the wide applicability of Merton's conception.

Our first example comes from the streets of inner-city Washington, D.C. During the summer of 1988, police, parents and community leaders were watching children 10-years old and younger imitating the role of the get-rich-quick drug hustler. The children are very much aware of the dealers' financial success because

---

[15]Lewis A. Coser, "Merton's Uses of the European Sociological Tradition" In Lewis A. Coser (ed), *The Idea of Social Structure* (New York: Harcourt, Brace, Jovanovich, 1975).

[16]Robert K. Merton, "Social Structure and Anomie," in *Social Theory and Social Structure* (New York: Free Press, 1949, 1968), p. 129.

they see the hustlers flashing large wads of bills and driving around in luxury cars. The emulating children crush chalk to resemble cocaine and place it in plastic bags smuggled from home. Their bankrolls are wads of Monopoly money wrapped in rubber bands. "You see them playing and you hear, 'All I want is my cash, Jack,' or 'Give up the stash, sucker.' "[17]

Dramatically different examples have been taken from research laboratories. There are procedural norms that encourage scientists to act in a reserved manner, express humility concerning their work, and carefully follow the scientific method. The most valued goal in science is an original discovery. Those who receive credit for an important discovery receive medals, grants, and public esteem. These ends can lead scientists to abandon any pretext of humility and claim the priority of their own work while slandering their competitors. In some cases, the value of the rewards leads to unethical and illegal behavior as scientists commit plagiary or contrive their data.[18]

The preceding examples focus upon situations in which culturally sanctioned ends are stressed to the relative disregard of socially institutionalized means. The exaggeration of either, according to Merton, results in anomie. It should also be noted, however, that exaggeration is only one of the ways in which means and ends can get out of step with each other. In addition, compliance with institutionalized means may not lead to goal attainment; for example, scientists may faithfully pursue a promising research agenda, but not discover anything. Playing by the rules, in other words, does not have the anticipated (successful) consequence. As long as the means and ends do not fit together, the disjunction constitutes a state of anomie.

Durkheim's own examples of anomie tended to be more macroscopic, focusing upon disjunctions between (or among) large segments of society. He talked, for example, about increasing rates of business failures as evidence of a breakdown in organic solidarity. For the parts of a society—producers and consumers, in this instance—to be adjusted to each other, there must be contact between them. This has not occurred in modern societies because the marketplace has become so large and impersonal. Over time, Durkheim is certain that a new form of economic organization, more attuned to modern markets, will occur. In the interim, production and consumption each continue unchecked by the other. Thus, there is a temporary condition of deregulation, or anomie.

CONCLUSION: MARX AND DURKHEIM COMPARED

In order to appreciate the fundamental difference between Marx and Durkheim, it is instructive to examine their views of modern capital and labor. Marx, it will be recalled, saw capital and labor as inherently in opposition because of their competing relations to the means of production. These groups were the modern contest-

---

[17]Rene Sanchez, "Learning to Play the Drug Game." *The Washington Post*, June 5, 1988, p. A19.

[18]Jonathan R. Cole and Harriet Zuckerman, "The Emergence of a Scientific Specialty," in Lewis A. Coser (ed), *The Idea of Social Structure.*

ants, but all of human history was regarded as involving such conflicts woven into the structure of society.

For Durkheim, however, the conflict between capital and labor is an example of a temporary rupture in organic solidarity.[19] Up until the fifteenth century, he argues, masters and apprentices worked at the same workbench. Conflicts were rare. However, occupations then became the sole possessions of masters, leading journeymen to form independent associations, and the level of conflict increased. This struggle was characterized, in Durkheim's view, by the journeymen's desires to improve working conditions or wages. Their objectives were specific and were not prompted by a view of the employer as a natural enemy.

The beginnings of a large-scale industry, in the seventeenth century, separated workers and employers. Corresponding to the increasing complexity of the division of labor, work became regimented and overspecialized. Then labor strife became more violent, but only in large firms. Labor relations remained relatively harmonious in small firms. The working class everywhere, he continued, was dissatisfied to some degree with wages and working conditions. However, acute conflicts did not occur in small shops. The source of serious tensions, therefore, must be large-scale industry.

Durkheim also noted a number of other more recent contributions to labor conflict. There was the "contagious influence" of urban life, the replacement of people with machines, the decline of pride in craftsmanship, and still greater specialization. The result is conflict rather than solidarity because the differentiated organs of a society (for example, capital and labor, workers and their families) are not sufficiently interconnected, hence regulated. Durkheim concluded: "these new conditions of industrial life naturally require new organization, but as these changes have occurred with extremely rapidity, the conflicting interests have not yet had the time to reach equilibrium."[20]

During the transition period, regulation is lacking. This is ironic because it is precisely during a state of anomic deregulation that human aspirations are most in need of discipline. The result is that the "collective mood" is characterized by melancholy, pessimism and sadness; and suicide rages. Such anomic periods are, in themselves, pathological but entirely normal from a long-term view in that such periods are bound to occur. In the long run, industrial society can and will be characterized by organic solidarity, in Durkheim's view. Thus, social classes in industrial society are inherently interdependent rather than inherently in conflict.[21] This is the most profound disagreement between the two theorists and accounts for why Marx concluded his diagnosis with a call to arms while Durkheim advocated pains be patiently endured until normalcy returns.

In sum, both Durkheim and Marx explained estrangement and despair as a function of the substance structure of society, whether called the division of labor or

[19]Durkheim, *The Division of Labor in Society*, pp. 353-357.

[20]Ibid., p. 370.

[21]Emile Durkheim, *Socialism and Saint Simon*, edited by Alvin W. Gouldner (London: Routledge and Kegan Paul, 1959).

the means of production. Both also recognized highly similar alienating forces in contemporary societies: overspecialization, regimentation, and excessively large-scale firms.

Marx and Durkheim also were alike, according to Mizruchi, in that both viewed the Industrial Revolution as producing large numbers of marginal or unattached people. To Marx, they were an unemployed "surplus" population that kept down the cost of labor by providing the bourgeoisie with a ready pool of replacement labor. To Durkheim, they were a weakly integrated segment of society whose behavior would be difficult to regulate.[22] However, while Marx saw conflict between labor and capital as the endemic source of the problem, for Durkheim they were symptomatic, rather than causal, and temporary, rather than enduring.

Their differing conceptions of human nature were an important basis for their different diagnoses and prescribed therapies. Marx stressed the self-actualizing needs of human beings as a species and the way they were thwarted by the social structure. Durkheim, by contrast, polemicized against the dignity of the individual arguments, regarding the needs of individuals as derived from the social structure. Therefore, they possessed no autonomous existence that could come into inherent conflict with any social structure. In addition, individuals were viewed by Marx as poor, exploited objects, robbed of spontaneity, feeling, and imagination; in short, dehumanized. Durkheim, however, held a much more callous and cynical view of people. He was essentially distrustful of unregulated passions and presented a picture of greed and lust as characterizing the essential human condition.[23]

Finally, let us return to where we started and imagine both theorists responding to Peggy Lee asking, "Is that all there is?" Yes, Marx might argue, because all previous societies have thwarted the human soul, denied people the opportunity to experience all they could. Durkheim would probably also argue that there was nothing more to life but attribute people's dissatisfactions with what there was to a state of anomie.

SUGGESTIONS FOR ADDITIONAL READING

JEFFRY C. ALEXANDER, *Theoretical Logic in Sociology,* Vol 2 (Marx and Durkheim), Berkeley: University of California Press, 1982.
HERBERT J. GANS, *Middle American Individualism,* New York: Free Press, 1988.
MARC SILVER, *Under Construction: Work and Alienation in the Building Trades,* Albany, NY: SUNY Press, 1986.

[22]Ephraim H. Mizruchi, *Regulating Society* (New York: Free Press, 1983).

[23]For example, society must "call the individual to a moral way of life." Ibid., p. 69.

II

SOCIAL STRUCTURE, PROCESS, AND CHANGE

INTRODUCTION TO PART TWO

If we knew nothing at all about a phenomenon, but wished to understand it, we would probably find it useful to begin by examining its structure. This entails identifying its major elements, or components, and the way in which they fit together. The ceilings and walls of a house or the valves and arteries of a heart provide familiar illustrations. Thus, the description of structure is like a stop-action photograph. It portrays form, or organization in space, at a single point in time. Also like a photograph, descriptions of structure can be closeups, full of detail, or distant views that are deliberately set back to be totally encompassing at the expense of detail.

Many of the most important sociological theories have focused upon social structure. To pursue this issue, they have had to identify the major components of society, such as institutions, and then further dissect them into successively smaller components, such as organizations and statuses. The first three chapters included in this section (that is, Chapters Five, Six and Seven) examine varied aspects of social structure. Chapter Five presents an ecological view with a telephoto lens. It focuses upon structure as embodied in the spatial distributions of people and activities. Chapter Six also uses a telephoto lens, but it emphasizes social, rather than geographical, space. The distributions of wealth, status, and power are examined, and these patterns of social stratification are regarded as a crucial aspect of social structure. Chapter Seven moves in for a more detailed examination of organizational structure, describing the nature of bureaucratic organizations and their relationship to the larger social structure.

Comprehension of any phenomenon is greatly aided by an analysis of its structure, but such an analysis is rarely sufficient. It leaves unanswered fundamental questions about how the phenomenon developed and the processes by which it will be either maintained or changed. To extend the previous analogy we may note that while a still photograph provides useful information, it is limited to a single point in time. More insights would result if there were a series of photographs and an analysis of what did or did not change as well as *how* the structure was either changed or maintained.

Chapters Eight and Nine are devoted specifically to an analysis of social processes. The former examines behavioral exchanges, that is, the ways in which people reciprocate favors, insults, praise, and other kinds of rewards and punishments. The latter chapter examines conflict at both the interpersonal and aggregate levels. The more specific foci are upon the conditions under which conflict occurs, the reasons for its varied levels of intensity, and the ways in which conflict contributes both to the stability and change of social structures.

The final segment of this section, Chapters Ten and Eleven, explicitly examines social change. Chapter Ten first views the form and rate of deviance as determined by the social structure and then examines patterns of deviant behavior as both the cause and effect of changes in that structure. Chapter Eleven focuses upon the place of people's values and questions the degree to which structural features of a society change in response to changes in values.

5
STRUCTURE
Human Ecology
Park, Burgess, Hawley

In 1948, nearly 50 percent of all the money spent anywhere in metropolitan Detroit in restaurants, bars, department and clothing stores, specialty shops, and so on, was spent in the downtown shopping area. By 1960, downtown Detroit's share of total retail purchases in the city and its suburbs had been reduced to about one-half of its 1948 level. In the years since, downtown has continued to decline as the place where residents of the Detroit metropolitan area do their retail shopping, though the rate of decline has slowed.[1]

Most of the department stores, restaurants, and specialty shops that were formerly located downtown have either gone out of business, or moved. Many of the latter are now located in suburban shopping centers. For the downtown area and for the city (as opposed to the entire metropolitan area), this change has resulted in the loss of both retail jobs and city revenue in the form of sales taxes. To refer to the store closings, the loss of jobs and of revenue as the "death" of downtown Detroit is an exaggeration. It is not quite lifeless; but, the retail exodus out of Detroit prompted people facetiously to ask, "Will the last one out please turn off the lights?"

It is unfair to single out downtown Detroit in these respects because substantial declines in retail sales have also occurred in the downtown shopping areas of many cities. In fact, it is the exceptional downtown that has not declined as a retail shopping center. However, this trend would probably be very surprising to the sociologists who were analyzing cities at the turn of this century. Downtowns were then vibrant areas whose functions in a city were described as analogous to the functions of the nucleus in a cell; that is, centers of growth and development. "Quite

---

[1]Between 1977 and 1982, the latest figures available show that retail sales in Detroit's central business district declined an additional 8.8 percent. U.S. Bureau of the Census, *1982 Census of Retail Trade* (Washington, D.C.: Government Printing Office, 1985).

naturally, almost inevitably," Burgess wrote, "economic, cultural and political life are concentrated in the downtown area."[2]

What has happened to downtowns? One apparent change is that many people moved to suburbs and preferred to do their shopping closer to home. They have also gone out to eat, drink, or attend movies closer to their suburban homes. People have "voted" with their feet and their wallets for suburban shopping centers rather than downtown stores. However, the population growth of suburban areas does not, in itself, adequately explain what happened to downtown areas. For example, why did the downtown not remain a multi-funtional nucleus for the expanded metropolitan area?

An enduring perspective on the interdependence of the components of metropolitan areas was developed, between about 1915 and 1925, by sociologists at the University of Chicago. The central figures were Robert Park, Ernest Burgess—a student of Park's, then his collaborator—and Robert McKenzie, also Park's student. These men, their students, and collaborators are collectively referred to as human ecologists. While they would be surprised at what has happened to downtown business districts, they developed a perspective with which ensuing sociologists can provide explanations.

Competition and a struggle for existence were the conceptual cornerstones of their ecological approach to the social organization of cities. They were directly influenced in this regard by Darwin's evolutionary theory, formulated during the latter half of the nineteenth century. This influence is reflected in an introductory textbook compiled by Park and Burgess for University of Chicago students in 1921. They included in this collection four excerpts from Darwin's writing and several other essays which attempted further articulation of Darwin's writings.[3] Therefore, let us begin our examination of the ecological perspective by looking at the nature of Darwin's influence.

STRUGGLE FOR EXISTENCE

Darwin's view of evolution stressed a continuing struggle for survival among plants and animals. One basis for the struggle was Malthus's doctrine that the reproduction rate of any species would tend to increase geometrically, unless checked by external forces. In order to illustrate the consequences of such reproduction rates, Darwin projected growth rates of elephants, deliberately selected for their slow breeding rate. Assuming that all elephants will breed from the ages of 30 to 90 years, a pair of elephants will normally produce six offspring in their lifetimes. Darwin further assumed that all offspring would survive and continue to breed at

[2]Ernest W. Burgess, "The Growth of the City," in Robert E. Park, Ernest W. Burgess, and Roderick McKenzie, *The City* (Chicago: University of Chicago Press, 1967). (Originally published in 1925.)

[3]Robert E. Park and Ernest W. Burgess, *Introduction to the Science of Sociology* (Chicago: University of Chicago Press, 1970).

the same rate. If this occurred, then 750 years later there would be almost 19 million *living* elephants descended from that first pair.[4]

Among plant species, producing thousands of seeds each year, the possibility of rapid growth rates is even more pronounced. However, the enormous reproductive capacities of most species are rarely attained. For example, in Malthus's view, unchecked human populations would outgrow their food supplies; that is, they are able to reproduce faster than they can increase their production of food. Starvation then serves as a check upon population increases. For many species, a temporary increase in their numbers may also lead to an increase in the numbers of their natural predators, resulting in no permanent increase. Thus, there are a number of restraining forces—external to a species, but endemic to the web of interdependence among life forms—that serve to check rapid growth potentials. If there are more cats, there may be fewer mice, for example; fewer mice, Darwin reasoned, leads to more bees because mice prey on bees' nests; more bees lead to more red clover because bees fertilize the clover, and so on. Park summarized Darwin's view by noting the ultimate dependence of red clover on the number of cats.[5]

In the writings of Darwin, Park, and others a struggle for existence was regarded as very pervasive. "Winning" in this struggle presumably meant that a species grew in size and, correspondingly, expanded within a community of interdependent species. To lose, by contrast, meant a species was unable to reproduce, and therefore, became extinct. However, Darwin was aware of ambiguities in the criterion "success in leaving progeny" and did not uniformly employ it. Ensuing sociologists seemed to be even less certain of how to conceptualize success, or winning.[6] Thus, sheer survival was utilized as a criterion as frequently as growth or expansion.

Park and Burgess viewed the human community, and cities in particular, as socially organized geographical units in which at least a metaphorically similar struggle for existence was occurring. In all instances, changes in the social organization of human life were seen as continuously occurring and forcing every role, institution, or area to continuously adapt or face extinction.

A highly systematic and influential contemporary statement of how adaptation occurs in human societies was presented by Amos Hawley. He began by emphasizing the *environment* (defined as all that is external to a society, but capable of impinging upon it). An environment would, for example, include the physical resources, such as raw materials, that were available to a population. It is difficult to operationalize environment precisely because modern technologies are literally able to transform it. However, Hawley insists that the environment must still be regarded as a separate phenomenon because the major adaptations required of a population are to forces (environmental) that are external in origin.[7]

[4]Charles Darwin, *The Origin of Species* (New York: Macmillan, 1927).

[5]Robert E. Park, "Human Ecology," *American Journal of Sociology*, 42 (1936).

[6]For further discussion, see Chapter six in Pitrim A. Sorokin, *Contemporary Theories* (New York: Harper and Row, 1964). (Originally published in 1928.)

[7]Amos H. Hawley, *Human Ecology* (Chicago: University of Chicago Press, 1986).

Adaptation to an environment, Hawley continues, involves a system of interdependent relationships (i.e., organization) among members of a population. It is through the establishment of such relationships that a population can act as a unit. Individuals are of interest to this ecological model only in so far as they behave collectively. The focus is upon a population whose system qualities (i.e., modes of organizing) transcend the lifetime of individual members.

In recent research there has also been an explicit emphasis upon organizations (such as business firms, universities, voluntary associations, or the like) as the units of analysis. They too can be viewed as comprising populations that compete with other organizations for environmental resources; for example, consider savings banks and commercial banks as competing populations of organizations. Each type of bank tends to have some distinctive qualities reflecting the fit of each to the demands of its environment.

It is assumed that environments select for or against populations of organizations based upon organizational attributes. However, the adaptation potential of organizations is often viewed as more limited than that of populations of individuals. Limitations to the organizations' adaptation arise from the *structural inertia* of internal arrangements. For example, a company may have large investments in equipment that is not easily transferred to other purposes. There are also external pressures toward inertia, such as legal barriers against entering some markets. Thus, organizations seem to follow a Darwinian principle of survival of the fittest with somewhat limited possibilities of adaptation.[8]

Park, Burgess, and their students similarly analyzed how a variety of social roles and institutions were facing extinction as a result of changes to which they could not adapt. Examples included: hoboes, traditional neighborhoods, and ethnic newspapers. Perhaps because Park was a newspaper reporter before becoming a sociologist, some of his essays were on newspapers. They have been a favored object of ecological analyses from the 1930s through the most recent analyses of populations of organizations. Our attention now turns to analyes of newspapers conducted over the decades, beginning with Park's.

THE NEWSPAPER'S CHANGING ROLE

Park's premise was that newspapers, like any other part of human society, evolve under changing conditions. To comprehend the contemporary newspaper, he wrote in the 1930s, requires an account of the entire "natural history . . . of this surviving species."[9] He noted that during the first decades of this century the circulation of newspapers in cities was rapidly increasing and Park explained this increase as due

---

[8]Michael T. Hannan and John Freeman, "The Population Ecology of Organizations," *American Journal of Sociology*, 82 (1977). By the same authors, see also "Structural Inertia and Organizational Change," *American Sociological Review*, 49 (1984).

[9]Robert E. Park, "The Natural History of the Newspaper," in Park and others, *The City*.

partly to the simple increase in literacy of urban populations. The newspapers' struggle for existence, he stated, is a struggle for circulation. The more people who can read, the more people who can read newspapers. However, the economic viability of the newspaper—like any other cultural form—requires that it be congruent with the larger social organization. In this regard Park noted changes that were occurring among the immigrant groups that were settling in American cities.

The Italian, Polish, and other immigrants had typically left rural European villages. In American cities they initially established ethnic communities, like the ones they had left (for example, "Little Italy"). Many of these communities still exist today, but none of them could persist unchanged because they were part of a larger industrial and urban context. In preurban villages, gossip carried the news that mattered among people who knew each other intimately; for example, "Sophie's daughter is getting married in April." Nobody had to ask, "Sophie who?" Informal communication networks continue to function effectively in conveying information of this type. However, to the immigrants settling in New York, Chicago, or other cities, it was not all the news that mattered. They also needed to know whether war was breaking out in Europe, if jobs would be available at a new factory, when a ship might arrive carrying their relatives from the old country.

The point is that in the American Cities extracommunity events impinged upon the lives of the immigrant. Gossip and other informal community networks could no longer adequately disseminate all the important news. Newspapers filled this need which was not present in European villages; therefore, circulation increased. In addition, the modern newspaper helped to shape public opinion among culturally diverse people, to focus attention upon the same issues across ethnic lines. Thus, Park concluded, while newspapers are a response to changing conditions, modern city life also would not be possible without the newspaper.

American cities in the 1990s are, of course, very different from the cities Park described in the 1920s. As noted at the onset of this chapter, for example, the relative size of suburban areas relative to central cities has increased enormously. This is another way of noting the transformation of cities into metropolitan areas. We will have more to say about this later because it is obviously relevant to our questions about downtown Detroit. For now, however, we may simply note the continuing growth, first of cities, then of metropolitan areas.

Because of the historic and continuing civic emphasis upon growth, Molotch describes the city as a "growth machine."[10] Growth has been one of the few objectives, he observes, that business and political elites can all agree on for their city (or metropolitan area). They also have a variety of competing interests though, and the contemporary newspaper plays a unique role in this modern context.

Moloch states that every parcel of land is associated with certain people's vested interests. Those who own the land, of course, want it developed in the way that will maximize their potential profits. Those who own nearby land are also

---

[10]Harvey Molotch, "The City as a Growth Machine," *American Journal of Sociology*, 82 (1976).

interested because of the ways in which they can be affected. For example, if odorous factories are built in one area, then an adjacent piece of land no longer presents a good site for private residences. Both direct and indirect interests in land are the basis for the formation of interest groups. Writing very much in the tradition of the Chicago ecologists, Molotch proceeds to describe how both conflict and the potential for joining together characterize increasingly larger geographical units.[11] Store owners on the same street, for example, may compete with each other over where a bus stop is to be placed. They may form a coalition, however, to obtain a bus line for their street. Still more encompassing coalitions may be formed when store, hotel, and restaurant owners attempt to influence where in a city a new convention center is to be built. Thus, conflicts and alliances make up the city as a growth machine.

In this context, the contemporary newspaper has a unique role to play. It is, Molotch states, the voice of the entire community, and it is viewed as taking a "statesmanlike" position that transcends special interest. Why is this so?

Are newspapers somehow exempt from the land-based competition that characterizes other enterprises? Yes, in one sense, Molotch answers. Newspapers are relatively unique in that they do not care where in the metropolitan area growth occurs, just so long as it occurs. Growth entails the potential for increased circulation, hence increased revenue. Therefore, when newspapers urge civic and business leaders to rise above selfish interests and prepare plans that will enhance the long-term growth of the metropolitan area, the newspapers are promoting their own special interests, regardless of the sincerity of the people who write the editorials. Newspapers are nevertheless able to play a key role because their sole commitment—growth—is the one objective which otherwise competing groups can support.

At the same time, however, there is competition among newspapers, themselves. As metropolitan areas have grown in size, it has been argued that the start-up costs for new general interest newspapers, that could serve the entire metropolitan area, have become prohibitive. The environment poses difficult economic barriers to entry. The founding of new newspapers that survive beyond infancy has correspondingly been very infrequent and as casulties have mounted among existing papers the result has been more and more metropolitan areas that have only a single general interest daily newspaper.[12]

As described in the preceding pages, competition among diverse entities was considered by the ecologists to be a fundamental characteristic of human societies. Competition was seen only as one cornerstone, though; the other was interdependence.

---

[11]However, the Chicago ecologists emphasized a "natural" view which underplayed the role of political intervention while Molotch views decision-making as an explicitly political process. For further discussion of this important difference, see John Logan and Harvey Molotch, *Urban Fortunes* (Berkeley: University of California Press, 1987).

[12]For more analyses of birth and death rates among populations of newspapers, see Glenn R. Carroll and Yangchung Paul Huo, "Organizational Task and Institutional Environments in Evolutionary Perspective," *American Journal of Sociology,* 91 (1986).

INTERDEPENDENCE AND UNANTICIPATED CONSEQUENCES

Darwin noted that in their struggle to reproduce every plant or animal is dependent upon others of the same, and other, species. Competition and interdependence are, therefore, simultaneous conditions. For example, seedling mistletoes growing on the same tree are in competition with each other for space; but, Darwin continued, in order to spread, the mistletoes are dependent upon birds to disseminate their seeds. A large concentration of mistletoes on a tree may better attract birds. Therefore, the success of the mistletoe in the struggle to survive may be enhanced by the very crowding that threatens each individual mistletoe. The competition that results from the location of many automobile dealers on the same street may analogously threaten the survival of each individual dealer. However, their concentration attracts car buyers to the area and may enhance the probability of the street persisting as an automobile sales area.

The clustering of highly similar, or identical, activities is due to a variety of forces. Maximum access is one such consideration. In order to attract sufficient customers, workers, or markets, an activity might require easy access to an entire metropolitan area. An opera house is an example of such an activity. Activities which attract overlapping clienteles—such as ballet companies or symphony orchestras—might be attracted to the same location. Joint ventures, such as a common box office, might then entail economies of scale for all of the operations.[13]

Noncentral locations might also lead to agglomeration if a particular site is associated with access to specialized labor pools or specialized business services. Thus, "automobile rows" typically develop in proximity to banking and credit agencies upon whom they are dependent. A clustering of smaller firms also produce economies of scale for the labor pools or specialized services upon whom they are dependent. The resultant concentration is efficient for the entire system, and an individual firm's ability to survive may be better within the agglomeration than outside of it; however, the survival of individual firms within a concentrated area almost inevitably requires that they be more specialized than scattered firms. On automobile row, for example, a firm may have to sell only used foreign cars in order to differentiate itself sufficiently from competitors. A suburban dealer, by contrast, may sell several types of new cars.

Because the evolutionary theorists examined all forms of plant and animal life, they were dissuaded from inferring motives on the part of individual members of species. Mistletoes were not regarded as clustering on trees because they wanted to attract birds! Events and outcomes were regarded as the result of complex natural processes. Intentional, rational planning was not seen as an important variable in the equation. Mistletoe, like red clover, birds, bees, mice, cats, and elephants do not deliberate over the long-term consequences of their actions.

---

[13]Edgar M. Hoover, "The Evolving Form and Organization of the Metropolis," in *The Modern City* edited by David W. Rasmussen and Charles T. Haworth (New York: Harper and Row, 1973).

And yet, many species displayed an elaborate social organization. Coordinated activities within ant and bee colonies, for example, were particularly pronounced; but they were not explained by attributing rationality or intentionality to individual ants or bees. The implications of this approach for the study of human society were profound. Specifically, it meant that the sheer existence of social organization was not in and of itself a sufficient reason to infer (human) rationality or a variety of other distinctive (human) motives.

The unwillingness to view human social organization as the result of distinctively human qualities did not entail a denial of these qualities. To the contrary, Park elaborately described the processes by which people acquired the distinctive qualities of human beings. In this regard, he stressed the difference between behavior and conduct. The latter includes an actor's judgments about the appropriateness of his or her behavior. Only human beings do this, Park stated, so we are the only creatures who feel self-conscious, blush, and the like.[14] Thus, the ecologists did not deny the existence of distinctively human judgment and understanding. Rather, they argued that these special qualities did not need to be inferred in order to explain (human) social organization. In other words, social organization evolves and changes *apart* from people's sentiments, judgments, intentions, and so on. The influence of Durkheim's view that society, or social organization, is a "separate thing" is apparent. (See Chapter Twelve.)

A clear example of this separation is provided by Burgess's description of the basic necessities of urban life. Millions of people in Chicago, he noted, are dependent upon one water system, one gas company, and one electricity plant. "Yet, like most of the other aspects of our communal urban life," he concluded, this interdependence occurs, "without a shred of the 'spirit of cooperation.'"[15]

Evolutionary theory, then the dominant perspective, stressed the similarities among all life forms. By separating human social organization from the distinctive qualities of human beings, the ecologists achieved a degree of congruence with the dominant perspective of the time. It also permitted sociological analyses to parallel biological analyses, enhancing the academic and intellectual stature of the newer discipline. Thus, the ecologists appreciated the distinctiveness of human "conduct" but at the aggregate level, viewed people as "behaving," just like other life forms.

In order to reconcile their recognition of conduct, at the individual level, with their view of behavior, at the aggregate level, the ecologists stressed the unanticipated consequences of human activities; that is, the way individual conduct contributed to social organization without the intent or awareness of the individual. During the eighteenth century a group of Scottish moralists articulated a view of human society which stressed such unanticipated consequences. Their perspective provided basic tenets that later became central both to the evolutionists and the ecologists.

---

[14]Robert E. Park, *Principles of Human Behavior* (Chicago: Zalas Corporation, 1915). Portions are reproduced in the Park-Burgess *Introduction*.

[15]Ernest W. Burgess, "The Growth of the City," in Park and others, *The City*, p. 53.

The Scottish Moralists[16]

The philosophers who are categorized in this school all shared a distrust of the role of reason. Within the psychological make-up of people, they considered reason to be subordinate to "passion." David Hume, for example, argued that reason, by itself, should never be viewed as the cause of people's behavior. Whether people's motives are learned or instinctual, they can not be seriously altered by reason because reason is "the slave of the passions."[17] So, for example, if a scientist claims to be motivated by a dispassionate search for knowledge, do not believe it. You will more likely be correct if you assume the motive is a desire for personal fame or some other compelling emotion.

Given the subordinated role of reason, the Scots questioned, how is social order possible? They answered that it was the result of unanticipated consequences. People—like ants or bees, in this regard—have little conception of the larger social order. Further, whatever conception they may have does not detour them from pursuing their own highly limited goals. However, from each individual's selfish pursuit of restricted objectives, a coherent whole develops.

Park and Burgess presented this view of unanticipated consequences to their University of Chicago students in an excerpt from the writings of one of the best known Scots, Adam Smith. In this paper, the "father of laissez-faire capitalism" describes how every employer and employee pursues those ends that each considers to be to their own personal advantage. The result, however, is that capitalists create the maximum number of jobs and workers wind up in the positions that are of maximum benefit to society. They are all led by "an invisible hand" into a more nearly perfect order than planners could ever devise.[18] Smith's notion of an invisible hand had numerous counterparts among other Scottish moralists. Thomas Reid, for example, described the geometric movements of bees as based upon knowledge that was held only by "that great Geometrician who made the bee."[19] The, there is both order and ultimate purpose to the social worlds of ants, bees, and people. Individual "members" of a society all contribute to this order in some way, despite their ignorance of it and despite the selfishness of their personal motives.

It should also be noted that social order that resulted from unanticipated consequences, in the Scots' view, was not inferior because it was unplanned. To the contrary, they viewed it as more perfectly organized and/or efficient than any intentionally created system. This view provided another important precursor to the Park, Burgess, McKenzie emphasis upon urban social organization as resulting from "natural" processes.

In summary, the eighteenth century writings of the Scottish Moralists and the late nineteenth century evolutionary theories provided a number of abstract assump-

---

[16]For further, general discussion of this school, see the "Introduction" in *The Scottish Moralists,* edited by Louis Schneider (Chicago: University of Chicago Press, 1967).

[17]David Hume, "Some Limitations of Reason," ibid.

[18]Park and Burgess, *Introduction to the Science of Sociology,* pp. 232-233.

[19]Quoted in Schneider, *The Scottish Moralists,* p. xxxi

tions which influenced the human ecologists. The most important of these can be summarized as follows:

1) Competition and interdependence are the pervasive and natural features of social organization.
2) In order to persist, every institution, role, or geographical area must adapt to changes which are continually occurring.
3) Aggregate actions determine the form of social organization independently of individuals' intentions.

With these background assumptions in mind, let us turn to the ecological analyses of how cities grow.

HOW CITIES GROW

The immigration-induced growth of turn-of-the-century American cities was pronounced. Between 1880 and 1910, for example, Detroit's population increased from slightly over 100,000 persons to nearly one-half million persons. Philadelphia, Chicago, and many other cities doubled, or more, in size during this period.

When the population of a city increases, the area encompassed by the city will typically expand, unless rivers, mountains, or other topographical features present barriers. Most of the rapidly growing turn-of-the-century cities were following this growth-expansion rule, and explaining how these processes occurred provided the major set of concerns for the human ecologists.

Burgess viewed fluctuations in the size of a city as indicative of a process that was analogous to the metabolism of a body.[20] A decline in the natural rate of growth (births minus deaths), for example, would be akin to a physiological pathology in which cells fail to reproduce. The then major source of population change, however, was international migration; but it was occurring so rapidly that Burgess feared newcomers would not easily find new roots. If they were "foot loose," they would probably not be under social control, either. Thus, great movement was associated with insufficient regulation and high rates of murder, robbery, promiscuity, and vice. The equilibrium of the entire social organism was threatened.

McKenzie called attention to the crucial role of mobility, or movement, in contrasting the theoretical underpinnings of plant and animal ecology. The important difference, he stated, is that animals have the power of locomotion. The human animal is further distinguished by the capacity to deliberately modify an environment. However, McKenzie concluded, planning capacities do not significantly alter the form of human communities making them, theoretically, subject to the same type of analysis as other animal communities.[21]

[20]Burgess, "The Growth of the City."

[21]McKenzie's adherence to the Scots' perspective in this matter is clearly indicated in the following footnote: "Although the actions of individuals may be designed and controlled, the total effect of individual action is neither designed nor anticipated." Roderick McKenzie, "The Ecological Approach to the Study of the Human Community," *American Journal of Sociology,* 30 (1924), footnote 5.

Concentric Zones

The typical city, Burgess proposed, will expand from its downtown outward, in a series of circular zones; circular because all parts of a circular zone (north or south, east or west) remain equally distant from the centrally located downtown. The central location and the central role of downtowns natually go together. With respect to their central role, Burgess noted that it was in the downtown area of every city that department stores, skyscraper office buildings, art museums, great hotels, theatres, and city halls tended to be located. With respect to their central location, he noted that modes of transportation, such as bus lines or subways, tended to converge in the downtown.

Sociology graduate students at Chicago, during the 1920s and 1930s, further examined downtowns—Chicago's, in particular—in minute detail. Earl Johnson, for example, documented its role as the focal point of transportation and communication by noting telephone and telegraph patterns, commuting rates, and so on. To illustrate, he noted that almost one-half of all telegraphic messages sent from anywhere in the city of Chicago originated in the downtown area. From telephone company records, he reported that 25 percent of all local calls were made from downtown Chicago even though it contained only about 5 percent of all the telephones in the city. During a 24-hour period (in 1931), he tallied over one-half million automobile and truck trips between sections of the metropolitan area and found that downtown was either the origin or destination of over 70 percent of them. He concluded that patterns of transportation and communication, fix the downtown at the ecological center of the city and entire metropolitan area.[22]

Encircling the downtown, Burgess continued, there is typically a transitional zone. Its deteriorated buildings ring downtown, extending out for as little as a few blocks or as much as a number of miles. One of the principal characteristics of this zone is heterogeneity. It contains light manufacturing plants, small businesses, rooming houses, vice centers, racial or ethnic ghettoes, and slums. Both its physical deterioration and the great heterogeneity of its occupants detracts from its desirability: New immigrants would not likely choose to live adjacent to whore houses; owners of small businesses would probably prefer not to be located in slum areas, and so forth. However, all the conditions which make the area undesirable make it affordable for socially and/or economically marginal residential or commercial uses.

The Chicago ecologists regarded the zone of transition as a socially disorganized area. It attracted persons who were marginal in some ways, to begin with; but the general immorality of the place further contributed to its high rates of delinquency, prostitution, addiction, crime, and the like. While the inner city of Chicago, like most other cities, has undergone transformations since the 1920s, a diversity of life-styles still characterizes many portions of this zone. Aged brownstone and modern high-rise apartments share the same streets today, adjacent to "fun houses," stand-up singles bars, and strip joints.[23]

[22]Earl S. Johnson, "The Functions of the Central Business District," in *Contemporary Society* (Chicago: University of Chicago Press, 1932).

[23]Joyce R. Starr and Donald E. Carns, "Singles and the City," in *Cities in Change*, edited by John Walton and Donald E. Carns (Boston: Allyn and Bacon, 1973).

Beyond the zone of transition, Burgess described a zone of "workingmen's homes." It is primarily an area of second-generation immigrants, living in two flats and working in factories. Encircling this zone, further out from the downtown, is a residential zone containing private homes and more exclusive apartment buildings. Finally, there is the suburban, or commuter's zone, beyond the city limits.

Invasion-Succession

Burgess wrote that Chicago's downtown once contained most of the varied activities and social types that, by 1920, were spatially distributed across the five zones. With the growth of a city, types of activities and people expand outward, dominating particular locations, in a process termed, "succession." Both the term and the process had been previously described by botanists, and their formulations were adapted to cities by the human ecologists. Specifically, the plant ecologists had described stages through which plant communities passed in the course of their development. For example, many different plant species would simultaneously occupy an area prior to the invasion of pine trees. Then the area would become (exclusively) a pine forest.

By analogy, human communities were also viewed as growing in stages, or successional sequence. In small towns in the state of Washington, for example, McKenzie described a recurrent sequence as entailing first a grocery store, then a restaurant, followed still later by a bank, and then other specialized stores.[24] In other words, as the size of a community's population increased, there was increased specialization in the kinds of services offered, and it occurred in a predictable order. With continued population growth, the location of specialized activities also becomes increasingly differentiated. Ultimately, specific specialties dominate in particular locales, as illustrated in the concentric zones.

Growth eventually results in differentiation of location because it increases competition for space at the center. Only in a small town is it possible for all commercial-retail activities to be concentrated on Main Street. As the town grows in size and new land uses emerge, competition for space in the center is intensified. Central locations are almost always most accessible due to the tendency of human communities to grow centrifugally, that is, by spreading outward from the center. Lines of transportation and communication both lead to and follow this population expansion. Therefore, central locations remain the most accessible, making them the most desirable and expensive. However, only those activities or land uses that can most profit from a central location can afford it. Those activities which would benefit less are forced into less accessible, lower priced locations. (Remember, according to the ecologists, this highly efficient sorting of activities and land uses is a natural process, requiring neither the awareness nor intent of individuals.)

Invasion and succession referred not only to types of activities, but to types of people, especially to immigrants who generally tended to move as groups. Later arriving immigrants were described as invading the neighborhoods occupied by

[24]Roderick D. McKenzie, *The Metropolitan Community (New York: McGraw-Hill, 1933).*

earlier arrivals. The latter would slowly leave and be succeeded by the newcomers. Land uses might remain constant, however; that is, buildings that formerly served as apartments, churches, or stores would continue to function in the same capacities. Only the ethnicity of the tenants and owners would change.

The nature of this invasion-succession process is illustrated by shifting residential patterns in New York City. Prior to the 1880s, German, Irish, and other Western European immigrants predominated. Then the number of immigrants increased in number and involved Italians, Russian Jews, and others from Eastern Europe. In each instance, newcomers to the city settled initially wherever they could afford to live; typically in less desirable and overcrowded tenements near the center of the city.

Adjustment to an American, urban way of life was frequently associated with upward mobility, especially for the children of immigrants, and a desire for better and more spacious housing. This meant moving from Manhattan to Queens, Long Island, and eventually beyond state boundaries into New Jersey and Connecticut.

Mobility often entailed changed identifications and aspirations which made people want to move. However, those who wished to remain were faced with an invasion of new immigrants. In effect, the "costs" of staying were increased, both psychologically and economically. It meant being engulfed by a different ethnic community which led to changes in the character of stores and schools. Maintaining the same way of life also became economically unfeasible. After 1880, for example, German and other Western European Protestants found the membership in their Manhattan churches declining so rapidly that Sunday schools and other church activities dramatically increased in cost for those who remained.[25] Thus, persons of any given ethnicity typically wound up migrating in mass, its collective nature resembling a flock of geese or a colony of ants.

The movement of immigrant groups was a centrifugal process. Newly arriving groups could typically afford to reside only in the deteriorating and disorganized zone of transition. As they became better educated, more skilled, and assimilated into the main stream of American life, they also became better able to afford more desirable neighborhoods. Thus, they were pulled outward by more attractive residential areas as well as pushed outward by newly arriving immigrants.

In sum, moving up has traditionally meant moving out, and moving out has traditionally meant moving into communities where the residents are predominantly either natives or/and members of earlier arriving ethnic groups. Thus, there has been a strong association among: status attainment, geographical mobility and assimilation.

In many contemporary cities, the experience of blacks appears to provide an exception to this pattern. Specifically, as blacks move up socially and move out geographically, white flight has tended to keep down the amount of residential integration that results. However, in general, the status-movement-assimilation

---

[25]Oscar Handlin, *The Newcomers* (New York: Anchor, 1962). For further discussion, see Stanley Lieberson, *A Piece of the Pie* (Berkeley: University of California Press, 1980).

pattern seems to be even more true now than it was during the early part of this century; and it does seem to describe the experience of other non-white (Hispanic) groups.[26]

Expansion and Integration

The spatial form of a city is largely determined by the modes of transportation and communication that are available at any given time. Beginning in the 1920s, mass-produced automobiles permitted city dwellers to move further and further out from the inner city but still commute daily to inner-city jobs. High speed commuter trains permitted still further expansion. There were simultaneous increases in the strength of radio signals, the circulation radius of daily newspapers, and the like. Thus, even in highly dispersed metropolitan areas, transportation and communication mediums continue to tie distant areas to the inner city. (Of course, the very meaning of distance changes with these developments. How far five miles is really depends upon whether one has to walk it, take a bus or cab, and so on.)

If the central city, in general, and the downtown, in particular, is coordinating and integrating activities across an extended metropolitan area, it ought to be reflected in the city's labor force distribution. Specifically, Kasarda has reasoned that transportation, communication, and public administration are the major occupational categories that provide coordination. Therefore, the greater the percentage of a city's labor force employed in these occupational categories, the more the city is likely to provide metropolitan area integration. His hypothesis was: The larger the population of the suburban area relative to the city, the larger the percentage of the city's labor force that will be employed in the coordinating occupations.[27]

Using census data from 1960, he proceeded to trichotomize a large sample of American cities according to the relative size of their suburban population. If 70 percent or more of the total metropolitan area resided in the city, the suburban area was considered small. If 30 percent or less of the total population resided in the city, the suburbs were considered large. A medium category involved between 30 and 70 percent.

Kasarda then examined city occupational patterns in relation to the relative size of the city's suburbs. His findings show, as expected, that the larger the suburban area, the larger the percentage of city employment in integrating occupations. For example, as the relative size of suburban rings increases from small to medium to large, the proportion of city employees in transportation and communication occupations increases from 29 to 36 to 43 percent. While Kasarda did not attempt to locate these employees more precisely, it is clear from other studies that a large proportion of them are employed in downtown areas.

With respect to coordinating activities within extended metropolitan areas, it appeared that downtowns were still functioning analogously to the nucleus of a cell

[26]Douglas S. Massey and Brendan P. Mullan, "Processes of Hispanic and Black Spatial Assimilation," *American Journal of Sociology*, 89 (1984).

[27]John D. Kasarda, "The Theory of Ecological Expansion," *Social Force*, 51 (1972).

in 1960. There were, however, some results which suggested that coordination might be in the process of becoming less centralized. For example, Kasarda noted that as the size of the suburban ring increased, *suburban* employment in transportation, communication, and other integrative occupations also increased. The suburban increase was smaller, and it occured after the city increase; but Kasarda felt that it might increase more dramatically after 1960.

Beginning in the late 1960s, for the first time, there was an increase in population growth outside of metropolitan areas; to be more specific, it was in areas adjacent to, but just outside of, metropolitan areas. With this greater decentralization, more of the coordinating function seems to have moved from central cities to suburban areas. The latter became more important centers, integrating the central city with residential populations located outside of the previously established metropolitan area.[28]

The decentralization of retail centers appears already to have occurred in response to changes in the distribution of urban populations. As early as the 1920s, Burgess noted the development of retail centers outside of Chicago's downtown, or loop. He referred to them as "satellite loops" and noted that they were then controlled from within the central business district.[29] The chain store (then just beginning) was presented as the best example of centralized decentralization.

However, as the urban population grew in size and expanded in territory, patterns of retail trade have become increasingly decentralized in organization as well as location. The movement of integrative functions from central city to suburb was, from one perspective, simply the last of many functions to move out.

CONCLUSION

The location of retail centers is determined primarily by accessibility to potential shoppers. As the population of large metropolitan areas, like Detroit, has become dispersed, so too has the location of retail centers. It was, of course, the automobile that led to the large-scale dispersal of urban populations. Affordable, mass-produced automobiles made people free to live almost anywhere. They no longer had to live within walking distance of work sites or else close to trolley or street car lines.

The entire social organization slowly accommodated to the privately owned automobile. Not only were commuting patterns altered, but patterns of courtship, shopping, family visiting, and so on. As the ecologists had noted, every institution, role, and geographical area had to adapt to the changes or face extinction. Downtown shopping centers, such as Detroit's, have tried. For example, associations of down-

[28]David F. Sly and Jeffrey Tayman, "Metropolitan Morphology and Population Mobility," *American Journal of Sociology*, 86 (1980). For further discussion of the limitations of the earlier theory of ecological expansion, see Harvey Marshall and John Stahura, "The Theory of Ecological Expansion," *Social Forces*, 65 (1986).

[29]Burgess, "The Growth of the City."

town merchants have become increasingly active in trying to lure shoppers back to the downtown. However, they have not been able to compete successfully with suburban shopping centers. The latter possess an almost insurmountable locational advantage as well as much more abundant parking facilities.

Thus, despite the nostalgic sentiments that surround downtown shopping and regardless of the inducements offered by downtown merchants, downtown retail centers continue to decline.[30] The generally unplanned, "natural" dispersal of metropolitan populations, in conjunction with the automobile, has resulted in the formation of numerous retail nuclei across metropolitan areas. Moreover, this pattern now seems irreversible as the spatial dispersion of metropolitan areas continuously prompts changes in the larger social organization to which all elements must adapt.

Hawley makes a distinction between types of cumulative change that may be helpful to us here. Specifically, he identifies *growth* as the development of a system to the largest size and maximum complexity that can be supported by existing means of transportation and communiction. Put in other words, growth entails the gradual maturation of an adaptive system. Hawley terms the second type of change, *evolution*. It tends to be a response to forces that are external in origin that lead to the development of new information/knowledge that increase the system's potential. Thus, evolution is more dramatic than growth because it results in new forms of social organization.[31]

The data we have been describing with respect to residential dispersal, retail decentralization, and so on—viewed from Hawley's framework—may be better regarded as producing evolutionary changes rather than growth. At some point, probably around 1970, many larger metropolitan areas simply outgrew the capacity of their formerly centralized organizations.

SUGGESTIONS FOR ADDITIONAL READING

BRIAN BERRY and JOHN KASARDA, *Contemporary Urban Ecology*. New York: Macmillan, 1977.
AMOS H. HAWLEY, *Urban Society*, New York: Wiley, 1981.
BILL MCKELVEY, *Organizational Systmatics*. Berkeley, CA: University of California Press, 1982.

---

[30]There are a few central business districts whose retail sales have revived in recent years, but not due to the traditional ecological variables. For an analysis of the variables related to CBD sales, see Judith J. Friedman, "Central Business Districts," *Social Science Quarterly*, 69, 1988.

[31]Hawley, *Human Ecology*.

6

STRUCTURE
Social Stratification
Marx, Weber, Davis and Moore

Throughout California and parts of several other western states, farm workers have historically received meager wages. Their financial returns have been barely enough for them to continue to toil in the grape and lettuce fields. A large proportion of the farm workers are foreign born, or the offspring of foreign-born parents. Mexican descent is especially common, but Filipinos and many other nationalities are also represented. In general, they are members of minority groups whose ethnic or racial status is relatively low in the United States. The farm workers have historically lacked political representation or organized lobbies as well. They have, therefore, been able to do little to change the conditions under which they live.

In sum, farm workers have generally been (1) poor and economically dependent, (2) members of low-status minority groups, and (3) without political power. These three conditions often go together and, when they do, they tend to persist from generation to generation.

Their persistence was illustrated by an exchange between Phillip Veracruz, then a vice president of the United Farm Workers and a group of owners of grape fields in Delano, California. The meeting was called in response to the owners' insistence on deducting ten cents an hour from the wages of Filipino workers. If the union would not agree, the owners threatened, then reduced profits would force them to close the labor camps in which the farm workers lived. Veracruz responded by noting how much more the owners and their children would have to lose from such a shutdown. "I remember when he was a very small boy," Veracruz said, pointing to one of the owner's sons across the table. He had since become wealthy, Veracruz added. It appeared that the offspring of the owners had much to show for their efforts, he concluded, then asked, "But what do the Filipinos have?"[1]

---

[1]Quoted in Mark Day, *Forty Acres* (New York: Praeger, 1971), p. 178.

It is interesting to question how different the historical experiences of farm workers would have been if they had not simultaneously been characterized by poverty, low social status, and no power. Suppose, for example, the farm workers had somehow managed collectively to acquire wealth. Would they have remained just as powerless? Or, suppose they were able to attain political power. Would their social status have been affected?

Our ability to provide answers to speculative questions, such as those raised above, is enhanced by the intellectual debate that began between Max Weber and Marx's "ghost." At the crux of this debate are profound sociological questions about the dimensions of stratification and the relationships among them. Specifically, Weber contended that economic, social, and political dimensions of stratification were analytically distinct from each other and that each was at least somewhat autonomous. This view was formulated by Weber in reaction to Marx's (earlier) argument that the social, political, and other dimensions of stratification were little more than "redundant manifestations" of the economic order.

MARX ON THE ECONOMIC ORDER

Marx offered a critique of social and economic classes throughout history. Much of his analyses was devoted to an analysis of change, specifically the process by which emerging economic systems selectively retained features of previous forms. The capitalistic system drew most of his wrath, however, and it also provided the immediate point of departure for his radical program of change. It is enlightening, therefore, to begin by briefly examining the origins of capitalism and the kinds of theoretical statements, including Marx's, which it elicited.

Adam Smith: "Leave us alone"

The feudal period in Europe was very slowly and fitfully coming to a close around the turn of the eighteenth century. Serfs, lords, and knights were being replaced by factory workers, bankers, and farmers. While entrepreneurial activities were growing, they were impeded by lingering vestiges of the feudal period. This included a harsh and corrupt system of taxation and a set of very burdensome commercial regulations. Those who wished for rapid "modernization" were frustrated. It was within this context that Colbert, the finance minister of France, asked of the entrepreneurs, "How may we help you?" One leading French merchant, late in the seventeenth century, replied, "Nous laissez faire"; that is, "leave us alone!"[2]

The classic justification for laissez faire capitalism was offered, during the late eighteenth century, by Adam Smith. About 50 years later Marx formulated his theories which led to the *Communist Manifesto*. Their ultimate commitments could hardly have been more different. In many respects, the unregulated pursuit of

---

[2]Quoted in Robert L. Heilbroner, *The Economic Problem* (Englewood Cliffs: Prentice-Hall, 1968), pp. 72-73.

profit—laissez faire capitalism—and communism are polar opposites. What is intriguing about Smith and Marx, however, is that their descriptions of stratification in (then modern capitalistic) societies are very much alike.

Smith contended that in all modern societies people are divided into three basic categories according to their primary sources of income. He specifically described the three groupings as those whose livelihood rested upon[3]

1) Rents from land and buildings (that is, landlords).
2) Profits from the ownership of businesses (that is, merchants and stock holders).
3) Wages from labor (that is, employees or laborers).

Interspersed in Smith's description were some very harsh criticisms of these categories. For example, he regarded the landlords as tending to be lazy and ignorant because they had it too easy. He viewed the business owners as often willing to deceive the public in order to further their own selfish economic interests. These shortcomings were seen more as flaws in character than as defects in the system, though. Correspondingly, they did not call for fundamental changes in his view.

Like the other Scottish Moralists (see Chapter Five), Smith was reluctant to equate appearance and reality. Any system of social organization was assumed to serve "divine intentions" which individuals could not be expected fully to comprehend.[4] They should, therefore, be very reluctant to try to change the system. This perspective led Smith to regard the three income groupings as a "natural" consequence of modern economic systems. As such, they were expected to be enduring.

In sum, Smith's writings clearly provided a powerful philosophical defense for laissez faire capitalism, unregulated commerce dominated by the profit motive. Despite agreeing with much of Smith's empirical description, Marx obviously felt very differently about what he observed.

Marx: Naked, Callous Calculation

The underpinning of a society, in Marx's view, was provided by the means of production and by people's relationship to these means of production. (See Chapter Four for elaboration.) In capitalistic societies, Marx continued, this produced the three groupings described also by Smith: landlords, business owners, and laborers. However, Marx saw these categories as a by-product of human actions, rather than divine intentions. Because he rejected the "naturalness" of the system and its groupings, deliberate change seemed both more possible and desirable to Marx.

Marx saw the distinction between landowners and business owners as declining in importance in the more highly developed capitalistic nations. The two groups were in the process, he wrote, of becoming parts of a single class, the bourgeoisie. The distinguishing characteristic of this class is its ownership of capital, or productive wealth in the form of machines, land, factories, and the like. Profits or interests

---

[3] Adam Smith, *The Wealth of Nations* (Edinburgh: Adam and Charles Black, 1863).

[4] For example, he stated that the system serves, "beneficent ends which the great Director of nature intended." Adam Smith, *Theory of Moral Sentiments* (London: G. Bell and Sons, 1892), p. 110.

or rents generally accrue to the owners of capital when labor is added to their capital; for example, people are hired to work the machines. This introduces the second class (both chronologically and symbolically), the proletariat. These are the people who have only their labor to sell: the machine operators, clerks, tenant farmers, and so on.[5]

While Marx recognized that small merchants, highly skilled crafts workers and others could be placed into distinct subgroups for purposes of stratification, he argued that the trend in capitalistic societies was toward a bipolar division into bourgeoisie and proletariat. By comparison to the fundamental difference in their relationship to the means of production, all other distinctions seemed minor.

Measuring Marxist Classes

Relations to the means of production must be a core feature of any Marx-inspired measure of social classes, but Erik Olin Wright has argued that Marx's dichotomy (i.e., the bourgeoisie and the proletariat) is not adequate for classifying classes in modern capitalistic societies. One important reason for its inadequacy is that several large occupational categories appear to occupy contradictory locations within a capitalistic system of production. For example, managers clearly dominate workers in the workplace. Managers may also have some ownership rights in their companies and, thereby, exploit the workers, as well as dominate them. However, managers typically own little or none of their employing companies. They are then like the workers they dominate in that they are exploited and dominated by the true bourgeoisie.[6]

Wright's social class typology includes, of course, the bourgeoisie and the proletariat, and managers as described in the preceding paragraph. In addition, it includes three other categories of workers:

1) *Petty bourgeoisie*—as described by Marx, people who own and use their own means of production (i.e., self-employed business persons).
2) *Small employers*—petty bourgeoisie who also employ fewer than ten workers.
3) *Semi-autonomous professionals*—experts who do not own the means of production, but have substantial control over their own work activity.

One of the most distinctive features of Wright's classification is that it emphasizes social relationships; that is, buying and selling labor and patterns of domination and control within the production process. Specifically, he classified nearly 50 percent of an American sample as working class (essentially proletariat), because they lacked significant control and decision-making authority over their own work, and they did not control anyone else. Another 20 percent of the labor force (consisting of semi-autonomous employees and low-level managers), were considered to be predominantly working class, as well. Thus, nearly 70 percent of the population was classified as working class, rather than middle class.

[5]Karl Marx, *Capital,* vol. 1 (Chicago: Charles H. Kerr, 1906).
[6]Erik Olin Wright, et al., "The American Class Structure," *American Sociological Review,* 47 (1982).

Wright's classification procedures and results stand in marked contrast to conventional practices. The latter generally assign people to a class location according to the amount of education, prestige, or some other attribute they possess. The result is a gradational scale in which the middle class is much larger than in Wright's relational scale.

Class and Interest

Contractual ties between capital and labor were, in Marx's view, regulated by a legal code. This code appears to dispense justice; but, in fact, it reflects and perpetuates the inequities of capitalist society through its protection of private property. Marx believed, therefore, that the study of law was one of the best ways to disclose the class structure of a society. Why, for example, are there so many more restrictions on the renter of an apartment than on the landlord?

As a result of the differences in their relationship to the means of production, Marx contended that the bourgeoisie and proletariat have objectively different class interests. Only the owners of capital benefit from the continuation of a capitalistic mode. However, the proletariat have generally failed to recognize their objective class interests, as Marx defined them. Criminal and civil law, the mass media, and "traditional values" all reflect the class interests of the bourgeoisie. The laboring class is thereby diverted from developing an awareness of its class position and related interests. Thus, Marx concluded, the oppression of the proletariat is based upon both deception and coercion.

Put in other terms, Marx was distinguishing between a class "in-itself" and a class "for-itself." The former referred to an objective relation to the means of production, apart from any feelings of one-ness that might or might not characterize those whose positions were the same. A class for itself, by contrast, implies a recognition of the objective commonality, leading a class to act in accordance with its interests.

As the interests of the bourgeoisie molded political, religious, and other institutions to meet its class-based needs, Marx and Engels described how occupations were "stripped of their honor." The priest, the poet, the scientist, and so on were no longer looked up to in awe. All were reduced to wage laborers. In other words, modern bourgeois society created a world in its image, and honor had no place in this world; it had room only for production, exchange, and property.[7]

Weber's Reply

In many respects Weber's theory of stratification was a reply to Marx's view. While it is possible to view Weber's treatment as an explicit polemic against Marx, this position fails to recognize the many areas of agreement between them. In the following pages we shall note both their agreements and their disagreements, and then reexamine the situation of the farm workers in light of this comparison.

[7]Karl Marx and Friedrich Engels, *The Communist Manifesto* (New York: International Publishers Co., 1948).

One of the most fundamental disagreements between Marx and Weber followed from the latter's view that stratification entailed three orders, or dimensions: economic, social, and political. Within each order, he continued, people are divided into classes (economic), status groups (social), and parties (political). The relationships among these orders was, at least potentially, reciprocal in Weber's view; that is, in any concrete society, any one dimension could influence the form of the others. By contrast, Marx's view was more one-directional, since it regarded the economic dimension as determining the others.[8]

CLASS

Weber defined a class as people who have the same life chances in so far as these life chances are determined by their economic position. By life chances he meant their living conditions, their life experiences, and their opportunities to acquire goods and services. This includes such things as people's ability to buy a home or a business, take a European vacation, and so on.

Weber wrote that he intended to define class in terms of possessions which he recognized were ultimately matters of people's market situation. Very much like Marx, he saw the capitalistic market as excluding the nonowners of capital "from competing for highly valued goods."[9] In Marx's terms, Weber argued that the bourgeoisie had a monopoly on certain kinds of opportunities. Those who "have nothing to offer but their services"—the proletariat—are closed out of the competition. However, Weber differentiated class positions more than Marx did. The bourgeoisie vary, he argued, according to the kind of property that people own. Those who own mines, cattle, buildings, factories, and the like, are all different from each other, and similar kinds of differences also characterize those without property; that is, who have only their labor to sell (as miners, ranch hands, janitors, machine operators, and so on).

A more significant difference between Marx and Weber can be found in the latter's sharp distinction between class position and class interest. First of all, Weber contended, class interests are ambiguous, People in the same class situation, as classified by an outside observer, may not regard themselves as being in the same situation. Thus, Weber concluded, neither possessions nor life chances necessarily "give birth" to class actions.

This difference between Marx and Weber may not be as great as it initially appears to be, though. Marx also thought that the proletariat had not recognized its true class interests. He merely thought that they *should,* and he believed that they would, in the long run. By placing more emphasis upon a subjective construction of circumstances, Weber simply called attention to one of the impediments to class action. Moreover, Weber also agreed with Marx's contention that class actions

---

[8]The following discussion is based primarily upon H. H. Gerth and C. Wright Mills, *From Max Weber: Essays in Sociology* (New York: Oxford, 1958).

[9]Ibid., p. 181.

would be more likely when people recognized that their diminished life chances were due to the economic order. However, Weber regarded status considerations as an additional impediment to collective action based upon class position, and in this regard the difference between Weber and Marx was more substantial.

STATUS

Status, according to Weber, involves life-style, matters of honor and privilege. If class is ultimately related to the production of goods then, Weber stated, life-style is tied to the consumption of goods. The relationship between class and status was, for Weber, a crucial question. On the one hand he acknowledged that status can be based upon property and that it typically is, in the long run. "It may be that only the families coming under approximately the same tax class dance with one another."[10] On the other hand, he sharply distinguished between status and "mere economic acquisition." He also contended that the same status group sometimes included persons of different class situations; for example, bosses and their employees might belong to the same club.

In general, life-styles imply restrictions on social interaction. This typically entails routine avoidance of persons in lower ranked status groups and an attempt to confine the marriages of offspring to others of the same circle. The boundaries of a status group are usually amorphous, but they can become rigid, or castelike. When this occurs, status honor becomes a matter of legal privilege; that is, laws confine the eating of certain kinds of food, wearing special clothing ("uniforms"), carrying arms, or the like, to certain status groups.

Weber specified several conditions under which a status group was most likely to become castelike. The most important of these was when status honor and class position coincide and persist congruently for a long period of time. If status distinctions are related to ethnic or racial differences, then Weber proposed that castelike groups were also more likely to form.

An excellent illustration of the kind of issues Weber raised in his discussion of status is provided in a study reported by DiMaggio and Mohr. They developed a scale to measure people's interest in prestigious cultural resources. It was based upon attendance at symphony concerts and art events, literature readings, and so on. The investigators hypothesized that young people who scored highly on this scale would prefer more highly educated spouses because such spouses would be "more presentable" in high-prestige circles. Their analyses of a national sample supported the hypothesis even when the class position of both the respondents and their spouses were held constant. In other words, the correlation between people's cultural interests (at age 18) and their spouses' educational level (at age 30) was due to status considerations independent of class.[11]

---

[10]Ibid., p. 187.

[11]Paul DiMaggio and John Mohr, "Cultural Capital, Educational Attainment and Marriage Selection," *American Journal of Sociology,* 90 (1985).

Class or Status: Coats of Arms

In some concrete situations, it is difficult to tell the degree to which class and status genuinely involve separate spheres. Depending upon whether one is more inclined to follow Marx or Weber, very different interpretations can be applied to the same situation; for example, the rights of families to claim coats of arms in Britain during the late middle ages.

No one is certain, but it was probably during the twelfth century that coats of arms were first displayed in Britain. Arthur C. Fox-Davies, an expert in "pedigrees and heraldry," describes three functions that were initially served by the granting of arms:

1) to honor families for the special service to the nation of their (male) members.
2) to distinguish the meritorious so they could better serve as a model to others.
3) to differentiate families with noble ancestors.

The right to display a coat of arms was largely confined to males who could prove (legitimate) male descent from a person to whom such a grant had been made. If the family of a man's wife had this right also, he could incorporate her family's emblem on his shield if—prior to marriage—he was entitled to transmit arms by virtue of his own noble birth. A woman could transmit arms only if she were an heiress, a position whose medieval meaning differs from current usage. Specifically, an heiress was a woman, without brothers, born to a father who had been granted arms. Under these limited conditions, she could transmit arms. "Neither land nor money have anything to do with it."[12]

By the late middle ages, however, "abuses" began to multiply. Merchants and monks encroached upon the privileged few. The trend has continued, with faked claims to noble lineage outnumbering the legitimate claims. For this reason, Fox-Davies and others have attempted to codify the rules and establish the precedents. His two-volume work, for example, contains over 2,000 pages devoted to description of legitimate arms, their crests, colors, mottos, and origins.

Armorial bearings provide an excellent example of symbols which set apart a status group, in Weber's terminology. Through high rates of intramarriage, these noble families have persisted as a more or less distinct status group for several hundred years. It is precisely this type of stratification that Weber is better able to account for than Marx. At the same time, while the right to transmit arms characterized only some of the medieval landed aristocracy, it was almost completely confined to this segment. Thus, Marx would be quick to point out that arms-rights were a class privilege, and Weber would have to concede that it was a situation in which a status group was based upon class position.

PARTY

Parties, according to Weber, are associations that explicitly attempt to influence collective decisions, usually in the face of opposition. Examples include political

[12]Arthur C. Fox-Davies, *Armorial Families* (Rutland, Vt.: Charles E. Tuttle Co., 1970), p. xxxiii.

groups, such as the Young Republicans, as well as such varied associations as the Women's Christian Temperance Union and the Chamber of Commerce.

Class interests can lead to the formation of parties, to attempt to determine the price of labor, for example. Status groups can also lead to the formation of parties, to protect a group's exclusive use of certain symbols, for example. In most instances, however, Weber viewed parties as based partly upon class and partly upon status; but any combination was regarded as possible.

Weber considered it very important to distinguish among: (1) the distribution of people into varied types of strata, (2) social relationships among persons within a stratum, and (3) associations, or organizations, designed to influence collective decisions. His discussion of parties was meant analytically to distinguish the third activity from the former two. Thus, a class or a status group, in and of itself, may try to exert influence, he conceded, but "parties live in a house of power." In contrast to Marx, Weber stressed that dealings in the house of power were separate from class and were usually based upon both class and status considerations, rather than class alone.

Class *and* Status: The Antisuffrage Party

An interesting illustration of the way in which class and status variables can come together to influence political decisions is provided by Marshall's analysis of the antisuffrage movement. During the early decades of this century, while feminists were organizing to try to extend voting rights to women, another group of women was organizing in opposition. The latter group was known as the National Association Opposed to Woman Suffrage, and between 1912 and 1918 it put out a monthly journal. Marshall's study was based upon an analysis of all the published issues of that journal.[13]

Marshall's analysis of all the published issues indicated that the major opposition to suffrage centered around the defense of the "homemaker lifestyle." The antisuffragists argued that the special status of American women was due to the separation of the home from other institutional spheres of activity. This separation was regarded as the source of women's spirituality, modesty, moral superiority, gentleness, and so on. Because voting would increase women's outside-the-home involvement, the home would decline as a separate sphere, and the source of women's status would be adversely affected. Marshall concludes that one basis of opposition to women's suffrage may be termed *status politics* because it involved a group's effort to enhance or defend the prestige (or honor) of its style of life.

A second major theme in the antisuffragist publications concerned the perceived effects of voting upon the economic interests of women as a class. They feared that voting would increase political competition between the sexes, leading men to renounce their legal responsibilities for financial support of female dependents. They also feared that political competition would foster economic competition between the sexes. An influx of women into the labor force could lead to a lowering of everyone's wages, especially the wages of women relative to men. One article in 1913 put the matter this way:

[13]Susan E. Marshall, "In Defense of Separate Spheres." *Social Forces*, 65 (1986).

"The married woman who lives on her husband's wages is a public benefactor in more ways than one. By refusing to compete, she keeps up both men's and women's wages."[14]

The antisuffragist movement largely ended when the nineteenth amendment was passed in 1920, giving women the vote. Particularly between 1911 and 1916, however, the movement constituted an effective *party* in Weber's sense of the term. Woman suffrage referenda were defeated in about three-quarters of the states that held them between 1911 and 1916, and the antisuffrage movement made a major contribution to the defeats. It also seems clear that the movement was a good example of a party whose adherents were attracted on the basis of both class and status considerations.

Class, Status, and the Power of Farm Workers

Before turning to other issues, let us briefly return to the situation of the farm workers with which this chapter began. The main features of Marx's and Weber's theories, as well as the differences between them, are illustrated by the contemporary farm workers. As wage workers with only their labor to sell, the farm workers are in a subordinated class position, and both theorists would probably agree on this. However, Weber would also emphasize their relative subordination as a status group. Moreover, because ethnic-racial differences are related to their status, this presents the kind of condition under which Weber thought castelike status groups were particularly likely to form.

A critical question for differentiating between the theories involves the degree to which these class and status considerations are independent of each other. Are the Mexican-American and Filipino-American farm workers a low status group because of their subordinated class position—as Marx would argue? Alternatively, following Weber, are these dimensions somewhat independent of each other? It is exceedingly difficult to answer this question because the class and status of the farm workers are so highly correlated. The existence of this strong relationship is certainly consistent with Marx's view that status is derived from class, but it is also consistent with Weber's view that class and status will tend to be congruent, in the long run, even though they are analytically separate.

The political and economic efforts of the farm workers, aimed at changing the conditions under which they live, are our final consideration. On the one hand, following Weber, these efforts seem to illustrate the "prototype" situation in which a party is formed partly upon the basis of class and partly on the basis of status. Correspondingly, farm workers' associations have attempted to increase wage rates[15] (that is, class interests) while simultaneously trying to manipulate symbols of status; for example, by pressuring local schools to recognize the cultural heritage of their children.

[14]*Ibid.*, p. 342.
[15]Even if they were able to increase the price paid to labor, their relationship to the means of production would be unaltered. Thus, from Marx's perspective, the change would be more cosmetic than real.

It seems to me that Weber's class-status-party typology provides the better conceptual framework from which to analyze the actions of the farm workers. However, it must be recalled that Marx called attention to the discrepancy between how people act and how (from his perspective) they ought to act. Thus, it is unfair to judge Marx's theory too harshly because it fails to account for empirical observations. In other words, Marx presented an ideology as well as a theory, and only the latter is amenable to conventional empirical assessment.

THE FUNCTIONAL THEORY

Both Weber and Marx regarded the form of stratification as varying in different historical periods. Both recognized that *stratification* reflected the social organization of a society, and would, therefore, vary as a result of differences in social organization. An explicit interest in such variations is one of the cornerstones of the functional theory of stratification.

However, at the heart of Marx's theory was the view that all of history, if properly understood, was the history of class conflict. Because any system of production involves different relationships to the means of production, there will always be classes whose interests are inimical to each other, whether the people involved recognize it or not. An opposite conception is built upon assumptions that the components of society are alike in important respects or that they share significant interests in common.

Both of these latter assumptions were very pervasive in sociological theory during the early-middle decades of the twentieth century. They helped to spawn a functional theory of stratification which, while not explicitly offered in opposition to Marx, rested upon a very different conception of society. Correspondingly, many of the most severe critics of the functional perspective have been conflict theorists.

Parsons's View[16]

Talcott Parsons's view of the social system was extremely influential during the middle of this century. His fundamental concern was with how social order was possible; specifically, the Hobbesian question of what prevented continuous "warfare" among persons in a society. To a substantial degree, as discussed in Chapter Three, he saw the answer amid the interpenetration of the cultural, social, and personality systems. This entails the institutionalization of cultural values into the norms and rules of the social system. People find it easy to comply, as a result, because the rules are "harmonious" with their shared values. Furthermore, the institutionalized expectations of the social system are, according to Parsons, internalized in personality systems. This provides people with a personal motivation for complying with expectations.

[16]Portions of the following section are adapted from, Mark Abrahamson, *Functionalism* (Englewood Cliffs, NJ: Prentice-Hall, 1978).

When shared values shape the social norms and people's personalities, the society will be stable and there will be very little conflict. For all of this to occur, however, there must first be shared values within a society. Where do they come from? In large measure, though not exclusively, Parsons saw shared values emanating from within religious institutions. This was regarded as an important function of religion, despite great cross-cultural variations in the form of religious institutions. In this regard Parsons's position was, of course, very different from Marx's view of religion as the "opiate" of the proletariat.

The assumption of consensus played an important part in Parsons's theory of social stratification. Specifically, he believed that everyone's evaluation of an individual's social status would be highly congruent. If they were not, he argued, the stabilizing influence of shared normative expectations would be disrupted, producing, "a functionally impossible state of lack of integration of the social system."[17]

The primary criterion of an individual's status, he continued, is the individual's occupation. Of greatest relevance to stratification is the wealth that is associated with an occupation, but Parsons also noted other potentially important occupationally related attributes, such as prestige and influence. The occupationally based stratification system was also seen as resulting primarily from individual achievements. Parsons recognized the possibility of high status—or any of the specific attributes that could result in high status—being based upon ascription; for example, inherited wealth or inherited social standing. In modern societies like the United States, however, such occurrences were viewed as sporadic and of very minor significance. Thus, in Parsons's view, the stratification system was based on consensual evaluations of achievements in the occupational realm.

If evaluations of individuals are based primarily upon their occupations, then logically the next question is, What accounts for the consensual ranking of specific occupations? Parsons offered several answers to this question. For example, he identified the amounts of skill, required education, and authority over others as being potentially associated with the ranking of a position. Parsons's primary emphasis, however, was upon economic reward and value consensus. Thus, his major answer to the question of what accounts for an occupation's rank is "the more highly valued jobs are the best paid." Visualized in this way, wealth was a symbol of high ranking rather than a cause, an assertion later stressed by Davis and Moore.

DAVIS AND MOORE

The single most succinct presentation of the *functional theory of stratification* was offered by Davis and Moore in 1945. This article later came to be the "conspicuous statement" of the theory, and it partially accounts for their two names being used almost interchangeably with the theory itself. During the early 1940s, they devel-

---

[17]Talcott Parsons, "An Analytic Approach to the Theory of Stratification," *American Journal of Sociology*, 45 (1940), 843.

oped a rather lengthy manuscript to present the theory, and Davis alone published a brief article that outlined many of the major points.[18] Unfortunately, in light of the ensuing debate, they condensed the monograph into the brief, seven-page article in 1945.[19] Extensive criticism, accompanied by rejoinders and still more criticism, followed the presentation of the 1945 article, which was viewed not as concise, but as unqualified and dogmatic.

In the 1945 statement, Davis and Moore posed this central question: "Why do different positions carry different degrees of prestige?" It is a different question, they insisted, to ask how specific individuals obtain those positions. Much of the subsequent criticism failed to appreciate the difference, however. Before considering this, though, let us first consider how the two theorists answered their basic question.

Differing degrees of prestige (and other types of rewards) are universal, they began, because every society must place the "proper" people into the most important positions and then motivate them to perform the duties associated with the positions. Like Parsons, they saw this distribution of rewards as giving rise to a stratification system. Unlike Parsons, though, they did not equate functional importance with consensual values. Rather, following Durkheim, they viewed society as the sui generis, with stratification linked to its (that is, the society's) needs. Thus, in what was to become perhaps the most problematic phrase in the essay, Davis and Moore asserted that stratification was an "unconsciously evolved" mechanism through which societies went about assuring that the best qualified people wound up in the most important jobs.

One of the fundamental arguments made by Parsons is that stratification is necessary, and also desirable, for a complex, achievement-oriented society; necessary because it allocates rewards and "connections" to positions according to the amount of collective responsibility entrusted to them and desirable because this arrangement permits the entire system to function effectively. Thus, Parsons noted that industrial managers in Russia were part of the "intelligentsia" and received more of all types of rewards than ordinary workers. Their greater rewards are not valued as legitimate within the Soviet system, and the same inequities in the United States would be considered "capitalistic." Nevertheless, unequal rewards accrue to managers in both societies, and "a sociologist is at least entitled to be skeptical" that any ideology could change this pattern given "the essential structural situation" in a complex society.[20]

In addition to functional importance, Davis and Moore also proposed that the ranking and rewards of a position were determined by the relative scarcity of qualified personnel. If the obligations of a position require substantial amounts of innate talent or extensive training, then greater rewards will have to be associated with the position in order to induce a scarce pool of potential incumbents to seek the position.

[18]Kingsley Davis, "A Conceptual Analysis of Stratification," *American Sociological Review*, 7 (1942).

[19]Kingsley Davis and Wilbert E. Moore, "Some Principles of Stratification," *American Sociological Review*, 10 (1945). A later elaboration was provided in Kingsley Davis, *Human Society* (New York: Macmillan, 1948).

[20]Talcott Parsons, *The Social System* (New York: Free Press, 1951), p. 160.

Much to the credit of the theory, Davis and Moore did explicitly recognize that although stratification was universal, its specific form would vary in relation to "major societal functions." Here Parsons's influence is most apparent as Davis and Moore begin by considering the universality of religion and how increasing secularization is related to changes in the ranking of religious practitioners. They proposed that in medieval types of societies the organized priesthood was very high in prestige. This high rank is due to the functional importance of religion in such societies, where an "unlettered" population is highly "credulous." Given the importance of religious ritual in these "sacred" societies, it may be surprising, they note, that the position of the priest is not ranked even more highly than it is. What tempers their status, Davis and Moore note, is the ease with which anyone can claim to be in communication with deities, without fear of rebuke. Thus, there is a limited pool of eligibles in such societies only if literacy is a prerequisite. Therefore, the highest ranking of priests occurs when the priestly guild itself rigidly controls access to the profession.

Similarly, Davis and Moore go on to describe other possible variations in ranking due to changes in government, relations to the means of production, and technical knowledge. They conclude that actual stratification systems can be a number of polar types, varying in equalitarianism, opportunities for mobility, degrees of stratum solidarity, and so on. However, even though the form may vary, functional importance and relative scarcity are seen as the basic principles of stratification.

There have been numerous attempts to test the Davis-Moore, or functional theory of stratification. Most of them have only been partially satisfactory, though, because of measurement problems created by the abstract nature of some of the key concepts. For example, how is the functional importance of a position to be measured in a concrete way? One research project turned to professional baseball teams.

Baseball Players' Salaries

This study proposed that the performance of a major league team was reflected in 1) its place in the standings, and 2) its total attendance. As might be expected, the two are strongly related, and indicators of each were combined into a single measure of team performance. Then measures were developed to describe the offensive (batting) and defensive (fielding) performances of each position on a team, except pitchers. Because their position is unique, the measure of pitchers' performance was also unique (including the number of hits, walks, runs, and so on that they permitted).[21]

To measure the functional importance of positions, the performance of all positions was correlated with the performance of the team. The stronger the correlation, the more the position affects the entire team, hence, the greater the functional importance of the position. (As baseball fans would expect, pitching had the greatest effect, independently accounting for about 40 percent of teams' success in the seasons that were examined.)

[21]Mark Abrahamson, "A Functional Theory of Organizational Stratification," *Social Forces*, 58 (1979).

The second Davis-Moore variable, the scarcity of skills required by a position, would ideally be measured by vacancy rates; that is, positions so demanding that they are regularly unfilled. However, baseball teams—like many other organizations—can not have vacancies. The best available person must be placed into the position. Therefore, scarcity or the uniqueness of abilities may be better conceived in terms of the interchangeability of persons and positions. If a position is exclusively filled by people who sometimes fill other positions as well, it implies that their regular position requires skills that are in scarce supply.

For example, persons who regularly play center field may sometimes play left field, but the reverse is very uncommon. Similarly, professors who regularly teach advanced graduate seminars may sometimes teach introductory courses, but the instructors who regularly teach introductory courses are not likely to teach graduate seminars. These patterns of interchangeability were utilized to assign each position a scarcity of skills score.

Finally, rewards in this study were measured by the minimum, maximum, and average salaries paid to players, which were then grouped by position. Recall that the functional theory leads us to predict that the rewards allocated to people will vary according to the functional importance of their positions and the scarcity of personnel qualified to fill the positions. The results of the analysis strongly supported the functional theory. For example, functional importance and scarcity-interchangeability, in combination, explained almost one-half of all the variations in minimum player salaries.

IS STRATIFICATION FUNCTIONAL?

One of the major criticisms of the functional theory is directed at the inevitability and desirability of stratification that is presumed by the theory. Tumin claims that the more stratified a society is, the more likely are talented, lower-standing persons to go "undiscovered." Because their access to mobility channels often is denied, they are not likely to develop their talents. From the standpoint of the society, he concludes, this is hardly functional.[22] Furthermore, Tumin questions whether rewards must be viewed as the best way or the only way to motivate people: What about intrinsic work satisfaction as an alternative?

These motivational assumptions are at the heart of the criticism offered by the Polish sociologist, Wlodzimierz Wesolowski. The view held by Davis and Moore concerning the indispensability of rewards is based, Wesolowski contends, on the assumption that human nature is characterized both by selfish, materialistic drives and by laziness.[23] Rewards are correspondingly viewed as the necessary energizing mechanisms. Davis and Moore have disregarded, he concludes, the

---

[22]Tumin's various papers criticizing the functional theory are reproduced in *Readings on Social Stratification,* edited by Melvin M. Tumin (Englewood Cliffs, NJ: Prentice-Hall, 1970). By the same author, see also: *Social Stratification,* second edition, (Englewood Cliffs, NJ: Prentice-Hall, 1985).

[23]Wlodzimierz Wesolowski, "Some Notes on the Functional Theory of Stratification," *Polish Sociological Bulletin,* 3–4 (1962).

impact of cultural values. This leads them to be insensitive to the possibilities, in some cultures, of training people to fill important positions without their reckoning on future material advantages.

The most important issue raised by this line of criticism has been termed, "the strangulation of talent." For Davis and Moore and other functionalists, stratification was viewed as having positive consequences, and society was identified as the beneficiary. The "strangulation-of-talent" argument contends that stratification is dysfunctional because it leads to the underdevelopment and underutilization of potential ability. This strangulation occurs particularly among groups in a society that lack access to high-ranking positions (and intervening institutions that offer mobility) by virtue of ascribed characteristics: birth into low-standing (and hence, low-resource) families, minority group status, and so on. The critics contend that in the long run, any institutional structure (such as stratification) that limits the pool of eligibles must be dysfunctional to the society.

This strangulation-of-talent argument has elicited two kinds of replies from Davis and Moore; one a concession, the other a clarification. They have conceded that their theory might be partially limited in applicability to achievement-oriented societies. However, along with the concession came an important clarification. The Davis-Moore theory was primarily an attempt, the critics were reminded, to account for the ranking of positions. It did not purport to explain how individuals or groups attained such positions, and it remains a separate issue. (Parsons, it will be recalled, did treat these two issues simultaneously but the critics were specifically addressing the Davis-Moore version.) Thus, even in a highly ascribed caste system, the differential ranking of specific castes can be explained by the theory, even if individuals are sorted into castes ascriptively.

Functional or Powerful?

By placing a greater emphasis upon conflict, Collins has endeavored to demonstrate how erroneous functional interpretations of stratification provide ideological justifications for the status quo. He began with the commonplace observation that in modern societies, such as the United States, many positions are requiring increased levels of education as an employment prerequisite. Why does this happen, he asked. According to the functional theory, increasingly complex technology has increased the skill requirements of jobs, thus necessitating more formal training. However, Collins doubts this interpretation and examines a number of surveys whose data suggest a more cynical interpretation; namely, that increased prerequisites are the arbitrary imposition of organized and powerful groups who are trying to dominate jobs.

Collins's historical examination of many jobs suggests that the amount of skill necessary for their performance has increased only very slightly. However, the educational levels required for these same jobs appears to have increased greatly, far in excess of the actual skills needed. Similarly, Collins questions whether formal education does, in fact, provide job skills, even if increased performance abilities could be demonstrated. His answer is again negative and is supported by studies which report only weak relationships between productivity and level of education. The learning of most relevant skills seems to occur on the job, not in classrooms.

Thus, Collins concludes, the demands of occupational positions are not fixed by functional requirements. Rather, they are determined by "negotiations" among organized groups. For example, various medical "specialists" are not produced in six-month training schools because of the power of the American Medical Association to limit access and not because the skills required for the positions could not be acquired in that period.[24]

CONCLUDING POSTSCRIPT

The student-reader should not feel dismayed if he or she feels perplexed at this point. The functional theory of stratification does appear to have the unique capacity to seem useful at one moment and useless the next. Perhaps we can put the mixed blessings of this theory into some perspective by briefly returning to our analysis of the farm workers.

The functional theory offers the following guide: If the contribution of a position is small, or the number of people who could perform the activity is great, then the prestige of the position will be low, and financial remuneration will be small. Does this account for the position of the farm workers? One immediate obstacle concerns how to measure functional importance. How indispensable are lettuce, grapes, or the people who pick them? These are extremely difficult questions to answer. However, the theory also states that if many people are able to perform the activity, that in itself is sufficient to produce a low ranking for the job. While working in the fields is physically demanding, it is nevertheless likely that a great many people posses the requisite stamina. Both prestige and wages should, therefore, be low, and they are, in line with the theory. On the other hand, few people possess the requisite capital and the organizational-administrative skills with which to carry out a large-scale planting-harvesting-marketing operation. Because of the greater scarcity of these skills, the financial return of owners-managers should exceed that of laborers. Again, in line with the theory, it does.

Is this stratification of positions functional, though? Does such stratification, as Davis and Moore contend, benefit the society? The answer depends largely upon how we choose to define society. The farm workers are, after all, part of society, and it is difficult to see how they benefit from this form of stratification. Part of the value of Marx's theory is that it immediately sensitizes us to the structural basis of the farm workers' subordinate position. It also leads us to ask, are the values which support

---

[24]Randall Collins, "Functional and Conflict Theories of Educational Stratification," *American Sociological Review*, 36 (1971). Collins' own stratification views combine a little of Weber with a little of Marx and place more emphasis upon the links between macro stratification structures and everyday interaction. See also, Randall Collins, "On the Microfoundations of Macrosociology," *American Journal of Sociology*, 86 (1981).

their subordinated position anything more than ideological justifications of bourgeois privilege? Furthermore, is not the continuation of such privilege based largely upon power; that is, bourgeois control over production?

SUGGESTIONS FOR ADDITIONAL READING

RICK FANTASIA, *Cultures of Solidarity*, Berkeley: University of California Press, 1988.
ANTHONY GIDDENS and GAVIN MACKENZIE (Eds), *Social Class and the Division of Labour*, New York: Cambridge University Press, 1982.
JAMES R. KLUEGEL and ELIOT R. SMITH, *Beliefs About Inequality*, New York: Aldine de Gruyter, 1985.

7

STRUCTURE
Bureaucratic Organizations
Weber

If a student wishes to drop a course, he or she can consult the college catalogue for instructions. At most colleges the student will be directed to the registrar's office to complete the appropriate forms. The student's academic status and the time during the semester that the request is made will then determine whether it is granted. Who the student happens to be is irrelevant. This university example illustrates the major features of bureaucratic decision making. Specifically, it involves an organization following formal, written rules and conducting its affairs in a spirit of detached impersonality.

If the student feels like a square peg being pushed into a round hole, it is because that is precisely what is happening. Individuality is suppressed because bureaucratic decision making cannot cope with unique cases. Every specific case must be evaluated according to general rules, irrespective of the personal attributes of the parties involved. Thus, people feel squeezed, pushed, and molded in dealing with a bureaucracy. These same feelings can be provoked, not only in dropping a course in college, but in applying for a driver's license, a job at McDonald's, or benefits from an insurance company because most large corporations in the United States and throughout the modern world are bureaucratic.

On the other hand, we typically want organizations to behave in a bureaucratic manner, and deviations from this regimen are generally considered deviant or immoral. For example, suppose the Internal Revenue Service deliberately selected political opponents of the president as subjects for audits, or that all the good jobs at Sears went to relatives of people in the personnel department. Actions of this type would lead most people to be upset because there are widely held values in this society concerning how organizations ought to operate; and the model against which actual procedures are implicitly judged is bureaucratic. That is, people expect organizations (whether the Internal Revenue Service or Sears) to reach decisions in accordance with universal rules and to do so in a spirit of detached impersonality.

Because people often value and expect bureaucratic procedures, it is apparent that their feelings of dismay, when they are personally pushed and squeezed by bureaucratic organizations, are only one side of the coin. Bureaucratic procedures, it appears, are not inherently bad, or wrong, at least to judge from peoples' values.

In sociological theory, bureaucratic procedures have tended to be regarded explicitly as inevitable and implicitly as desirable. These two attributes are clearly separable. Future wars may be inevitable, for example, but hardly desirable. An end to provety would be desirable, but it is certainly not inevitable. Therefore, we will separate these two qualities, focusing upon the issue of inevitability first, and examining desirability at the end of this chapter.

Viewed briefly, sociological analysis of bureaucracy began, on a large scale, in the early nineteenth century. It was analyzed in relation to the modern system of social organization which was then seen to be emerging. The most influential analysis of bureaucracy was offered, early in this century, by Max Weber. His views, because they have continued to provide the point of departure in contemporary sociology, will be emphasized in this chapter. Especially since the end of World War II, there have been a large number of very diverse empirical studies covering most aspects of Weber's work. Representative studies of this type will also be examined.

BUREAUCRACY AND MODERN SOCIAL ORGANIZATION

The late eighteenth century and the first half of the nineteenth century were times of intense, and sometimes violent, turmoil in France. Extensive social changes were occurring as an old regime battled newly formed interest groups. The general turmoil and the recurrent revolutions provided the background against which social theory and social criticism were formulated. Analysts tried to envision what the new social order that was emerging would eventually look like; and they were very interested in what would provide the basis for social cohesion in this new social order. Most historians of sociology contend that the modern discipline of sociology also emerged at the time, though there is not complete agreement as to who ought to be called the father of the discipline. The two men most frequently nominated are Henri Saint-Simon (1760-1825) and his secretary-assistant, Auguste Comte (1798-1857). It seems most likely that Saint-Simon was responsible for more original ideas than his younger collaborator, though it was Comte who apparently coined the name, "sociology," for what they were studying.

According to the future projections of both Saint-Simon and Comte, an enlightened elite of diverse scientists and scholars were destined to be in positions of great power. Their rule, it was claimed, would be both more rational and more humanitarian than that of the traditional elites.

The new social order they envisioned was viewed as the result of two principal forces: science and modern industry. Both of these forces were producing a new rationality that would replace national politics, warfare, and traditional Christianity with a new world order based upon competence and "positive" morality. Thus, as theological thinking diminished and scientific thinking increased, scientists would replace priests and inherit the previously held "spiritual power" of priests because they (that is, the scientists) would best embody the predominant mode of thinking in the society. Correspondingly, the new class of industrialists would replace the warriors as the most highly rated group in the society and they would direct and administer activities in the society that was emerging.[1]

The decline in religion and the growth of rationality, epitomized by modern science, were the key changes emphasized by Max Weber (1864 to 1920). Before we discuss detailed aspects of Weber's theories, however, it may be helpful to examine a concrete example of the changes noted by all the major theorists. The changing features of American college football, in the late 19th century, provide an interesting example of both the impact of rationality and the emergence of a new industrial class.

The Rationalization of College Football[2]

Until the 1870s, American college football strongly resembled British soccer and was characterized by a relative absence of formalized rules. The recreation and enjoyment of genuinely amateur participants, as in the British universities, was its reason for being. All of this changed, though, primarily as the result of changes which were sweeping American society and, for some reason, had their greatest initial impact at Yale. One indication of their impact is provided by changes in Yale's trustees during the last half of the nineteenth century. Increasingly, the trustees represented the newly emerging industrialists and bankers, men of modest origins who attained great wealth in a rapidly industrializing society. (They were representative of the larger group of industrialists that have been termed "the robber barons.") At Harvard, by contrast, the late nineteenth-century trustees were still selected exclusively from an old guard, predominantly involving Boston's aristocratic families.

Many of Yale's trustees had attained great wealth by following highly rational "scientific methods" in industry. The same approach was attempted at the stadium by Yale's famous football coach, Walter Camp. He revolutionized the game in the 1880s through a number of innovations. Perhaps most importantly, he defined a clear hierarchy of responsibility and authority among assistant coaches. Some worked on offense; others, on defense; still others with linemen and with running backs; but Camp stood at the apex of the hierarchy. He coached the coaches. Meanwhile, at Harvard, like many other schools, 30 or more assistants would clutter the practice field, arguing among themselves and working at cross-purposes.

---

[1]Gertrud Lenzer (Ed), *Auguste Comte and Positivism* (New York: Harper, 1975).

[2]The following discussion is based upon David L. Westby and Allen Sack, "The Rationalization and Commercialization of College Football in the Late Nineteenth Century" (paper presented at the *American Sociological Association,* San Francisco, August, 1975).

Camp was also a serious student of football, without peer at this time. He faithfully recorded and analyzed statistical profiles of team performance, both Yale's and its opponent's. Then he utilized this information to introduce new offensive and defensive systems which were highly effective. Furthermore, he carefully recruited both players and coaches to fit into his system. However, Yale's ultimate success was contingent upon wider reaching changes which Camp was also able to innovate. Specifically, this involved formalizing the rules of football. British soccer, at this time, was a "loose" game, haphazard in character. He systematized the American game by introducing rules concerning the line of scrimmage, the number of downs, and so on. Thus, Camp formalized the game and then developed techniques to make Yale's team standardized and precise.

The result was enormous success. Between 1875 and 1900, Yale beat arch rival Harvard almost every year, and often by very wide margins. One such defeat led a Harvard observer to liken Yale's football team to a machine and Harvard's to "hand labor." Thus, the values of the newly rich industrial class that were now governing Yale were clearly expressed in Yale's football teams.

Camp's formalization and systematization of the game at Yale also had long-term consequences for ex-players. For many of them, coaching college football became a career. Between 1876 and 1910, for example, over 65 Yale graduates became college football coaches compared to fewer than 20 Harvard graduates.

By the 1920s, other schools had copied Camp's successful formula at Yale, and Yale was not able to continue quite the same degree of domination. However, during the late nineteenth century, several of Camp's innovations are important to note:

1) Formalization of the rules.
2) Systematizing role performance.
3) A hierachical staff with clearly defined authority.
4) Selection of personnel (that is coaches and players) according to specific competencies.
5) Orientation to football as a career.

All of the above are important characteristics of bureaucracy in Weber's view. Moreover, their apparent association with increasingly rational views, associated with modern industry and science, illustrate key aspects of the perspective we have been discussing.

WEBER ON LEGITIMACY

Weber, like Saint-Simon and Comte, regarded the increasing rationalization of everyday life as one of the exceptionally important trends in Western societies. He viewed rationality as involving a self-conscious, deliberate evaluation of alternatives and saw it as replacing "the unthinking acceptance of ancient custom."[3]

[3]Max Weber, *The Theory of Social and Economic Organization,* trans. by A. M. Henderson and Talcott Parsons, edited by Parsons (New York: Oxford, 1947), p. 123. For further discussion of the importance of rationalization to Weber's theory of social organization, see George Ritzer, "The McDonaldization of Society," *Journal of American Culture,* 6, 1983.

However, it was Weber who uniquely tied bureaucratization with rationalization. In fact, he defined bureaucracy by its reliance upon rational legitimation of authority.

The legitimation of authority, in general, refers to why, in any association or organization, subordinates comply with the orders of superiors. Thus, Weber defined discipline as, "the probability that a command will receive prompt and automatic obedience."[4] Unless there was some reasonably high probability of compliance occurring, Weber felt it was difficult to view the relationships among participants as constituting an organization or a relationship. In analyzing a compliance-to-commands continuum, he described the prompt obedience of slaves and the generally reluctant obedience of people in voluntary associations as constituting polar types.

Given any degree of compliance by subordinates, Weber questioned how the authority of superiors was legitimated. In other words, why do people follow orders? He answered this question in a penetrating essay on domination. Whether in the context of a total society, an organization, or a simple relationship, people are not equal. They differ, Weber noted, in wealth, in status, or in some other regard. Even though these differences may be purely accidental, people rarely regard them as such. Those who are in the favored positions tend to seek justification, that is, to view their advantages as legitimate. The continuation of every form of domination, Weber concludes, always requires self-justification which ultimately involves some basis of legitimation. The dominated, on the other hand, tend to think little about justification; that is, they tend to accept the justifications of the privileged so long as the situation is stable.[5]

It has been proposed that legitimacy is especially important in restraining the earliest stages of protest. When a number of individuals initially come together because of dissatisfaction with some rules or procedures, the legitimacy of the rules is likely to make alternatives seem either foolish or wrong. The opposing individuals are likely to be viewed as disruptive deviants rather than as agents of beneficial changes. Thus, legitimation reduces the possibility that a collectivity will mobilize to try to change a rule or practice.[6]

Questions about how superior power is legitimated could be applied to large organizations, family relations, or the relationships among different segments of a society. If Weber were writing in the contemporary United States, this interest might well lead him to ask how Supreme Court decisions become implemented. The Court decides that public schools in Arkansas must be racially integrated, or that Standard Oil must divest some of its holdings because its huge size interferes with (that is, is a restraint of) trade. So what? That is, why do Arkansas schools desegregate or Standard Oil divest?

[4]Ibid., p. 152.

[5]Max Weber, *On Law in Economy and Society*, edited by Max Rheinstein, trans. by Edward Shils and Max Rheinstein (New York: Simon and Schuster, n.d. original copyright by Harvard University Press, 1954). See pages 334–337.

[6]For further discussion of the issue and an experiment that supports the hypothesis, see George A. Thomas, Henry A. Walker, and Morris Zelditch, Jr., "Legitimacy and Collective Action," *Social Forces*, 65, 1986.

Any order may be regarded as valid—with compliance ensuing—in a limited number of ways. One of them is by coercion, if the individual or group giving the order can force others to comply. This alternative could fit if the Supreme Court had an army at its disposal to enforce its decisions. (It does not.) A second type of legitimation is based upon affect or loyalty. Recognizing the crucial role of the Court in the American political system, compliance with its orders might be regarded as patriotic. A third possibility is that people might agree with the order, that is, find it to be an expression of their own values. A fourth possibility noted by Weber, but irrelevant to this example, is because of religious conviction. Failure to comply with some orders might be regarded as interfering with salvation or a religious state of grace. Finally, compliance can be based upon self-interest, peoples' perception that they will gain, often in an economic sense, by complying.

Weber made a distinction between the types of motives that were involved in maintaining a legitimate order, once it was in force, and those which lead to assigning legitimacy to a new order.[7] The motives discussed in both contexts are largely the same, but not identical. Presented here, in the preceding paragraph, are the motives which maintain legitimacy. They are more appropriate to a discussion of the Supreme Court. However, I have added coercion, or force, to the list because Weber treats it elsewhere as a motive. The most important motive Weber lists only in the context of a new order is tradition; that is, a view that it is legitimate because it has been so in the past.

Now, let us consider any real or ʊ.ʌpothetical Supreme Court decision and ask how legitimacy becomes attributed to it. Can the Supreme Court force compliance? Not directly, but the attorney general or the president could bring force to bear, either with the army or federal marshals. In addition, even the defendants might regard the right of the Supreme Court to make such decisions as legitimate and feel morally bound to comply. Alternatively, people might comply because they fear economic sanctions if they do not; for example, consumer boycotts or the withholding of federal grants.

In any actual situation, Weber recognized that there might be a variety of motives involved. However, he felt that it was typically possible to infer one as predominating, and he developed an "ideal type" analysis for this purpose. An appreciation of his use of ideal types is indispensable to an understanding of Weber's conceptual methodology. Therefore, we must examine it in some detail before tying the preceeding discussion of legitimacy to his view of bureaucracy because he treated both of them as ideal types.

IDEAL TYPES

Any concrete situation, as we have noted, is likely to involve the simultaneous existence of diverse meanings and intentions. People differ in their subjective interpretations of symbols (for example, the Supreme Court) and in the way they

[7]Weber, *The Theory of Social and Economic Organization*, pages 126-132; see especially footnote 51.

act toward them. To Weber, the task of sociology was to understand the *shared* subjective meanings and relate them to behavior. Note that Weber's definitions of phenomena do exactly that. A state of marriage exists, for example, to the degree that there remains a probability that certain types of meaningfully oriented social action will take place. Thus, to the extent that each party ceases to take the other's hurt feelings into account subjectively, and respond accordingly, and to the extent other such actions do not occur, then the social relationship of marriage ceases to exist sociologically. Similarly, to the degree the charter of a government or the vows of priests no longer insure that certain meaningfully oriented activities will occur, then to that degree there ceases to be a government or a church, sociologically. (In a legal sense, the marriage, the government, or the church could still be recognized.) In sum, Weber defined sociology as the study of social relationships which, in turn, are defined by the presence of common orientations and the probability of reciprocal behaviors occurring. Social relationships—between citizens and a court, or between partners in a marriage—exist, therefore, to varying degrees, sociologically speaking.

In addition, Weber defined sociology as a generalizing science which meant that it should be directed at typical motives, typical subjective intentions, and typical modes of conduct. Thus, excluded from the proper province of sociology were the study of purely psychic phenomena (such as a person's day dreams), specific historical events, or any other non-shared or nonrecurrent phenomena. This dictum meant that sociological analysis would necessarily be abstract and require extensive inferences. How else could one attempt to describe typical motives?

The very notion of typical intentions (or typical anything, for that matter) is very problematic because of the previously described tendency for diverse motives to be present simultaneously, even within the same actor. For example, we speculated that compliance with a Supreme Court order might be based upon fear of coercion, moral claims, anticipated economic losses, and so on. Each actor's compliance, or probability of compliance, might be based upon a slightly different weighing of specific motives.

The task of the sociologist—in fact, the very activity upon which the discipline of sociology rests—is to abstract from reality, to construct "pure types" which are understood to be exaggerated. These pure, or ideal, types are mental constructs, but they are indispensable for the type of comparative historical analyses that most interested Weber. To illustrate the notion of ideal types, suppose you were going to try to compare the social organizations of the North and South prior to the Civil War. Before any comparison would be logically possible, you would have to extract certain key features of each region. In the South, for example, you might focus upon plantations, slaves, and a rural way of life, and the (white) woman as a traditional Southern belle. Then this image of the South could be contrasted with an urban, industrial image of the North. In reality, however, everyone realizes there were Northern farmers too, that all Southern women were not very representative of Southern belles, and so forth. In short, there were many exceptions, in reality, to the constructed images; but, by exaggerating certain *distinguishing* features of each region, it becomes substantially easier to compare them.

This regional example illustrates both how and why ideal types are constructed. They are, in sum, deliberate exaggerations of more subtle trends which are exaggerated in order to abstract out the form of the pure, unadulterated phenomenon. Virtually all of the major concepts Weber dealt with were treated as ideal types. (In this context, ideal is not meant to imply perfection or desirability. The closest synonym would be "pure.")

THE IDEAL-TYPE BUREAUCRACY

Social relationships obviously exist in very different contexts. There are clear differences among the relationships of husband and wife, priest and parishioner, boss and secretary. Our main interest here is with relationships that occur within formal organizations. As defined by Weber, such organizations are characterized by the presence of a head or chief, an administrative staff, and a continuing, rather than short-run, purpose. (Examples of such purposes include the elimination of birth defects, selling cans of soup, or delivering mail.)

The modern type of formal organization, bureaucracy, is distinguished mostly by the fact that claims to the legitimacy of authority are on rational grounds. In general, as previously discussed, Weber defined rationality as a deliberate, or self-conscious, evaluation of alternatives. In the context of a formal organization, however, the rational legitimation of authority rests upon participants' belief in the "legality" of both the rules and the persons who issue them. Thus, bureaucratic rules have a lawlike quality; for example, sophomores in good academic standing may drop a course, without consent of the instructor, until the third week of the semester. Moreover, the persons who issue these legal orders (for example, the registrar) are in positions appropriate to such issuances. Thus, despite the lofty sounding title, a vice president for institutional research could not "legally" formulate rules governing the dropping of courses.

Because rational legitimation stresses legal considerations, pertaining both to rules and rule makers, Weber frequently referred to this characteristically bureaucratic mode of legitimation as rational-legal. Its major feature, as noted from the onset of this chapter, is a system of abstract and impersonal rules. Weber also noted a number of additional organizational and interpersonal qualities which were characteristic of bureaucracy, and we will consider them in the following pages.[8]

Individuals employed by the organization enter into a limited contractual (that is, legalistic) arrangement. They are hired to fill a position, and the rights and obligations they inherit are tied to the position. The "totality" of a person is not involved. Thus, if a woman is hired (by a bureaucracy) to supervise the 11 P.M. to 7 A.M. shift, then her roles at other times are technically irrelevant. She is subject to the organization's rules only in her role as supervisor; that is, the rules circumscribe the behavior of a supervisor, rather than a person, per se, because the person and the position are not synonymous. (She may be, in addition, a wife, mother, member of a church, a bowling team, and so on and unaffected by the rules of the bureaucracy in these other positions.)

[8]Ibid., pp. 329-336.

In the abstract this feature of bureaucracies is sufficiently unambiguous, but in actual situations, organizations which otherwise conform to the pure rational-legal model appear to violate this feature. For example, the "off-hours" conduct of police officers, college professors, and many public officials has, at various times, been considered relevant to evaluations of their official performance. Thus, police officials or professors have been dismissed—by bureaucracies—because they exhibited, in their "private life," behaviors which were considered morally unacceptable for someone in their (official) positions.

If it is argued that persons in certain positions may never engage in certain kinds of activities, then the role and the person are virtually equated. Thus, if Caesar's wife could never even give the hint of any impropriety, then being Caesar's wife was not just a role. It can also be argued, in role terms, that the requirements of one position are incompatible with those of another; hence, persons are excluded from playing both, even if the times and places of their role performances are segregated from each other. In either case, however, such formal rules or informal expectations violate the bureaucratic notion of limited contractual obligations.

According to Weber, recruitment into a bureaucracy involves the matching of an individual's expertise with a position's responsibilities. These responsibilities are frequently explicated in a job description. For example, candidates may be expected to type 60 words a minute and take shorthand. The qualifications of candidates, in the ideal type bureaucracy, are objectively assessed. This may involve examination (for example, a typing test), requiring proof of technical training (for example, a certificate or diploma), or both. The person who displays the greatest degree of competence relevant to the requirements of the position is then appointed, as opposed to elected. Thus, it is ideally what a person knows, rather than whom, that matters.

There are, of course, many deviations from this purely bureaucratic regimen. Personnel decisions may be influenced by subtle or overt perferences which lead to discrimination against some candidates and favoritism toward others. In addition, secretaries hired on the basis of demonstrated typing and shorthand abilities may, in fact, spend most of their time making coffee and straightening executive offices. However, the likelihood of such "deviations" occurring within an organization is markedly reduced, in principle, by compliance with a bureaucratic model. (It should be noted that our very notion of what is a deviation is very much shaped by our conception of a pure bureaucracy.)

Remuneration in a bureaucracy is according to a fixed salary, paid in cash (or equivalent). An incumbent's services are, therefore, neither honorific nor subject to regular fluctuations according to the whims of senior officials. At the same time, incumbents have no right to expropriate from the organization either services or property. Thus, subordinates may not be asked to cut the lawn at the home of a superior. Also, neither superior nor subordinate may take pencils and paper out of the office or use corporate holdings for personal enjoyment or personal gain. Finally, the fixed salary is usually the officeholder's principal source of income, the position is usually the sole occupation of the incumbent, promotion within the organization usually constitutes a career for the incumbent, and incumbents may not be arbitrarily dismissed.

As previously noted, people are recruited for positions according to demonstrated competence. Virtually by definition, such skills are reasonably specific. Correspondingly, the authority of positions is limited, circumscribed by the sphere of competence. Hence, in a pure bureaucracy, officials in the marketing department do not establish salary scales, and officials in personnel do not make advertising decisions. Attempts to make such decisions, because they violate spheres of competence, would be regarded as illegal (within the context of a bureaucratic organization).

Each of the clearly defined positions is organized within a clearly defined hierarchy of positions. This means that each office is under the control of a higher one. Typically, such organizations take the shape of a pyramid because they contain more lower than higher positions at each succeeding level. Thus, there are many professors for each department head; many department heads for each dean; many deans for each vice president; and so on.

To summarize, Weber viewed a bureaucracy as an organization with a formal head, an administrative staff, and an on-going purpose in which:

1) Decisions are made according to formal rules, in an impersonal manner.

2) People are subject to authority only in regard to their official (or role-related) obligations.

3) The competence of positions is clearly defined, and positions are organized hierarchically with higher positions supervising lower ones.

4) People are hired and promoted on the basis of demonstrated competence, paid a fixed salary, and are free from arbitrary dismissal.

5) The position is the incumbent's primary occupation and constitutes a career, but the incumbent's work is strictly separated from ownership and involves no rights of expropriation.

The characteristics described in the preceding list were offered by Weber as the distinguishing features of the pure bureaucratic form. The degree to which any actual organizations exhibit all of these characteristics is an intriguing question and one which has been studied in substantial detail.

The Existence of Ideal-Type Bureaucracies

A number of studies have examined whether the organizational features noted by Weber are found empirically to occur together. If the ideal-type characterization of bureaucracy is a useful model, then it ought to indicate something about the form of actual organizations. More specifically, Weber's ideal-type conception suggests that organizations will be of two polar types: those in which all the elements of a bureaucracy are highly developed and those in which all these elements are absent. Thus, some organizations should be found to be simultaneously high in formalization of rules, impersonal relations, hierarchical control, and so on while other organizations score very low on all these features. The former would then be termed pure bureaucracies, and their existence would indicate the empirical usefulness of Weber's conception.

Studies have approached this question with two different strategies. In the earlier studies, a highly diverse assortment of organizations were simultaneously examined and findings indicated that only some of Weber's major characteristics were correlated with each other and that some of the relationships were only moderately strong.[9] These findings provided only limited support for Weber's thesis. However, the rationale behind including hotels, manufacturing firms, government agencies, and so on in a single sample is subject to mixed reviews. It can be argued, on the one hand, that Weber's theory was meant to apply to organizations, in general. Therefore, the usefulness of the ideal-type conception ought to be manifest in the very heterogeneous samples of organizations taken by the investigators.

On the other hand, however, it must also be recognized that extrinsic considerations may cause different types of organizations to differ from each other in a variety of ways, including the nature and amount of technology they utilize, the kinds of environmental uncertainties they must confront, and so on. These differences may, in turn, be associated with differences related to bureaucratization. For example, some types of organizations routinely encounter certain recurrent problems which facilitate their development of formalized decision-making procedures. Other types of organizations, by contrast, regularly face non-recurrent problems which lead to less formalization. Differences of this kind might very well be totally unrelated to differences in impersonality, career orientations, or the like. Thus, to compare hospitals and tire manufacturing firms, for example, may be analogous to comparing apples and oranges, and therefore, represent an unwise way to test Weber's assertions.

Several studies have followed the alternative strategy of examining homogeneous types of organizations, and they report findings that are more congruent with Weber's notion. In a study confined to colleges in Canada, for example, many of the characteristics expected to be associated with pure bureaucracies were found to be highly correlated with each other.[10]

In summary, the reviewed studies suggest that Weber's ideal-type model does not provide a useful standard against which to evaluate specific organizations—if organizations in general are simultaneously examined. Weber seems to have overly assumed that any or all organizations were equally subjected to bureaucratization in every respect. When organizations are categorized by type, however, the ideal-type conceptualization appears to be applicable; that is, organizations that provide like services or products can largely be categorized in relation to an overall degree of bureaucratization.

---

[9]Richard H. Hall, "The Concept of Bureaucracy," *American Journal of Sociology,* 68 (1963), and Hall and Charles R. Title, "A Note on Bureaucracy and Its Correlates," *American Journal of Sociology,* 72 (1966).

[10]Edward A. Holdaway and others, "Dimensions of Organizations in Complex Societies," *Administrative Science Quarterly,* 20 (1975).

TYPES OF AUTHORITY

In a society where rationality predominated—envisioned by Saint-Simon, but more realistically described by Weber—the bureaucratic form of organization was regarded by Weber as virtually inevitable. The certainty of bureaucracy was due largely to the fact that its rational-legal mode provided the means for legitimating authority that was most compatible with rational orientations.

While authority could be legitimated in a variety of specific ways, according to Weber, they could all be placed into one of three pure types: traditional, charismatic, and rational-legal. His inevitability argument was based both on the congruence of rationality with rational-legal legitimation and the default of the other two types. Specifically, traditional legitimation was viewed as incompatible with rationality, and charismatic legitimation was viewed as inherently unstable, with rational-legal legitimation its usual successor. Each of the other two types will be discussed, in turn.

Traditional

Weber regarded premodern authority, both in social relationships and in large organizations, as legitimated primarily on traditional grounds. With traditional legitimation the "sanctity" of rules is a function of the fact that they have been handed down from generation to generation. Correspondingly, the authority of persons in positions of power is legitimated by virtue of their occupancy of traditionally justified statuses.

These features of traditional authority can be illustrated by the hacienda system in Mexico. Prior to the revolution in 1910, most Mexicans were illiterate farm workers, employed and "owned" by large haciendas. They were bound to patrons (that is, estate owners) by historical family ties to specific patrons and by their debts to the hacienda-operated stores. Because there was no effective government outside of haciendas, the peasants could be kept in virtual serfdom by the threat of force. During most of the prerevolutionary period, however, the hacienda system was stable and required little force. Children were socialized into the system in a context in which widely shared values emphasized such intergenerational continuity. Thus, the authority of patrons and the rules of the hacienda were legitimated on traditional grounds.[11]

The arch nemesis of tradition is people's calculation of what is in something for them. Traditionalism provides a stable system of order so long as those subjected to it do not think to calculate their benefits and their costs. Once old ways are seriously questioned, they often fail to survive. This type of examination of alternatives is exactly what is involved in the deliberate, self-consciousness evaluations of a rational orientation. Thus, rational orientations tend to lead to the discarding of traditional legitimations and their replacement with rational-legal legitimations.

---

[11] For further discussion, see Rodolfo Stavenhagen, "Social Aspects of Mexican Agrarian Structure," *Social Research*, 33 (1966).

Charismatic

Frequently intervening between tradition and rational-legal legitimation is the charismatic form, Weber's second pure type. Defined literally, charisma is the "gift of grace." It rests on subordinates' belief that charismatic leaders possess qualities that set them apart from ordinary people. The origins of these qualities are typically moot; it is rarely clear where such powers come from; hence, their "giftlike" bestowal. Historically, great religious leaders (such as Jesus Christ), revolutionaries (such as George Washington), and political rulers (such as King Solomon) were assumed, by their followers, to possess special qualities that set them apart. The salient issue is not whether they actually can heal, protect, or perform miracles, but the fact that such abilities are attributed to them.

Like traditional authority, charismatic authority is highly personal. That is, loyalty is sworn to an individual rather than an office. This differentiates both types from the rational-legal mode in which loyalties are impersonal, that is, to positions. The major difference between the traditional and the charismatic is that the former stresses stability and continuity while the latter tends to be revolutionary, or at least change oriented. Thus, charismatic leaders attempt to establish new orders, new regimes, new religions, and the like. In addition, tradition circumscribes the latitude of a leader whose authority is legitimated on traditional grounds. However, charismatic leaders have greater freedom to behave impulsively. Neither tradition nor legalistic orders establish tight boundaries in which they must operate.

The Achilles' heel of traditional legitimation was seen to be the self-conscious deliberation of rational orientations. Charismatic authority does not hold up well in this light either, but its fatal flaw is endemic; it is intrinsically short lived. The nonpermanence of organizations based upon charisma rests on the fact that irrespective of their other perceived attributes, all charismatic leaders share one feature in common with everyone else; they are mortal. Their eventual death almost necessarily creates a crisis for the organization they have built. How can a successor be chosen? By definition, charisma is a gift. Therefore, how can it be transmitted to another? A protege, an offspring, or a new revealed leader may emerge, or perhaps two or three will claim to be the rightful or logical successor. In any case, the decision is likely to involve establishing rules for handling successions. The existence of such rules, in and of themselves, makes authority within the organization less charismatic and more bureaucratic. In addition, once the original leader passes on, some of the bloom is off of the rose. The successor is not likely to be regarded as equally exceptional in special abilities, and the followers may be concerned with their investments. Remember, when authority is charismatically legitimated, organizations tend to be revolutionary, or at least, antiestablishment. To be part of such an organization usually requires that followers sever their ties to some (or all) conventional institutions—whether a church, a political system, or the like. With a new leader they are likely to wonder whether the price they are paying is justifiable. Some will leave. Others will attempt to protect their investments by creating an administrative staff to help oversee the organization. Again, it has become less charismatic and more bureaucratic.

Another reason for the instability of charismatic authority is built-in concern that often leads followers to force a charismatic leader into a disqualifying action. Given the price they are paying to follow—religious persecution, being hunted as outlaws, and so forth—it is not surprising that they would like continually to be reassured that the leader still possesses the remarkable abilities that attracted them in the first place. In effect they say, "you walked on water, but that was yesterday; what can you do today?" Simply repeating former feats is not sufficient. With repetition they become ordinary. Regardless of how much talent a charismatic leader possesses, eventually such pressures will often lead to an attempt that fails. Unfortunately for charismatic leaders, a 99 percent success rate is not sufficient. With the first failure, many followers will become demoralized and quit. Others will want a successor found immediately while still others will want to hedge their bets and create a staff. In either case, the charismatic organization will either disband or become more bureaucratic.

From Charismatic to Rational-Legal

Weber argued that organizations in which authority was charismatic could not long endure. They could simply wither away or, if they were to survive, do so by changing their character; that is, become increasingly bureaucratic. Even organizations which began as antibureaucratic, he concluded, would ultimately become subject to the same bureaucratization forces. Thus, Christ's charismatic organization "survived" only through a formalized church structure; Castro's revolution in Cuba ousted a bureaucratic regime and replaced it with another; the movement to hire minorities resulted in formalized affirmative action programs.

In sum, Weber regarded bureaucratization as inevitable because 1) the rationalization of orientations destroyed tradition as a mode of legitimation and resulted in the greater appropriateness of rational-legal legitimation, and 2) charisma is a nonenduring basis of legitimation which, in modern societies, tends to be replaced by the rational-legal form (if the organizations initially based upon charisma are to survive). In addition, size and complexity were also viewed by Weber as conducive to bureaucratization. More specifically, the large size of modern societies is associated with complex administrative problems. Consider, for example, the difficulty of administering a social security system involving about 230 million participants. Thus, the sheer complexity of large-scale problems, in a rationally oriented society, leads to bureaucratization. He concluded:[12]

> For the needs of mass administration today, it is completely indispensable. The choice is only that between bureauracy and dilettantism in the field of administration.

The relationship between size and complexity, on the one hand, and bureaucratization, on the other, has been subject to a large number of empirical studies.[13] While the results of these studies are difficult to interpret for a variety of methodological

---

[12]Weber, *The Theory of Social and Economic Organization*, p. 337.

[13]For an excellent review of these studies, see John R. Kimberly, "Organizational Size and the Structuralist Perspective," *Administrative Science Quarterly*, 21 (1976).

reasons, most studies do report the expected relationship between size or complexity (however measured) and various indices of bureaucratization.

In this section we have examined the sources of the presumed indispensability of bureaucracy. While the how and the why have not always been clear, Weber does appear to have been correct in anticipating increasingly widespread bureaucratization. Our approach, in this section, has been descriptive rather than evaluative. However, Weber's own analyses were tinged with values that led him to regard bureaucracy as not only inevitable, but as desirable. Therefore, it may be that his use of ideal types, at least with reference to bureaucracy, was meant to imply not only pure types of legitimation, but desirable types as well.

EFFICIENCY OF BUREAUCRACY

Weber's praise for bureaucratic organizations stressed their efficiency and their stability. To a limited degree he was absolutely correct in lauding their efficiency and their stability. However, he seems to have employed a rather limited view of efficiency and may have implicitly taken some large assumptions about personality too much for granted. Before we consider these criticisms, however, let us briefly examine what prompted Weber to attribute efficiency and stability to bureaucratic organizations.

Their efficiency, according to Weber, is tied to the characteristically high probability of a bureaucrat's prompt obedience to commands. The rules are explicit, lines of authority are explicit, and people are placed into positions according to demonstrated competence. Thus, in the *pure* bureaucracy, there is little opportunity for "slippage" to occur. Moreover, the spirit of detached impersonality restrains incumbents, preventing favoritism or personality clashes from entering the picture and producing deviations from the rationally designed system.

One of the best known examples of bureaucratic efficiency, cited by Weber, was the development of a professional army in England under Cromwell, Lord Protector of England. While not a pure bureaucracy, Cromwell's Puritan army was highly bureaucratized by seventeenth-century standards. It fought in a rational, disciplined manner. The partisans of Charles I, the Cavaliers, still fought in a more gallant and heroic manner, reminiscent of the Middle Ages. When the two armies clashed, in the middle of the seventeenth century, Cromwell's Puritans were victorious. This triumph of discipline over heroism was regarded by Weber as indicating the effectiveness of a bureaucratized army.[14] However, he did not view the superiority of bureaucratization as limited to armies; they merely provided one dramatic illustration.

Meyer argues that Weber's favorable evaluation of bureaucracy arose because, in most instances, he was comparing fairly simple bureaucracies with complicated

[14]Hans H. Gerth and C. Wright Mills, eds., *From Max Weber: Essays in Sociology* (New York: Oxford University Press, 1946).

traditional organizations. Meyer concludes that the greater apparent efficiency of the bureaucracies was due to their great simplicity. Over the past 75 years or so, however, bureaucratic organizations have grown in size and complexity (because of the legitimacy of the bureaucratic form). As a result, they may no longer provide the most efficient form of organization.[15]

Further, Weber probably paid too little attention to the ways in which bureaucracies could be damnably inefficient. He recognized that strict adherence to the rules could lead to ridiculous decisions, shrouded in red tape. However, he viewed bureaucratic administrations as efficient, in net balance, over the long run; but in so doing he may have exaggerated its surplus of efficiency over inefficiency. An interesting example of the latter comes from Schwartz's analysis of hospital emergency rooms. One obvious criterion of their efficiency is the speed with which injured or sick persons are admitted for aid. The longer people have to wait, without receiving medical attention, the more inefficient is the emergency service.

Schwartz observed efforts to increase efficiency in a stylized bureaucratic manner. This entailed further specializing the roles of hospital admitting personnel and adding additional staff. This bureaucratic response to the problem did not reduce waiting time; hence it did not increase efficiency. It only produced more red tape and more lines for people to endure.[16]

This problem is, of course, not confined to emergency rooms. Students encounter it at college bookstores at the start of every semester; tax payers confront it every spring in government office buildings, long lines and abundant red tape. In situations such as this, it is common for people to pray for the emergence of one sane official to take charge and organize the chaos. (It rarely happens.) However, Weber's point would be that if such a person did emerge and straighten out the situation, what would happen next time? Dependence upon *an* individual's ability may result in short-run efficiency, but may seriously impede the organization's ability to perform long-term services.

THE STABILITY OF BUREAUCRACY

Wars and their aftermath also provided one of the examples Weber utilized to illustrate the stability of bureaucracy. Weber died, in 1920, shortly after the end of World War I, and one of his unfinished essays dealt with the transfer of power in postwar Germany. The defeat ended traditional authority in government, industry, the army, and so on. New leaders came into power along with a new system of order. Yet, while this was occurring, all of the mundane needs of the German

[15]Marshall W. Meyer, *Limits to Bureaucratic Growth* (New York: Walter de Gruyter, 1985). Adding support to Meyer's contention is a survey of the literature which suggests that larger organizations may be more productive than smaller ones, but are not more efficient in a cost-effective sense. See Richard Z. Gooding and John Wagner III, "A Meta-Analytic Review of the Relationship Between Size and Performance," *Administrative Science Quarterly*, 30, (1985).

[16]Barry Schwartz, *Queuing and Waiting* (Chicago: University of Chicago Press, 1975).

population still had to be met: police and fire services, mail delivery, and the like. It was therefore necessary for individuals to remain at their technical functions. Fortunately, most of them did. Apart from their selfish economic desires to remain employed, the bureaucrats felt a continuing sense of duty to their positions. If not, "the breakdown of administrative organization would have meant a breakdown of the provision of the whole population . . . with even the most elementary necessities of life."[17] Thus, Weber noted, bureaucracies could continue to operate without interruption despite profound social changes.

The most fundamental reason for bureaucracy's stability is the fact that organizational needs, rather than the personal needs of incumbents, are paramount. By contrast, consider a family or a small fraternal organization. In these less formal associations, tradition or external organizations (such as extended families or national societies) may impose certain restraints on members' behavior. For the most part, however, how they do things is in large measure a function of interpersonal accommodation. In other words, the pleasure of each other's company is at least as important as external accomplishments, so they may organize themselves in ways they find to be mutually satisfying. In a bureaucracy, however, the demands of positions prevail. If there is an incongruence between the demands of positions and the personal needs of incumbents, it is the incumbents who adjust. Thus, bureaucracies are stable because they are designed to be self-serving.

Weber also considered bureaucracies to be stable as a result of certain implicit assumptions he apparently held regarding human nature. In modern societies, he seemed to believe that most people would not resent being subjected to strict discipline so long as the rules were clear, that most people wanted the long-term security of stable careers and so on. In short, he felt that bureaucratic requirements and personal predispositions were largely congruent.

One eminent Weberian scholar maintains that Weber's frequent use of military illustrations was not accidental; that, in effect, a distinct stereotype of people led Weber to write about bureaucracies as ideal in an evaluative sense. Specifically, Weber is pictured as expressing a "Prussian enthusiasm for the military type of organization" which would preclude a "consultative, let alone cooperative, pattern."[18] Indeed, the establishment of varied types of worker cooperatives in parts of Israel, Yugoslavia and, to a lesser extent, in the United States suggests that all modern people are not predisposed to conventional bureaucratic employment. Their cooperatives, designed to be consultative, have been subject to the same pressures toward bureaucratization as other organizations. Weber was more right than wrong in asserting its inevitability. However, he was not sufficiently sensitive to the possibility of a widespread discrepancy between bureaucratic organizations and the personality orientations of incumbents. In other words, by implicitly overemphasizing a military model of organizations, he simply failed to recognize that many officials would find

---

[17]Weber, *The Theory of Social and Economic Organization*, p. 385.
[18]Carl J. Friedrich, "Some Observations on Weber's Analysis of Bureaucracy," in *Reader in Bureaucracy*, edited by Robert K. Merton and others (New York: Free Press, 1952), p. 31.

the system to be oppressive and would resist following orders. Their ability to be defiant might be very limited and therefore not seriously effect the stability of bureaucracies. However, to the degree that bureaucratic employment is experienced as oppressive, it is difficult to share Weber's assumption concerning its desirability. Perhaps the salient question is, how large a price, in human terms, should people pay for bureaucratic efficiency and stability?

Looking, as we have been, at the congruence between initial predispositions and bureaucratic demands is only part of the picture. For many people there is an excellent goodness of fit. For many others, the spirit within them protests ever so feebly before capitulating. Therefore, there need not be any continuing tension between personality and organization, hence, no personal costs. What are the consequences for a democratic society, though?

BUREAUCRACY AND DEMOCRACY

One potentially serious problem for the society is a large group of overly submissive people, people who, as a result of bureaucratic employment, become *generally* too apt to follow orders.[19] Nazi Germany was, in part, a horrifying example of what can happen if people are too ready to follow orders. Could it happen here? A fascinating study by Milgram suggests it could. Volunteers, under the direction of an experimenter, were told to give electric shocks to subjects who made errors in a learning experiment. Some of the shocks were of nearly lethal intensity, and volunteers could hear the painful consequences. (They pushed buttons to administer the punishment to subjects who were in other rooms.) In reality, pushing the buttons did not produce electric shocks; however, the volunteers did not know that. The main purpose of the study was simply to ascertain whether they would follow the experimenter's orders and "dispense" the shocks, even the very high intensity ones. The results were clear: Most volunteers (who were from all walks of life) were willing to follow orders.[20]

To be fair in our assessment it must be recognized that widespread bureaucratization is not the only force which produces submissiveness to authority in modern society. It may not even be the most important one. However, to the degree that bureaucratic employment generates a general predisposition to follow orders, it produces a cadre of people extremely capable of behaving in an antidemocratic manner.

Juxtaposed to is deleterious consequence for a society are other consequences of bureaucratization which Weber was able to associate with "mass democracy."[21] The most important of these was a levelling tendency which reduced or eliminated

[19]Robert K. Merton, "Bureaucratic Structure and Personality," ibid.

[20]Stanley Milgram, *Obedience to Authority* (New York: Harper and Row, 1973).

[21]Weber, *The Theory of Social and Economic Organization*, pp. 340-341.

class privileges in favor of more equalitarian opportunities. These equalizing effects are due to a number of basic bureaucratic features:

1) The emphasis on technical competence leads to an expansion of opportunities for training; that is, recruitment needs lead to an expansion of the pool of technically qualified persons.
2) The spirit of formalistic relationships leads to a disregard of personal characteristics, such as class background.
3) Functional positions, stressing merit, replace honorific offices and titles which were the exclusive domain of the wealthy class.

Partially offsetting these equalitarian forces is an oligarchical tendency in which a small number of people form a self-perpetuating group that remains in control of the organization. In a bureaucracy, knowledge is power leading the people at the top to guard their privileged access to knowledge. Thus, oligarchical tendencies in bureaucracies tend to involve the guarding of "official secrets."

In addition, Weber may have stressed the compatibility of bureaucracy and democracy because of his emphasis upon how bureaucratic government agencies would treat citizens equally in their people-processing functions. Meyer proposes, however, that Weber may not have been as sensitive to the ways in which bureaucratic red tape and rigidity could adversely affect citizens' *participation* in democratic governance. In essence, if we consider the problems of both control and governance, it may be that bureaucracy presents a satisfactory, but not optimal, solution.[22]

CONCLUSION

In final summary, we have examined Weber's view of bureaucracy as the formal organization which rests on a rational-legal mode of legitimating authority. The ideal or pure type of bureaucracy was seen to have some applicability to "real life" organizations; but even when it was not applicable, the dimensions of bureaucratization described by Weber continue to provide the models against which actual organizations are analyzed.

With increasingly rational orientations, and the growth of large-scale administrative problems, widespread bureaucratization appears to be inevitable. However, it is more of a mixed blessing than Weber recognized. It seems to provide long-term stability and continuity at the cost of red tape and short-run inefficiency. For the larger society, it creates the risk that prompt obedience to orders will become a generalized trait while at the same time generating pressures which level social classes and promote mass democracy. Thus, bureaucratization defies any simple evaluations as a force for good or evil. The problem that confronts us is how to design organizations that are more responsive to human needs and less likely to produce robot-people but are at the same time capable of providing stability and long-term efficiency.

[22]Marshall W. Meyer, *Limits to Bureaucratic Growth.*

SUGGESTIONS FOR ADDITIONAL READING

ROBERT T. GOLEMBIEWSKI, *Organization and Development,* New Brunswick, NJ: Transaction
     Books, 1988.
EDWARD B. PORTIS, *Max Weber and Political Commitment,* Philadelphia: Temple University Press,
     1986.
ALAN SICA, *Weber, Irrationality and Social Order,* Berkeley: University of California Press, 1988.

Solidarity and Conflict
Simmel

Consider the following colleges: the University of Kentucky, Indiana University and Duke University. What do they have in common? A sports fan might recognize that all of them tend to have outstanding men's basketball teams, almost every year; but only rarely do any of them excel in football. Now that you are on the right track, consider the following group: the University of Southern California, Penn State University and the University of Nebraska. What do they share? Football. These universities usually have strong football, but not basketball, teams.

Colleges that excel in football do not typically excel in basketball, and vice versa, though there are some exceptions to these long-term patterns. Even in the short run, when a university's football program begins to improve, its basketball program tends to become worse; and vice versa. Thus, over the long run or the short run, there is generally an inverse relationship between success in football and basketball.

There are many reasons for this inverse relationship. One of them involves the power of the football coach relative to the basketball coach. Each must attempt to persuade the athletic director to allocate more resources to his or her sport. This includes scholarships for athletes, recruitment related expenses for phone calls and travel, access to training equipment in the gym and so on. All of these resources tend to be limited. At some point, therefore, what is allocated to the football team must come at the expense of the basketball team, and vice versa.

It is typical for athletic directors themselves to be former coaches. They may "naturally" be partial to their ex-sport and such favoritism can be a basis for a school's continuing excellence in one sport rather than another. Alumni groups can also provide resources directly to a team, or indirectly, by pressuring athletic directors to increase the support given to a team. A variety of other interested groups can also influence decision making in the short run or the long run.

The football and basketball coaches belong to the same department in the same university. Their teams wear the same colors, and they share many facilities in common. From one perspective they also share common goals, namely, serving students and winning games "for the school." Despite all of this, the coaches do not typically feel a common bond. In fact, they often consider each other bitter rivals and continuously watch the other's moves to make sure they are not going to try to "steal" something of value—like an athletic scholarship.

The situation in which the coaches and athletic director find themselves is not unique. Two women simultaneously trying to get the attention of the same man or two men trying to court the same woman are classical examples of the same phenomenon: two parties competing with each other in order to influence a third party. The continuous strain that is built into such situations often produces antagonism, distrust, jealousy, even hatred. Mere mortals are not usually able to rise above such situations and keep from feeling animosity toward their rival, even when the competitive situation is of brief duration. Two perplexed students and one reference librarian, twin siblings on an afternoon outing with one parent, two hurried customers and one slow-moving salesperson are all examples of competitive situations that are temporary, but nevertheless capable of generating antagonisms.

The previously noted examples also suggest that it is commonplace for two people to compete for the attention or favor of a third person. Situations of this type seem, in fact, to occur in many different facets of life: at work, during courtship, in families, and so on. The people involved may continue to be friendly and supportive to each other, but they are more likely to perceive a conflict between their objectives and another's and respond with antagonism or hostility. From this perspective, conflict is structured into social life; it is a routine part of everyday experience. It follows, therefore, that sociological analyses should focus upon the conditions which generate conflict, its mode of expression, and its resolution.

Patterns of solidarity and conflict were two of the topics addressed in the highly instructive theories of Georg Simmel. He is the major theorist to be discussed in this chapter. Before examining his writings, however, let us pose another question, to be considered later. If conflict is as pervasive and unavoidable as the preceding discussion suggests, then how is social life possible? What prevents it from becoming what Thomas Hobbes described as a continuous war of all against all? We will examine some interesting answers to these questions at the end of this chapter.

SIZE AND FORM

Most of Simmel's life (1858-1917)—as a child, student, and professor—was spent in Berlin. As a professor he taught very popular courses and published widely and often; yet most of his career was spent in a marginal, unsalaried position. This was partly due to "accidents" of birth. His parents were of Jewish origin, and even though they converted and he was baptized, he could not escape German antisemitism which was very strong in Berlin. In addition, his lectures and writings may have been a little too popular, creating the suspicion that he was more of a showman than a scholar.[1]

Perhaps because his position was so marginal, Simmel was sensitized to subtle nuances of everyday life, subtleties that might have escaped the notice of people whose positions were more secure. Thus, he wrote penetrating essays on such apparently mundane topics as the human face and ruined buildings. Throughout much of his writings was an emphasis upon the forms of interaction which he viewed as defining the primary subject matter of sociology as a distinctive discipline. Solidarity and conflict were two of the forms he investigated in great detail, especially in relation to the size of groups.[2]

The Dyad

The smallest unit worthy of sociological attention, he stated, was the *dyad,* or two party group: husband and wife, two friends, and so on. In a dyad there is the greatest possibility of total immersion by each party. Each can give of himself, or herself, totally and directly. This quality is intrinsic to dyads. Because there are just the two of them, there is no one who can come between them. Thus, Simmel concluded, two can feel as one. Three, or four, or more can never share an equally intense feeling of intimacy, or "one-ness."

While great closeness can be attained by the parties in a dyad, rampant conflict is also very likely to occur. This propensity for conflict can be due to the strong personal involvements of the parties to the relationship. Their feelings are on the line, and actions which in other situations might be ignored can be matters of serious consternation. In addition, the absence of other parties to the relationship virtually precludes impersonal orientations from acting as a buffer. Neither party can ever view the other's denial of anything as due to formal rules that would apply to anyone. The denied party must feel *personally* rejected; no one else is asking! (If there were somebody else, it would no longer be a dyad.)

Once hostile feelings are aroused, there is also a clear tendency for them to escalate in a two-party relationship. The angered or hurt parties can voice their complaints only to each other, eliciting emotional replies and spiraling anger. The absence of a third party is responsible for the intense intimacy of the dyad, but once conflict begins, a third party may be sorely missed. If there were such an "outsider," the quarreling parties would have someone, beside each other, to beseech. With such a third party, Simmel noted, each would also be more likely to offer more rational and less emotional appeals. The possibility for reconciliation would be enhanced.

Now, suppose our hypothetical football and basketball coaches, in the earlier example, were alone in the athletic department just the two of them. Each would

[1]For further comments, see Anthony Giddens, "Georg Simmel," in *The Founding Fathers of Social Science,* edited by Timothy Raison (Baltimore: Penguin, 1969).

[2]The following discussion is based upon two of Simmel's essays: "The Number of Members as Determining the Sociological Form of the Group," and "1 and 2," *American Journal of Sociology,* 8 (July and September, 1902).

then be more likely to feel responsible for, and committed to, the athletic program of the college. Simmel observed that the larger the group the greater the probability that members will conceive of the group as a superstructure and relegate concern for the whole to others. This is least likely to occur in a dyad.

On some days the coaches' shared concerns would probably lead to a bond between them. Sooner, or later, however, they are likely to begin to bicker over how to distribute athletic scholarships, or some other resource. Once it begins, the conflict between them might soon get out of hand. Thus, they might alternate between being the best of friends and the worst of enemies. This tendency toward extreme fluctuations that characterizes dyads has been depicted in numerous movies, plays, books, and television series. In the "Odd Couple," for example, the relationship between Felix and Oscar recurrently varied between solidary warmth and intolerable rage.

The tendency for dyadic conflict to spiral out of bounds was vividly portrayed by the older married couple in "Who's Afraid of Virginia Woolf." They would slowly become less and less of a loving couple as each progressively increased the aggressiveness of verbal assaults upon the other, until one of them was emotionally devastated. They recognized such attacks to be violations of their implicitly agreed-upon-rules; that is, each knew when he or she went "too far" in attacking the other. However, the intensity of the conflict seemed, of its own volition, to carry them beyond the boundary. Then they would make up, and move closer together until the same cycle would begin again.

The Triad

The addition of a third party dramatically alters the structure and form of relationships. In general the third party exerts a leveling, or moderating, influence. The degree of intimacy that is possible in a dyad is reduced; three cannot feel as one to the same degree that two can. At the other extreme, however, the tendency for conflict to reach spiraling heights is also reduced by the presence of a third party because of the possibility of the third party playing a mediating role.

Although it initially sounds ironic, Simmel noted that the third party unites by separating. Each of the three shares a common bond created by the relationship between the other two. For example, a married couple are initially a dyad. With the birth of a child, they become a triad. The child provides a common bond to the couple. Each now views the other, not only as a spouse, but as a parent of their child. While they are united in this way, the third party also separates. When the dyad terminates, so too does the intense intimacy that is uniquely characteristic of it. Three can not feel as one to the same degree. There are, however, compensations created at the other extreme as the result of the third party's possible mediating influence. Even before the child is actively able to play any role, his or her very presence may serve to restrain the level of conflict which occurs between the parents. Thus, they are simultaneously united and separated.

Simmel also proposed that triads tend to be unstable in the sense that inherent to their form was a continuing predisposition toward the formation of coalitions of two against one. The third party is, at least temporarily, rejected. Which of the three people is placed into the third party, or outcast, role varies over time, however. Today it may be mother and father against child; tomorrow it may be child and mother against father, and so on.

When there is a strong and enduring coalition between two members of a triad, the form of interaction can actually become dyadic; that is, involving two parties, though one of the parties is comprised of two persons. Within the coalition there is a dyad and, as within any other dyad, the persons can feel as one. In fact, their common opposition to the third party may make them particularly likely to feel as one under these conditions; but because solidarity within the dyad is at the expense of an outcast—even if the outcast keeps changing—a sense of intimate oneness is hardly likely to characterize such a triad in entirety.

Simmel provided a number of fascinating illustrations of the third party's effect. He noted, for example, a tendency for wealthy Europeans to hire only a single servant, despite their ability to afford more than one. A sole servant had been observed to identify personally with an employer and provide loyal service. When there were two or more servants, by contrast, their common status created a bond among them and separated each from the employer. A second servant would, therefore, mediate the relationship between each servant and the employer. Even if only one of the servants were physically present, the relationship implicitly retained this triadic quality, and hence tended to be less personal.

STRATEGIES AND TACTICS

The tendencies toward conflict that appear to be embedded in triads fascinated Simmel and subsequent generations of sociologists. This continuing interest is party due to the fact that there are many roles open to the parties that comprise a triad, and which is selected by any one of them has important consequences for everyone else. A third party, for example, may play a mediating role vis-a-vis two contending parties. Thus, the athletic director may intervene between arguing coaches. The coaches are then likely to present more rational and less emotional arguments to the director than either would to the quickly and with less personal strain. In many triadic situations, however, the third party may be inclined not to act as a mediator. This party may stand to gain from the conflict and therefore try to perpetuate it. Simmel called situations of this type "tertius gaudens," translated as third-party benefit.

The gains which accrue to the third party may be quite direct. In seeking the third party's approval or support, the two competing parties may offer services, gifts, or the like in excess of what would be offered if there were no competitor. The existence of a rival may spur a suitor to be more considerate or to give better gifts during a courtship than if there were no rival. The athletic director may generally be treated more deferentially by both coaches than if either coach were the only one in the situation.

The third party's benefits from the competition can also be indirect. While the two parties are preoccupied with each other, the third party may be free to act in ways which would otherwise be noticed. If parents are quarreling with each other, for example, a child may be able to take liberties without being observed. The liberties quietly taken by the third party might be attainable in any case, but if they were observed, they might require compensation, or some form of reciprocity. Under these conditions they are "free."

In all of the situations just described, the third party is likely to try to perpetuate the conflict. This often entails entering into temporary coalitions, or at least the appearance of coalitions, first with one rival, then with the other. Thus, each is given a "taste" of what winning would be like in order to keep each interested. Without some encouragement, either of the rivals may grow weary of the quest and drop out. The relationship then becomes a dyad, and the third party's advantages are lost.

The form of the relationship can also become dyadic if the two rivals form a coalition. This is an unlikely pairing, but it is probably the occurrence that is most dreaded by the party in the tertius gaudens position. Thus, the football and basketball coaches may stop fighting, form a united front, and demand more total scholarships. The athletic director then finds previous options closed; for example, the two coaches can no longer be played off against each other. Neither will be happy now just to have more than the other. Or, parents may suddenly stop quarreling, become as one, and thereby terminate the child's freedom. As these examples illustrate, tertius gaudens is dramatically terminated by a coalition among former competitors.

For the third party to maintain a triad for personal gains often requires very skillful manipulation. A premium must be placed upon keeping competitors sufficiently separated from each other to prevent them from forming a coalition. At the same time, however, they must be kept close enough to each other to remain aware of the continuing competition. Thus, sleepless nights of plotting can be required to maintain third-party benefits, but the rewards are sufficient to justify the effort. For the competitors, strategy can take the form of trying to alter the number of parties involved in order to change the form of relationships or else leaving the structure intact, but personally changing parties. One of the more insightful applications of these strategy perspectives is provided by Caplow's reanalysis of Shakespeare's *Hamlet*.[3]

Caplow's Hamlet

Shakespeare's *Hamlet* has been remarkably enduring. For generations it has been required reading in English courses and is recurrently presented by every imaginable kind of theatrical group. It has also been a favored object of literary criticism and analysis. The main character has become almost synonymous with procrastination. To risk tragedy by delaying action is to behave like Hamlet.

The popular view that Hamlet's fatal flaw was an inability to stop thinking and just act is due to the heavy hand of psychoanalytic interpretations of the play. Following Simmel, Caplow has offered a very different interpretation of Hamlet's

---

[3]The following discussion is adapted from Theodore Caplow, *Two Against One* (Englewood Cliffs: Prentice-Hall, 1968).

motives, a view which emphasizes dyadic and triadic forms of relationships. Before examining Caplow's theory, however, let us briefly outline the play. Hamlet's father, the king of Denmark, has recently died. His mother, Queen Gertrude, has married his uncle, Claudius, who has assumed the throne. Hamlet regards the marriage as hasty, incestuous, and opportunistic. He becomes convinced that his father was murdered by Claudius, that his mother's actions further shame his father's memory, and that he must avenge the murder. Instead of simply doing what he must, however, he feigns madness, directs plays, and offers endless soliloquies. (Otherwise the play would last for about seven minutes.)

Hamlet's deferred actions are not regarded as undue procrastination by Caplow, though. He notes that Hamlet could get at Claudius at any time but asks, How would he justify it? The only "evidence" that Claudius killed his father is a ghost's tale. If he killed Claudius on those grounds, he would be dishonored and probably be put to death himself. Certainly his apparent wish to succeed Claudius as king would be thwarted. What he needs is the support of his mother, the queen. However, while Gertrude seems not to have been in on the plot to murder her former husband, she now appears to be in a solidary coalition with Claudius, and Hamlet is unsure of her real feelings toward him.

Hamlet's basic problem, Caplow concludes, is how to alter the structure of palace relationships. At the opening of the play, there is a dyadic structure: Gertrude and Claudius are one party; Hamlet is the other. To avenge his father's murder without discrediting himself, Hamlet must force a wedge into their relationship. A triad, composed of Gertrude, Claudius and himself as separate parties, would be an improvement. A dyad, in which he and Gertrude were allied, would be better still. Most of the ensuing action in the play is interpreted by Caplow as Hamlet's attempts to convince Gertrude of his uncle's guilt (and her own shame) before taking revenge. The play-within-a-play, staged by Hamlet, is the final effort. From this perspective, Hamlet's behavior is deliberate, due mostly to external restraints, and there is little basis for the popular characterization of Hamlet as a weak and timid person.

These markedly different interpretations of Hamlet's behavior and personality are the result of expanding the conceptual emphasis. Rather than focusing solely upon Hamlet as an individual, Caplow has stressed the web of relationships in which Hamlet had to operate. Not only are the resultant personality inferences different, but the entire degree of emphasis upon personality is reduced in favor of greater attention to the form of association. In Simmel's view, this emphasis upon form was the most distinguishing characteristic of sociology as a distinct discipline.

Additional Numbers

Beyond a third person, the inclusion of additional numbers of persons sometimes has profound consequences for the nature of interaction within a group. With each successive addition, however, the consequences tend to decline in magnitude. Simmel illustrated this general principle by describing the changing situation of a man who slowly accumulates a harem of wives. With one wife the relationship is, of course, a monogamous dyad. The addition of a second wife converts the structure to a polygamous triad. All of the instabilities and conflicts to which triads are generally prone are especially likely to be pronounced in this specific triad.

The addition of a third wife is likely to reduce the friction substantially by leading to a more impersonal classification; that is, with respect to forms of interaction. The wives become like a category rather than a number of discrete individuals. To add a fourth wife, fifth, or more would probably have almost negligible additional effects upon patterns of interaction. In a similar way, the birth of a fifth, sixth, or later child would be likely to have a limited impact upon relationship patterns within a conventional family.

As groups grow larger, Simmel hypothesized a tendency for them to revert to a dyadic form of interaction. In the polygamous harem, as noted, the wives would eventually tend to constitute a single sociological entity, the same for the one (shared) husband. Relationships can, therefore, be dyadic even though one party to the relationship is comprised of numerous individuals, such as all of the wives. Both parties can also have multiple members; for example, mother and father may be one party, all their children may be the other party, and there may be a dyadic relationship between the two parties.

During the process of moving toward the dyadic form within larger collectives, each party (or category) tends to accept as members other people who are more-or-less like them. The similarity that is emphasized may be wealth, attitude, or anything else. At some point, however, the outer boundaries of a category are reached. Further distinctions become too complex, and a simple dichotomy is emphasized. Everyone is reduced merely to being either like us or different, for us or against us.

Race and ethnicity provide highly dramatic examples of the tendency to establish rigid dichotomies within larger collectivities. In the United States, for example, the historical pattern has been to classify people as either black or white; to be racially mixed, or partly both, has not been an alternative. To illustrate, in June, 1978, Dr. Doris Thompson was fired by Louisiana's governor from her job as an assistant secretary in the state's Department of Health. One reason for her firing, she later stated in an interview, was her negative attitude toward the "racial list" that had been maintained for years by the department. It contained the names of white families that, since about 1850, had partial black ancestry.[4]

When any "white" person in Louisiana wanted a birth certificate, it was the responsibility of a "race clerk" to check their name against the racial list. The historic practice was to tell applicants their race would have to be listed as "Negro" if they had any trace of "black blood." In 1970, any trace was dropped as the official criterion when the state legislature passed the current 1/32nd rule. Thus, people are identified as "Negro" on their birth certificates if the race clerk can ascertain one black great-great-great grandparent in an otherwise white lineage.

[4]Reported by Associated Press, in Connecticut *Journal-Inquirer,* June 16, 1978, p. 25.

Louisiana's policies may be extreme, but they are not unique. In Nazi Germany, for example, there was a similarly rigid dichotomy of people into categories: Aryan or Jew. Again, no intermediate or mixed categories were recognized. As noted earlier, these racial and ethnic categories are clear examples of the tendency, described by Simmel, for interaction within larger collectivities to revert back to a dyadic form.

SOCIOLOGY: THE STUDY OF FORM

Simmel was a pioneering sociologist who published widely both within and outside of sociology. The unclear boundaries between it and related disciplines, such as psychology and history, were a source of genuine concern to him. The then prevalent definitions—which actually have changed little over the years—were regarded by Simmel as terribly inadequate. One popular description of sociology as the "all-inclusive" social science only seemed to confound matters further. Other definitions which stressed the social nature of human life also seemed nearly worthless. He regarded this social-nature statement as true but argued that it was an assumption common to all the social sciences. As such, it could not help to clarify a distinctive subject matter for sociology.[5]

Simmel emphasized the difference between the form and content of social relations and differentiated sociology from other social sciences by its unique focus upon form. All the other disciplines are defined by their content. By content he meant the motives and other psychic states of participants, the proper subject matter of psychology, and the historical and institutional contexts—religion, economy, politics, and so on—that were associated with a particular discipline other than sociology.

By form Simmel meant the specific pattern, or style, that gave a kind of relationship its distinctive character. As examples of such patterns he noted: superiority and subordination, competition and solidarity, and others. Consider competition as a concrete example. Simmel was arguing that it is possible to conceptualize competition as a *form* of association, independently of participants' motives and apart from any particular context. To pursue this conceptualization further, recall how in many of the preceding examples the number of parties were differentiated from the number of persons. A party, we noted, could consist of one person or of many. The same form of relationship must, therefore, be able to occur in markedly different contexts. For example, Simmel described how the ancient Incas often divided a conquered society into two almost equal groups. The two divided entities typically proceeded to behave toward each other in a belligerent manner. There were then fewer threats to the Inca rulers because the conquered people were so preoccupied with each other. Thus, a tertius-gaudens pattern could equally well characterize a ruling nation, an athletic director, or a child. In each case the specific motives of participants might

---

[5]This discussion is primarily based upon "The Problem of Sociology," in Georg Simmel and others, *Essays on Sociology, Philosophy and Aesthetics,* trans. by Kurt H. Wolff (New York: Harper and Row, 1965).

be quite different, and the institutional contexts are clearly different; yet the same form of relationship occurs.

Simmel was unsure whether various forms were completely identical despite varying motives and contexts. However, he argued that they were at least nearly identical; in other words, sufficiently similar to be treated as alike. My own position is that it is unwarranted to assume precise comparability. In a dyad, for example, two lovers may feel as one; but I doubt whether two nations, in a dyadic relationship, can feel as one to a comparable degree, or whether there is an equally strong tendency for bitter, personal antagonisms to escalate. At the same time, however, the similarities in form which Simmel noted seem uncontestable.

By defining sociology as the study of form, Simmel recognized that he was building the discipline upon an abstraction. Content and form cannot be separated "in reality." Neither could actually occur without the other. In addition, he realized that it was not possible to prove the assumption that nearly identical forms could be abstracted from diverse contexts. Finally, Simmel recognized that an emphasis upon form would separate sociology from the other social sciences, all of which were organized around realms of inquiry, or contents. However, as defined, he felt that sociology was capable of addressing fundamental questions of human existence.

Simmel's interest in form and style blended over into an interest in "unusual" roles and interaction patterns. For example, he analyzed the distinctive role of strangers whose distance gives them a more objective view of a group and makes a group member more likely to share a confidence with them than another group member. From an analysis of this role, it was easier for Simmel to generalize about the generally overlooked place of strangeness in all social relationships. He similarly examined relationships between people who share secrets and the role of secrecy, the social role of the adventurer and the place of adventure in society, and so on. To further illustrate Simmel's contributions, we turn now to an analysis of secret relationships that his writing helped to inspire.

Secret Relationships

Simmel described all relationships as entailing a degree or type of secrecy. In some cases, people are hiding some information about their past, their motives, or the like from the other. The more that is withheld the more the relationship is circumscribed. The more that is revealed, the more the relationship is expanded. In other instances, aspects of a relationship, itself, are kept secret. For example, siblings may speak to each other in a private language only when no one else is present. To illustrate further: the nature of sexual intimacy, even where prescribed, as between a husband and wife, is usually kept private. When the intimacy is also forbidden, Richardson notes, there is a double emphasis upon concealment.[6]

Examples of sexual intimacies that are frequently considered forbidden, and hence doubly concealed, include relationships between persons of the same sex, professors and students, doctors and patients, and so on. One of the most common

---

[6]Laurel Richardson, "Secrecy and Status," *American Sociological Review,* 53 (1988).

secret, forbidden relationships in the contemporary United States occurs between single women and married men. In order to identify the *form* of these relationships, Richardson conducted private in-depth interviews with 65 single women who had long-term affairs (lasting one year or longer) with married men.

The general pattern described by these women involved two stages. In the first, the "outside world" is laid aside as the couple constructs their own world. Because the relationship is forbidden it must be conducted in complete privacy, providing opportunities for each to divulge secret information about him or herself. Much of this involves disclosing weaknesses such as fears, limitations, and so on. To reveal such secrets makes each more vulnerable; in a sense a "psychological hostage" to the other. Richardson describes stage one as the two people becoming confidantes.

Continuing affairs build upon the trust that develops in stage one and in stage two they become "We." Richardson chose this term because during the interviews women routinely talked about themselves and their lovers in terms of "we," "our," and the like. In stage two Richardson also noted a number of similarities between the couple's actions and the kinds of rituals Simmel described as characterizing secret societies in general; for example, ritual phone calls at the same time each day, coded messages, saving objects with shared significance, such as movie ticket stubs or a dried bouquet, and according them nearly sacred status. When relationships ended, many of the participants reported a ritualistic destruction of these objects. For example:

> "I spent New Year's eve, alone, burning our pictures, one-by-one in the fireplace, chanting, Good-bye, good-bye, over each one."[7]

INDIVIDUALS AND SOCIETY

In various writings, Simmel offered two different conceptions of society. On the one hand, he presented a Durkheimian view of society as a thing apart from individuals, primarily comprised of social institutions and institutional roles. On the other hand, he viewed society, like Weber, as resting upon individual consciousness.[8] When Simmel pursued questions about forms of interaction he typically stressed individual orientations; but in attempting to link the micro with the macro, he moved to an institutional emphasis.

When most people take on institutional roles, it is almost inevitable, according to Simmel, that some aspects of their individuality will be lost. Some people lose their individuality entirely as role and self become merged. For example, take the case of the physician who becomes only a physician; no role beside that of doctor has much meaning for this person. Other people remain outside of institutional roles; for example, strangers, as previously discussed. However, Simmel noted, even these outsiders' personalities are influenced by the social groups from which they are keeping their distance.

[7]*Ibid.*, p. 215.
[8]Georg Simmel, "How is Society Possible?" in *Essays.*

In one of his most penetrating essays, Simmel analyzed historical changes in people's relations to institutional roles. His basic thesis was that until relatively modern times, people's major commitments were to a single institutional realm. Soldiers, priests, and apprentices could not marry during the middle ages, for example, because marriage would have entailed familial attachments that could have conflicted with their primary roles. In the same way, women were largely precluded from making attachments to non-familial roles.[9]

Coser characterizes this historical pattern as involving "greedy institutions;" that is, institutional roles that were organized in a way that tended to engulf people. He also noted that they were not confined to one historical period. Thus, for many women, the role of housewife–mother has continued to absorb all of their time, energy, and commitments. In modern societies, however, role obligations tend to be more flexible, providing people with enough latitude to prevent their engulfment by a single role. The resulting pattern is one of multiple affiliations across institutional realms.

There are also formal rules, Coser notes, which protect people's commitments to institutions against trespass from other institutions. For example, child-labor laws protect the integrity of schools from the economic institution, and laws against forcing spouses to testify against each other guard the family against intrusions by the political institution. People tend, therefore, to be segmentally involved with many institutions, "all of which claim allegiance, while none makes exclusive demands."[10]

People's Commitments

Simmel offered two broad hypotheses to guide research in this area: 1) modern societies are more loosely organized, but people's commitments in different institutional realms are not entirely independent of each other, and 2) modern societies encourage individuality, but all configurations of multiple commitments do not necessarily occur with equal frequency. Any attempt to explore the multiple affiliation thesis must, therefore, begin by examining the consequences of people's commitments in one realm for their commitments in others.

In order to examine such consequences, one study interviewed a sample of adults twice, one year apart. The focus of the interviews was upon respondents' rates of participation, evaluations, and emotional ties to five institutions: economic, educational, familial, political, and religious. By allowing one year to elapse between interviews, it was possible to analyze how specific institutional commitments at time one apparently affected a range of commitments at time two.[11]

The results indicated that commitments to the economic, educational and political institutions tended to be interconnected at each time and across time. In other words, people who are attached to any one of these institutions tend to be attached to all three; and such persons were also found not to feel alienated from American society, in general.

[9]Georg Simmel, *Conflict and the Web of Group-Affiliations* (New York: Free Press,1955).

[10]Lewis A. Coser, *Greedy Institutions* (New York: Free Press, 1974), p. 3.

[11]Mark Abrahamson and William P. Anderson, "People's Commitments to Institutions," *Social Psychology Quarterly,* 47 (1984).

People's commitments to familial and religious institutions, by contrast, were more likely to be self-contained; that is, without implications for other institutional commitments (or for general alienation). Finally, when people appear to be engulfed by a single institutional commitment, the one set of institutional roles to which they feel a strong attachment tends to be associated either with their family or their religion.

SOCIAL CONFLICT

For a society to exist there must be interaction; more precisely, there must be mutual influence among the individual elements of the society. The sheer size of modern societies precludes direct personal relationships among all, or even most, of the individual elements. Therefore, the parts can affect each other only as members of larger associations or sociological categories: trade unions, religious organizations, social classes, or the like. For the most part such affiliations lay dormant during tranquil periods. Thus, there are almost no social relationships between the various groups. Different groups or categories come into contact with each other when there is conflict; then they become significant to each other. In this sense, Simmel observed, a total society becomes a sociological reality, rather than an abstractions, when there is conflict.[12]

Simmel also noted that for conflicts within a society to occur a degree of unity within factions is presupposed. The trade union, the religious body, or any other group must be unified in order to pursue its objectives against competing groups. In fact, it is the pursuit of such objectives in the face of opposition that frequently serves as a unifying force. It logically follows that if there were no opposition, shared goals would be less meaningful, hence they would provide less of a basis for relationships.

It does not follow, however, that all conflict is productive. Both sides must recognize and adhere to a set of norms or rules. When the conditions under which the conflict occurs is regulated in this manner, the competition can produce a "sense of honor" in both parties that is especially effective in uniting them to the larger social order. A prolonged conflict between union and management, for example, can create relationships among workers and consciousness of their common membership where neither previously existed. The same consequences may result for management. Thus, a factory with several thousand employees may become an actual sociological entity (relationship and consciousness) during periods of conflict. Labor conflicts may also spread beyond a single work site and become a general political conflict, as in Marx's formulation. When this occurs, relationships and consciousness of membership pervade the entire society. Such large-scale conflicts over impersonal goals tend to be particularly unifying within factions precisely because of their impersonality. Individual differences are relegated to the background as individuals, keenly aware of their common purpose, struggle for superindividual, or objective, goals.

---

[12]This discussion of conflict is based mostly upon Georg Simmel, "The Sociology of Conflict," *American Journal of Sociology,* 9 (1904).

Simmel also stated that even conflict can contribute to maintaining social life when conflict is highly personal. For example, modern city life squeezes together people who find each other to be intolerable. They display personal qualities which are so objectionable that others would simply retreat into isolation rather than interact with them. Coexistence—and social relationships of any kind—are possible only through opposition. Thus, conflict produces "the distance and buffers," Simmel concluded, without which social life would not be possible.

As previously noted, Simmel's theory differed from many of his contemporaries with its emphasis upon conflict as both pervasive and productive. It was not unique in this regard, but later generations of sociologists were more influenced by functionalist perspectives which emphasized social integration. In much of the functionalist writings society was viewed as a social organism. (See Chapter Four on Durkheim.) From this perspective, the parts of a society were expected to fit harmoniously together. The analysis of specific institutions focused upon their contribution to the maintenance of a unified social system, and this contribution was regarded as the institution's function. Within this conceptual framework, conflict was generally viewed as sporadic, rather than pervasive and as disruptive, rather than productive.

Simmel's view of conflict clearly ran counter to the functionalists' view which was particularly dominant during the 1940s and 1950s. During this period, Simmel's work on dyads and triads continued to be cited, especially by sociologists who were interested in small groups. However, his macrosocial view of conflict as a productive sociological force did not fit well with the dominant functional theories, and it exerted minimal influence. Beginning in the late 1950s there was a resurgence of sociological interest in theories of conflict, and much of the writing, then and now, paid tribute to Simmel's insights. Probably the most important work in "reintroducing" Simmel to social theorists was Lewis Coser's book, *The Functions of Social Conflict.*[13]

Coser's Formulation

The title of Coser's book, and its content as well, indicates the influence of functional theories at the time. Thus, Simmel's view of conflict was reintroduced from a functional perspective in which the maintenance of society was emphasized, and conflict—like any other practice—was (functionally) analyzed according to its contributions to the maintenance of a society. While many conflict theorists would prefer to work completely outside of a functionalist perspective, Coser's functional treatment of Simmel did not require extensive modification of Simmel's work, and it helped to bring out many of Simmel's insights.

The major consequences of conflict to a society, according to Coser, are reintegration and greater flexibility. When people question the legitimacy of a stratification system and/or experience a sense of unjustifiable deprivation, they are mobilized to address their grievances. Following Simmel, he proceeded to describe

[13](New York: Free Press, 1956). By the same author see also *Continuities in the Study of Social Conflict* (New York: Free Press, 1967).

the way in which the ensuing conflict integrates the opposing factions. For the entire society as a social system—if it is not too "rigidly" organized—the conflict—if it does not become excessively violent—can result in: the release of tensions, the revitalization of old norms, the innovation of new norms, and the reintegration of the system.

Coser notes many qualifying conditions. The courses and consequences of conflict are difficult to specify precisely. Under the conditions noted above, however, conflict is seen to make more likely the persistence of the (essential) system. Antagonisms are drained off, necessary accommodations are introduced, and the social system can be maintained. Without these effects of conflict, the system might develop such illegitimate deprivations that revolutionary changes would be instigated. Note, however, that these functions of conflict are limited to relatively unintense conflicts and to societies characterized by sufficient flexibility to permit minor changes to occur.

In conclusion, Coser's analysis is a decidedly nonrevolutionary treatment of conflict. It accurately calls attention to a nonrevolutionary quality in Simmel's theory, an important point of divergence between it and other conflict theories, most notably Marx's. (See Chapter Six.) At the same time, however, Simmel did not confine his analyses to minor conflicts of low-level intensity. In discussing Marx's view as an example of impersonal conflicts, Simmel described how personal embitterments were necessarily reduced. The individual capitalist ceases to be viewed as "a blood sucker" while the struggle moves toward "a vast impersonal end."[14] However, its intensity is not thereby reduced, he concluded. On the contrary, the struggle becomes more aggressive, more obstinate, and more irreconcilable. Thus, Simmel focused upon all forms of conflict, and did not confine himself to those forms which were of benefit to the persistence of a society, though clarification of such forms were certainly part of his impressive contribution.

SUGGESTIONS FOR ADDITIONAL READING

HOWARD S. BECKER, *Art Worlds.* Berkeley: University of California Press, 1982.
GUY OAKES (Ed. and Trans.), *Georg Simmel on Women, Sexuality, and Love,* New Haven: Yale University Press, 1984.
GEORG SIMMEL, *The Philosophy of Money.* (Trans. by Tom Bottomore and David Frisby), Boston: Routledge & Kegan Paul, 1978.

[14]Simmel, "The Sociology of Conflict," p. 500.

9
PROCESS
Behavioral Exchange
Homans and Others

In prisons and reform schools, alcoholism centers, old age homes, and diverse other institutions there is a tendency for inmates to refer to each other in kinship terms such as brothers or sisters, cousins, and so on. Family roles also provide a culturally prescribed model for the relationships they establish with each other. To illustrate: in women's prisons and reform schools, inmates try to recreate the relationships they had with boyfriends and husbands prior to their incarceration. They arrange dates and write love letters, for example. There is total sexual intimacy among some couples, but for most couples, physical contact is limited to holding hands or an occasional light kiss.[1]

Many of the couples are comprised of women whose behavior is complementary to each other. Specifically, one woman tends to initiate the relationship, exert dominance after it is established, and defend her partner from other prisoners. The other woman in the couple tends generally to be more passive and submissive. For some women, these prison roles are an extension of the roles they previously played outside of prison. Thus, to be the one who dominates a relationship may seem perfectly natural to some women.

Other women may be accustomed to having boyfriends or husbands "take care" of them, however. To initiate a relationship, act dominantly or defend a mate might be very difficult for them. The pain of being alone, with no one to care for, might motivate them to try to be more aggressive. Alternatively, they may be enticed into the role if they observe that the woman who is dominant within each couple is accorded higher status in the inmate community, or receives gifts (e.g., cigarettes) or services (e.g., having her cell straightened) from her partner.

---

[1] A survey of homosexual practices in U.S. and Canadian prisons is provided in Alice M. Propper, *Prison Homosexuality* (Lexington, MA: Lexington Books, 1981). For a general discussion of fictitious kinship patterns in institutions, see Jaber F. Gubrium and David R. Buckholdt, "Fictive Family," *American Anthropologist*, 84 (1982).

The notion that people's behavior is influenced by the amount and kinds of rewards they anticipate introduces the *exchange theory* of human behavior. One of the major assumptions of this perspective is that the rewards people expect to receive from others are an important determinant of how they will behave. The rewards can be tangible objects, such as cigarettes, or reciprocated actions; for example, people may be rewarded for acting tough if another shows deference to them in response.

For people's behavior to be influenced (called forth) by the responses of others, it follows that a reasonably high degree of behavioral flexibility must also be assumed. If past experiences or genetic endowments rigidly determine how a person will behave, then others' responses cannot logically serve as a decisive influence. However, in assuming flexibility it is not necessary to reject all the effects of past experience. Thus, as noted in the example of the women's prison, assuming a more aggressive role may come easier to some women than others. If an inmate is absolutely unable to bring herself to initiate relationships, then she is at a disadvantage in the sense that she enters a prison "marketplace" with one less behavioral "commodity" to exchange. The differential amounts of difficulty experienced by the women who are able to initiate such relationships account for differing amounts of cost on the left-hand ledger of this accounting scheme. Cost is also incurred by the value of alternatives foregone; that is, what opportunities are precluded by a woman when she initiates a relationship of this type.

In the following pages we shall discuss the varied assumptions of exchange perspectives and further examine cost, reward, and the related concepts upon which the perspectives are built. We shall also pursue some more general implications, with special attention to the notion of social justice. Finally, we shall periodically return to the women's prisons example and reanalyze the inmate community.

LEARNING STUDIES

The basic concepts and propositions which give form to modern exchange theories in sociology and social psychology have been adapted from many years of research in comparative experimental psychology. For decades these psychologists have been conducting learning experiments in which rats, pigeons, and other animals, including humans, serve as subjects. The basic terms upon which they have focused are stimulus, response, and reinforcement.

A stimulus is any external object which the subject of an experiment is capable of differentiating with any sensory mode. A tone of 50,000 cycles can serve as a stimulus to a bat, for example, but not to a rat. The latter appears to be incapable of hearing it. A response is any observable movement by an animal, such as pressing a feeding bar or running from an electrical grid. Reinforcements are the consequence of a response. They are ordinarily manipulated by the experimenter and provided after the subject's response to a stimulus. They can be positive (rewards, such as food) or negative (punishments, such as electric shocks).

Even in a controlled laboratory experiment, there are many potential stimuli to which a subject could respond and many potential responses to each stimuli. One particular stimulus and one particular response become associated with each other when a reinforcement follows closely on the heels of a stimulus-response sequence. To illustrate, a bright light is flashed (stimulus), a rat presses a bar (response), and pellets fall into a feeding dish (reinforcement). Most normal rats (or pigeons or monkeys) will soon learn to press the bar when the light appears because they are deprived of food for an extended period before serving as experimental subjects. Learning, in these experiments, is defined by a new association between a stimulus and a response. Thus, learning is said to have occurred when a stimulus-response pairing, not previously exhibited by the subject, can be consistently observed.

The animals' food deprivation motivates them which is overtly expressed by an increase in their activity levels. (The same phenomenon can often be easily observed among young children who become very active shortly before mealtime.) The heightened activity induced by the motivation is important because it leads the animals to move and be responsive to their environments.[2] Thus, they emit behaviors which the experimenter can reinforce leading to learning. By contrast, if the animals were not motivated they would be passive, and no behavior can be reinforced until after it is emitted.

The rats, pigeons, and other subjects of these experiments differ from human beings in a variety of ways. Within-species variation in the capacities and needs of humans is much more pronounced; that is, people differ from each other much more than rats or pigeons differ from each other. As a result, there is more error in predicting human patterns. In addition, the previously offered definitions of stimulus, response, and reinforcement are more problematic when applied to human subjects. For example, stimuli apparently need not be external because of humans' (unique?) capacity to be self-stimulating. In addition, human responses are not confined to overt movement because of their (unique?) capacity for nonovert responses. Finally, there is the related issue of people's ability to be self-rewarding.

Despite all of the issues just noted, learning curves and a variety of other phenomena have been shown to be remarkably similar across different species, including homo sapiens.[3] Therefore, if the theories and procedures developed in comparative experimental psychology were modified so as to become more congruent with sociological conceptions, the result could be very fruitful.

Human Subjects and Interaction

In order to bridge this gap, sociologists and social psychologists have attempted to place more emphasis upon people's subjective feelings. These internal and not-directly-observable sentiments have been viewed as potential stimuli and responses in addition to external and overt phenomena. It has also been necessary

---

[2]This is, of course, a distinctive view of motivation which, compared to most sociological theories, accords a smaller role to symbolic variables and to self-motivations. See Jonathan H. Turner, "Toward A Sociological Theory of Motivation," *American Sociological Review*, 52 (1987).

[3]For discussions of the similarities and differences among human and non-human primates, see the articles included in Rom Harré and Vernon Reynolds (Eds.), *The Meaning of Primate Signals* (Cambridge: Cambridge University Press, 1984).

to rework the typical rat or pigeon study in order to introduce the critical concept of interaction. In the usual laboratory experiment, lights, bells, and the like function only as initial stimuli. After an animal's response, they do not respond, in turn. True interaction is precluded because of this absence of mutual, or symmetrical, reactions.

In experiments with human subjects, there is necessarily some degree of interaction whenever the stimulus is presented by a person, rather than an external object. The "danger" is that subjects will develop feelings toward the experimenter, the experimental situation, or the like. Such sentiments constitute an additional variable that is extrinsic to the objectives of the study and is not experimentally controlled. Therefore, it may systematically distort the results of an experiment. The design of most studies, however, sharply limits the kinds of interaction that is permitted to occur between subjects or between subjects and experimenter. To illustrate: Marwell and Schmitt placed pairs of subjects behind panels in different rooms. By turning switches on their separate panels, the subjects could elect to cooperate with each other or work individually, and the decisions of each were mechanically conveyed to the other. Each subjects' panel also indicated the amount of money both they and the other were earning as they worked on the assigned tasks. The interaction between subjects was limited to turning the switches and knobs on the panel. In the next room an experimenter recorded all of their actions for later analysis.[4]

The researchers determined how reinforcements (i.e., money) would be allocated under varying experimental conditions. When subjects were rewarded more for cooperating than for working alone, they worked together on virtually every task. When individual effort was better paid, they worked alone. The exceptions occured during the very first tasks as subjects were figuring out how the system worked. Thus, we can conclude that the subjects quickly learned to cooperate or to work alone according to which approach led to greater reward.

Learning and Generalizing

It is hard to imagine that a simple experience, like serving as a subject in this cooperation experiment, would have any enduring effects. The stimulus-response associations that were formed almost certainly extinguished quickly after the experiment concluded. Outside the laboratory, however, in interactions with parents, teachers, and friends, reinforcements lead to more permanent stimulus-response associations.

Laboratory experiments also tend to be highly simplified by comparison to "real life." Their lack of complexity is intentional so that the researcher can isolate cause and effect relationships. However, from a behavioral exchange perspective, the experiments are essentially accurate, though simplified, models.

In more complex, real-life situations in which reinforcements (from parents, friends, and the like) lead to more enduring stimulus-response associations, there also tends to be a carry-over of learned behavior to other similar situations. This widely

[4]Gerald Marwell and David R. Schmitt, *Cooperation* (New York: Academic Press, 1975).

studied tendency is referred to as *stimulus generalization*. The more the stimulus in a new situation resembles one previously responded to by the subject and reinforced, the greater the probability that the learned response will be generalized to the new stimulus.

An interesting illustration is provided by studies of grade school children. Researchers have been interested in the effect of praise from a teacher (a positive rinforcement) on children's subsequent actions. Specifically, teachers as a question (stimulus) and children can raise their hands (response). If the children who are called upon are praised by the teacher, they are found to be more inclined to raise their hands the next time the teacher asks a similar question. What happens if the nature of the task changes, though, as when children are moving from one type of problem to another very different type? There is still a generalization of expectations as previous reward leads to a significantly higher rate of hand raising on subsequent tasks.[5]

THE CALCULUS OF EXCHANGE

Thus far, our discussion has been confined largely to an analysis of basic terms as they have been operationalized in laboratory experiments. Outside of the laboratory a richer vocabulary and more complex concepts are needed, especially if the focus is upon people interacting because this entails processes of mutual reinforcement; that is, on-going reciprocity of a kind not usually encountered in laboratory studies. The key terms that theorists and researchers have tried to define in this context are cost and reward.

Costs

George C. Homans, one of the pioneer exchange theorists in sociology, has defined the *cost* of a behavior as a "value foregone." In a woman's prison, for example, one inmate (call her Mary) may consider approaching another (call her Jane) to strike up a conversation. The cost of doing so includes all those rewards Mary could have obtained if she chose some other course of action. For example, she might approach Nancy rather than Jane, or avoid everyone and go read a book, take a nap, or so on. Each of these alternatives would potentially provide Mary with some degree of reward. In seeking out Jane, Mary denied herself these alternative possibilities. The greater their attractiveness, or potential reward value, the more costly it is for Mary to initiate a relationship with Jane. Correspondingly the more reward she will have to anticipate before she commits herself to this course of action. On the other hand, if no other alternatives are attractive to Mary at the moment, then it will not be very expensive for her to approach Jane. The rule is: "no alternative, no cost."[6]

---

[5]Doris R. Entwistle and Murray Webster, Jr., "Raising Expectations Indirectly," *Social Forces*, 57 (1978).

[6]George C. Homans, *Social Behavior: Its Elementary Forms* (New York: Harcourt Brace Jovanovich), 1974 p. 100.

An identical set of general considerations confront Jane and determine how she will respond if Mary walks up to her. Whether a more enduring relationship will form depends upon their abilities to provide rewards to each other that exceed the costs each of them are incurring.

To keep others in a relationship usually requires either being able to offer attractive rewards or the ability to keep the other's costs down. Homans notes numerous situations in which people deliberately manipulate others' costs (that is, alternatives foregone). A rather grim example is provided by Cortez who, after his soldiers landed, burned the ships that carried them. This strategy worked because fleeing, rather than fighting, was removed as an alternative. It thereby lowered the soldiers' costs of fighting. Cortez knew exactly what he was doing, of course. Burning the ships was a rational decision, calculated to increase the probability of a successful invasion. We need make no similar assumptions about Mary, Jane, or others in routine social relations. They may, or may not, be as conniving as Cortez.

While most sociologists have followed Homans's view of cost as entailing values foregone, a quite different view of cost has been suggested by Thibaut and Kelley. It involves the difficulty, or effort, experienced by a person in carrying out any sequence of behavior. For example, Mary may feel awkward, embarrassed, or anxious about approaching Jane. These inhibiting feelings are difficult to overcome, costly, according to Thibaut and Kelley. Mary can be expected to make the effort—pay the price—only if she anticipates commensurate rewards.[7]

Underlying the notion of cost as involving performance difficulty is the assumption of behavioral repertories. Most people have reasonably extensive repertoires, which is to say that they are capable of behaving in diverse ways. Observations of the same people in different contexts makes their variability apparent. Our hypothetical prisoner, Mary, may at different times or different situations act demure or aggressive, solicitous or rejecting, and so on. All these potentials are within her response repertoire. However, she probably can not act in all of these ways with the same degree of ease. As the result of prior experiences, she probably finds that certain ways of acting seem more natural than others; that is, she can emit certain kinds of behaviors with less effort, or less cost.

Look at the matter this way: We have all confronted situations in which another person expected us to behave in a way that did not come easily to us. Perhaps they expected us to be more considerate of their feelings than we would have been if left to our own inclinations. We may balk, squabble, even break off the relationship because of this expectation. If we continue in the relationship, we are likely to feel put-upon and make counter demands. In effect, we tell the other, verbally or by our actions, that we can be considerate, but that it will cost them. In return, we may expect our occasional temper tantrums to be overlooked. Now, they may balk and indicate, either implicitly or explicitly, that our price is too high. Therefore, further negotiations will have to occur, at least subtly, if our relationship with them is to continue.

[7]The first complete presentation of their theory was: John W. Thibaut and Harold H. Kelley, *The Social Psychology of Groups* (New York: Wiley, 1959). They revised and extended their perspective in: Harold H. Kelley and John W. Thibaut, *Interpersonal Relations* (New York: Wiley, 1978).

In addition to intra-individual variables, costs can also be affected by features of the interaction, itself. One such interaction contingency is *response interference.* It occurs when one party's actions instigate two or more responses in the other. The gestures of an approaching friend, for example, may indicate both an intention to shake hands and embrace. The other is unsure which stimulus to respond to first, and may try to reciprocate each gesture at the same time. The two behaviors interfere with each other, however; they can not be performed simultaneously and the conflict raises the person's costs in performing either one.

When one party is instigated to respond in two or more ways simultaneously, that person's actions tend to send conflicting stimuli back to the other. Thus, response interference tends to be a symmetrical process in which both parties' costs are increased.

The sequence of acts is another feature of the interaction, itself, that affects costs. Specifically, if a person has emitted the same behavior many times in succession, physical or mental fatigue may raise its cost. Thus, it is more difficult for a bride to say thank you to the seventy-third person in a reception line than to the first.

In sum, the costs of behavior may be conceptualized as values foregone or as performance difficulties.[8] Whichever type of cost is incurred, corresponding rewards will be expected or the persons incurring the costs will probably terminate the relationship, assuming they are free to do so. Nonvoluntary relationships present a special, but not necessarily limiting, case of the exchange perspective. For example, nonvoluntary relationships may be defined as those in which a person receives a lower net profit (reward minus cost) than the person would otherwise accept or a lower profit than the person would be able to obtain in an open market. The classic case of a nonvoluntary relationship involves the couple that are shipwrecked on a tiny deserted island. However, there are more common examples: low-status racial or ethnic groups whose opportunities for nonservile employment are restricted; married couples in societies where divorce is not permitted, and the like.

Rewards

Rewards, or positive reinforcements, are anything positively valued by a person: pleasures, gratifications, or need fulfillments. They can come totally from within (i.e., self-rewards), but most people are more-or-less dependent upon others for most of their rewards. Rewards are of great importance to the behavioral exchange perspective because they strengthen the association between a stimulus and a response. This basic principle of learning underlies the major propositions in the theory, namely, that the probability of a person acting in any way is a function of: 1) the frequency of past reward, and 2) the value of the rewards.

Rewards can be tangible objects, such as money or steak dinners. The exchange of behavior for such objects is commonplace, especially in the labor market. Less apparent, but of greater theoretical interest to us, are nontangible exchanges of

[8]For further discussions of the two types of cost, see J. K. Chadwick-Jones, *Social Exchange Theory* (New York: Academic Press, 1976).

behavior-for-behavior. Compliments, expressions of thanks, and pats on the back are all examples of frequently utilized behavioral rewards. However, any kind of behavior can be rewarding to some people, at least at certain times. Thus, a whipping may constitute a very gratifying positive reinforcement to a masochist.

It is not possible to discuss rewards for very long without wondering how to tell what people value. What will, so to speak, make Johnny run? Homans suggests two possible ways of deducing answers. First of all, he proposes direct observation of Johnny's reactions to alternatives, such as power, money or fame. Whichever of these possible goals acts as a reinforcer in strengthening a stimulus-response association may be considered to be of value to Johnny. The second way Homans suggests is by "measuring" the magnitude of a person's specific deprivations. For example, how long has it been since Johnny earned money? Homan's suggestions are developed by analogy to procedures routinely utilized in experiments involving nonhuman subjects. Thus, if a rat has gone 24 hours without feeding, it may reasonably be assumed that the rat now values food. It may correspondingly be assumed that a food reinforcement will effectively lead to a stimulus-response association.

Kelley and Thibaut also point out that rewards, like costs, can be a function of the interaction process, itself. For example, the reward value of the same behavior, repeated by another, may decline as the recipient either becomes satiated or takes the other's behavior for granted. Thus, a person will place less value upon a meal shortly after having just eaten one. Similarly, a student may be overjoyed to have lunch bought by his roommate on the first day. The second day, it is still pleasurable, but less so. By the third day, the student may be angry if the roommate does not bring lunch! The preceding examples illustrate the principle of *diminishing returns*.

EVALUATING OUTCOMES

Behavioral exchange theories are predicated upon the assumption that people will gravitate toward the relationships in which they are able to obtain the best *net* outcomes; that is, the greatest excess of rewards to cost. According to Thibaut and Kelley, two criteria are employed by people as they evaluate their outcomes from a particular relationship:

1) *Comparison Level (CL)*—an absolute standard for evaluating the attractiveness of a relationship. It is largely a function of what the person has come to expect from relationships of any given type in the past.

2) *Comparison Level for Alternatives (CLalt)*—an evaluation of the value of current alternatives. (It resembles cost in Homans' perspective.) It provides a standard against which people decide whether to remain in any given relationship.

CL and CLalt tend, over time, to be congruent with each other as a function of interconnected changes. To illustrate: Pat may have been one of the most popular kids in high school. In college, however, Pat may only be average. Pat's CLalt has probably decreased a great deal; people are no longer "lining up" to be with Pat. The decrease in CLalt means that Pat will have to remain in relationships that would previously have been terminated as unacceptable. This experience will eventually suppress Pat's CL, bringing it into line with the changed CLalt.

All the components involved in learning—motivation, stimulus, response and reinforcement—are measured most easily in a laboratory experiment when rats or pigeons are the subjects. People, especially outside of the laboratory, present a much more complex problem, and Homans realizes it fully. That is why, he says, he deliberately avoided the term "utility" as employed by economists. The problem with this term is that it implies that a reward is somehow good for the person who values it; but Homans notes, "Some men find some of the damndest things valuable."[9] However, it does not follow that they are therefore irrational. All that need be assumed is that people are capable of evaluating alternative means for reaching their ends. We may consider their ends to be idiotic, but that is another matter. So long as they calculate the probable efficacy of alternative means and behave accordingly, they are acting in a rational manner. Unless this sort of rationality can be assumed, the exchange perspective cannot be expected to offer accurate descriptions of interpersonal behavior.

Limitations on Rationality

Blau points out that there are some limiting conditions; that is, situations in which rationality, as described above, cannot be assumed. These limiting conditions generally include those "valuables that are not for sale."[10] Examples include love, approval, praise, and admiration. What they share in common is that they cannot be purchased or given in a calculated manner. Unless they are perceived as genuine statements of true feelings, expressions of love, praise, and the like are worthless to a recipient.

The reciprocal debts that accumulate in instrumental relationships may simply not work the same way when people are bound together in intimate relationships. For example, after helping a co-worker in an instrumental relationship, most people feel that the other is indebted to them. Reciprocity is expected at an appropriate time regardless of the sincerity with which the help was offered. By contrast, in an intimate relationship, a different calculus may be in operation. People's willingness to make sacrifices without expecting reciprocity is greatly increased. Further, actions, which might—in other situations—be regarded as entailing sacrifices may in an intimate relationship be regarded as pleasurable contributions to a relationship.

In sum, reward and cost perspectives may have serious limitations when applied to relationships between lovers, family members, or close friends. The limited applicability arises because expressions of love, admiration, or the like are not governed by the same norms of reciprocity. On the one hand, they cannot

[9]Homans, *Social Behavior*, p. 45.
[10]Peter M. Blau, *Exchange and Power in Social Life* (New York: John Wiley, 1964), p. 63.

usually be purchased. On the other hand, they cannot ordinarily be simulated; that is, offered cynically, independent of genuine feelings. Thus, rewards serve primarily to reaffirm and sustain intimate relationships, rather than as means for obtaining other ends.

At the same time, however, reward and cost considerations are not irrelevant to intimate relationships. Over time, the most devoted lover or dedicated friend may grow tired of a nonsymmetrical relationship. Unrequited love can be difficult to sustain. In fact, once either party adopts an exchange perspective and applies its notions to the relationship, their former degree of closeness may forever be reduced. In other words, calculation of costs and rewards can convert an intimate to an instrumental relationship.

It may also be prudent to consider mixed types of relationships; that is, relationships which are both intimate and instrumental and in which principles of behavioral exchange are partly applicable. This is the position proposed by Leik and Leik. They argue that the notion of Clalt implies that people have no special commitment to an exchange partner. Each party, it is implied, continuously monitors alternatives in a competitive marketplace. "The threat of taking one's business elsewhere always lurks in the wings."[11] However, they state, even in a ruthlessly competitive market there may still be room for trust, credit, and grace periods.

At the opposite conceptual extreme is the view that people are so commited to relationships that they never evaluate their outcomes or monitor their alternatives. If that were so, then people might never terminate a relationship once they were involved in it. In fact, however, once-happily-married couples later seek divorce, clergy recant their vows, and close friends later go their separate ways.

The principle seems to be that people's commitments vary from relationship to relationship and within the same relationship over time. Therefore, it seems most reasonable, the Leiks conclude, to treat commitment to relationships as a continuous variable, with principles of exchange considered applicable to the degree people's involvement in a relationship does not completely absorb them.

SOME PROPOSITIONS

Our discussion of the exchange perspective has, to this point, examined its most general assumptions. However, one of the real assets of formulations of this perspective has been the attempt to deduce specific propositions. Such propositions greatly enhance the utility of theory because they are more or less directly amenable to empirical assessment. Therefore, there is the long-term possibility of merging theoretical insights with empirical observations. Space precludes discussing, or even listing, all the propositions that have been deduced from the larger perspective.

[11]Robert K. Leik and Sheila A. Leik, "Transition to Interpersonal Commitment," in Robert L. Hamblin and John H. Kunkel (Eds.), *Behavioral Theory in Sociology* (New Brunswick: Transaction Books, 1977), p. 301.

Only a brief sample is presented here, along with some concrete cases that the propositions help to explain.

1) The more a person has recently received a rewarding activity from another, the less the person will value it in the future.[12] Over time, the recipient will come to regard as routine and expected those actions which were previously considered special and highly valued. There will be a corresponding tendency for the person to offer less in reciprocation, leading the other to cease providing the activity.

    For example, a husband may greatly appreciate and reward his wife for bringing him breakfast in bed on Sunday. The next Sunday it is still appreciated, but less so, because it is less of a novelty. By the following Sunday he may be peeved if she does not bring his breakfast on time.

2) The lower the status of people, the less selective they can be in withholding praise. Therefore, their judgment is respected less, and their approval is valued less.[13] It is the high value placed on the approval of high-status persons that enables them to dole it out more sparingly, thus keeping it in high demand.

    For example, if the general expresses admiration for a private's performance it will be valued more than the admiration of other privates. However, the privates' admiration for the general is not valued to a comparable degree by the general.

3) The greater the subjective salience of alternatives, the more difficult it will be for people to adjust to an involuntary relationship.[14] Therefore, people attempt to forget about or depreciate their alternatives in order to reduce their costs.

    For example, long-term prisoners often stop writing to their families and refuse to discuss them with other prisoners. Being reminded seems to make it more difficult for them to cope with the involuntary confinement.

These propositions, and the previously discussed examples, have all tended to focus upon interpersonal relationships. However, all of the major exchange theorists have been concerned with applying the perspective to macrosocial phenomena as well as to interpersonal relationships. Homans's conception of distributive justice is especially noteworthy in this regard.

WHAT IS FAIR?

Any theory of costs and rewards could be expected, sooner or later, to raise questions about fairness, to examine the social arrangements that would satisfy people's concerns for a just and equitable distribution of costs and rewards. It is a foregone conclusion that there will never be consensus about any concrete scheme. People will always disagree over what considerations, "should fairly be placed in the scales and at what weights."[15]

And yet, this profound issue has historically intrigued scholars, from Aristotle to Marx. One of the important contributions of the exchange theorists has been again

---

[12]Homans, *Social Behavior*, p. 55.
[13]Blau, *Exchange and Power*, pp. 64-65.
[14]Thibaut and Kelley, *The Social Psychology of Groups*, pp. 176-78.
[15]Homans, *Social Behavior*, p. 247.

to raise this timeless question. At the core of this contribution is distributive justice—Homans's analysis of how people decide whether rewards are apportioned in an equitable way. The immediate precursor to Homans's theory was formulated about the notion of relative deprivation.

Relative Deprivation

This earlier concept emerged out of a series of investigations of American soldiers during World War II. Stouffer and his associates were frequently surprised by the attitudes these soldiers expressed. The soldiers seemed to have more dissatisfactions and resentments when their conditions were objectively good (such as in the garrison) than when their conditions were objectively poor (such as in battlefields). For example, whites were more unhappy living with blacks than fighting with them. Enlisted men were more resentful of officers in the barracks than in the war zones. Similarly, there was more dissatisfaction with promotions in those branches of the military where overall chances for promotion were the highest.[16]

In sum, so long as everyone was cold and scared (for example, battlefields) or everyone did without (for example, promotions), no one seemed to mind very much. When everyone was better off, but some were more so than others, resentments emerged. In other words, soldiers apparently judged their own outcomes against those of others. They were personally satisfied, or not, by how they saw their comparative situations.

In subsequent analyses of the voluminous data generated by the war-time studies, Merton and Kitt appropriately shifted attention away from the notion of sheer deprivation to the notion of relative deprivation. They described how individuals' evaluations were influenced by the groups to which they belonged and the groups which served, psychologically, as their points of reference. In particular, they noted how individuals might simultaneously be influenced by multiple groups of each type.[17]

Subsequent studies of relative deprivation have focused upon the attributes that people evaluate and the types of comparisons that they make.[18] Homans's analysis of justice and satisfaction, which introduced the concept of distributive justice, began from this vantage point.

Distributive Justice

According to Homans, justice in the distribution of rewards is determined by three ratios. Specifically, people will be satisfied with the distribution when they perceive it as being proportional to contributions, status-investments, and costs. If

---

[16]Samuel A. Stouffer and others, *The American Soldier,* vol. 1 (Princeton: Princeton University Press, 1949).

[17]Robert K. Merton and Alice S. Kitt, "Contributions to the Theory of Reference Group Behavior," in *Continuities in Social Research,* edited by Robert K. Merton and Paul F. Lazarsfeld (New York: Free Press, 1950).

[18]For a review of this research, see Robin M. Williams, Jr., "Relative Deprivation," in *The Idea of Social Structure,* edited by Lewis A. Coser (New York: Harcourt Brace Jovanovich, 1975).

any of these ratios are regarded as disproportionate, people will feel resentment and, under some conditions, attempt to correct the incongruence.[19]

1) Contributions are what an individual or position provides to a relationship, group, or larger enterprise. Possible examples include protection, leadership, and planning. The more any of these are valued, the greater should be the reward of the person (or position) that provides them.

2) Status-investments involve prior attainments or positions. They may include past training or education, or past service, as reflected in seniority. Status-investments also include ascribed statuses, such as sex or race, when such considerations are viewed as appropriate bases for differential rewards.

3) Cost entails the amount of responsibility, danger, or other "sacrifices" made by people in certain conditions in-so-far as these costs imply superiority. (Other costs associated with a position, such as monotony, imply inferiority and hence do not lead to higher rewards.) The greater the relevant costs, the greater should be rewards in order to produce proportional profits.

In sum, people compare their rewards to others'—in relation to contributions, status-investments, and costs—in order to decide whether they are being treated fairly. Conflict emerges, Homans concludes, primarily because people differ in their evaluations of their own and others' contributions, status-investments, and costs.

Throughout his analysis, Homans attempted to "stay close" to people, emphasizing the psychological processes that underlie interaction. Correspondingly, he pays relatively little attention to those norms or values that sociologists often attribute to larger aggregates; for example, to social classes or to entire societies. Instead, his focus is upon those properties that emerge out of direct face-to-face interaction. As a logical result, Homans's analysis of distributive justice overly relies upon people's perceptions of the "going rate" of exchange. How much deference can be obtained in return for advice? How much special consideration in return for affection?

What is missing is any independent, or external, standard of justice. Therefore, the fair rate is, in effect, equated with the on-going rate. This is misleading, Blau states, because the very notion of justice implies a separate and independent standard of exchange. By disregarding the social structure within which exchanges occur, Homans does not confront situations in which there may be a discrepancy between the going rate and an external standard due to power and coercion in the exchange process.[20]

Despite this possible shortcoming, distributive justice has proven to be a very useful concept. It has been extensively studied, especially in laboratory experiments, and found to help to explain findings that would otherwise be puzzling. For example, in one experiment, subjects—who were equal in contributions, investments and costs—all expected to receive the same $2 payment. However, they were actually given one of three payments: $1, $2, or $3, and later asked how fair they thought the payment was and how contented they were with what they received.

---

[19]Homans, *Social Behavior*, Chapters 12 and 13.

[20]For further discussion, see Peter M, Blau, "Justice in Social Exchange," in *Institutions and Social Exchange*, edited by Herman Turk and Richard L. Simpson (Indianapolis: Bobbs-Merrill, 1971).

The theory of distributive justice predicted the results very well as those who received $2 considered the payment fairer and were more content with it than those who received either more or less.[21]

Similar findings have also been obtained by nonexperimental, nonlaboratory studies. Alwin's analysis of people's income and standard of living is illustrative. He examined several thousand interviews in which people had been asked how satisfied they were with their income, cars, housing, and so on; and whether they felt they deserved more or less. As might be expected, the better people's standard of living was, the more satisfied they were with it. However, even with actual levels of income held constant, there was a very strong relationship between satisfaction with any income level and the amount of income one felt to be deserved.[22]

THE MACRO–MICRO ISSUE

In formulating his behavioral theory, Homans criticized most of the conventional theories in sociology for focusing upon roles, organizations, social classes and other abstractions. These sociological abstractions do not really explain anything, he argued. They are just "window dressing." Only individuals act. Therefore, in order to explain why new technologies are innovated, why rates of crime increase, or the like, it is necessary to account for changes in individuals' behavior. Their behavior is governed, he concluded, by behavioral laws deduced from experimental psychology. Thus, "the only general propositions of sociology are, in fact, psychological."[23]

Homans's position is the antithesis of the position previously taken by Durkheim (as discussed in Chapter Four). Homans essentially argued against "elevating" individual facts to the social level. Durkheim, it will be recalled, argued against "reducing" social facts to the individual level. Blau's previously described criticism of distributive justice—namely that it fails to identify an independent standard linked to the social structure—is illustrative of the way many macro sociologists have responded to Homans and his followers.

To put the differences into stark contrast, consider the ways a sociologist could conceptualize (and measure) the concept of *anomie*. Following Durkheim and Merton (see Chapter Four), anomie can be described as a lack of congruence between cultural values and institutionalized rules. Note how this definition rests upon macro-level concepts such as culture and institutions. By contrast, behavioral theorists have experimentally defined anomie as the degree to which verbalized

---

[21]William Austin and Elaine Walster, "Reactions to Confirmations and Disconfirmations of Expectations of Equity and Inequity," *Journal of Personality and Social Psychology,* 30 (1974). For discussion of additional laboratory studies, see Guillermina Jasso, "Social Consequences of the Sense of Distributive Justice," in Karen A. Cook and David M. Messick (Eds), *Theories of Equity,* New York: Praeger, (1981).

[22]Duane F. Alwin, "Distributive Justice and Satisfaction with Material Well-Being," *American Sociological Review,* 52 (1987).

[23]George C. Homans, "Bringing Men Back In," *American Sociological Review,* 29 (1964), p. 817.

rules are enforced with rewards and punishments. For example, when teachers ignore rule-breaking behavior, the reinforcement contingencies faced by individual students become vague, and this defines anomie.[24]

In recent years, an emphasis upon *exchange networks* has helped to bridge the gap between micro behavioral approaches and more macro conceptions. Most behavioral theories tend to be limited to dyadic interactions. Exchange networks, however, begin with two or more connected dyads. Connected, in this context, means that exchange within either dyad affects exchange within the other dyad. These connections may be positive or negative according to whether exchange within one dyad facilitates or inhibits exchange in the other.

Within a connected network, positions have differential power based, in part, upon the importance of their link between dyads. Consider, as illustrative, two dyads comprised of A-B and B-C. Assume the two dyads are positively connected in a network. Both A and C are dependent upon B which makes B's position more powerful. How much more powerful depends upon the scarcity of the resources controlled by B.

The exchange networks approach readily permits the utilization of behavioral propositions in explaining within and between dyad exchanges. However, it is not confined to dyads (in isolation), because from the beginning of the analysis it is recognized that dyads are linked to other dyads. Further, units substantially larger than dyads can be introduced into networks. Finally, and of great importance to closing the micro–macro gap, notions like power and dependence can be conceptually separated from individuals and tied to structural characteristics of networks.[25]

CONCLUSION

In order to summarize the preceding discussion it may be useful to reconsider the women's prison example with which we began. Therefore, let us return to the prison courtyard where Mary is walking up to Jane. Perhaps consciously, perhaps not, Mary is making decisions about how to approach Jane. Should she act disinterested? Aggressive? Affectionate? What kind of response will each elicit from Jane?

When Mary finally reaches Jane, some action occurs, and the interaction begins. If Mary has considered forming a symbolic sexual relationship with Jane, her initial behaviour will probably indicate to Jane which role she expects Jane to play. Jane will then have to make an assessment, consciously or not, of what she could expect from such a relationship with Mary. Flattery? Deference? Cigarettes?

---

[24]For a review of behavioral measures of anomie, see Robert L. Hamblin and Paul V. Crosbie, "Anomie and Deviance," in Hamblin and Kunkel, *Behavioral Theory in Sociology*.

[25]For further discussion see, Toshio Yamagishi, Mary R. Gillmore, and Karen S. Cook, "Network Connections and the Distribution of Power in Exchange Networks," *American Journal of Sociology*, 93 (1988).

Whether a relationship will form and endure depends upon the value of the rewards each receives and anticipates receiving in relation to the costs each incurs and anticipates incurring. By costs, it will be recalled, we mean how difficult it is for Mary or Jane to play a given role, and/or the alternative rewards that each perceives as attainable but precluded by involvement in this specific relationship.

If each of their rewards are sufficiently great, or their costs are sufficiently low, the relationship will continue. Note, neither their rewards nor their costs need to be identical. It is profit (rewards minus costs) that is most salient, but it need not be identical for both, either. The concept of distributive justice sensitizes us to the fact that Mary may be willing to accept a smaller profit than Jane if she feels that Jane contributes more to the relationship, is more attractive to other women than she is, has more seniority in the inmate hierarchy, and so on. Mary is likely to feel dissatisfied only when her returns do not seem proportional to the above differences. If Mary's sense of proportionality is violated, she may ultimately become angry enough to break off the relationship. However, this calculus of exchange may be severely modified, or even irrelevant, if Mary loves Jane.

SUGGESTIONS FOR ADDITIONAL READING

KAREN S. COOK (Ed), *Social Exchange Theory*. Beverly Hills: Sage, 1987.
ROBERT FOLGER, *The Sense of Injustice*. New York: Plenum, 1984.
GEORGE C. HOMANS, *Certainties and Doubts*. New Brunswick: Transaction Books, 1987.

Deviance and Change
Durkheim, Merton, Erikson

In the middle of the seventeenth century, in the colony of Massachusetts, Ann Hutchinson was imprisoned, then excommunicated. She was charged with having craftily "seduced" the good citizens of Boston to follow her wicked teachings. She claimed her inspirations were based upon an "immediate revelation" from the Lord. The colony's leaders were shocked. They rejected her explanation and, in banishing her from the colony, intended to deliver her back to Satan.[1]

In order to understand how this came about, let us go back a few years before the trial. In the 1630s, the Hutchinsons' Boston home was a center of lively theological discussion. Community interest in Mrs. Hutchinson's biblical scholarship and view-points came to exceed interest in the minister's "official" sermons. Moreover, because she was critical of the theological interpretations imposed by the political-religious ruling body, the battle lines were soon drawn. The fact that the dissent was spurred by a woman—whose rightful place was believed to involve housework rather than scholarship—made her position still more tenuous. Her interpretations were threatening to the establishment because they denied the ministers' ability to utilize the covenant of grace as a political instrument; that is, the use of religious orthodoxy to keep people in line. Thus, while Ann Hutchinson and her followers appeared to be dissenting on theological grounds, she was initially charged with rebellion, rather than heresy.

The civil trial was a sham, even by seventeenth century standards. Her claim that her position was based on the revealed word of God was viewed by the court as a "devilish delusion." After polling the court, Governor Winthrop declared that, "the danger of her course among us . . . is not to be suffered . . . Mrs. Hutchinson is unfit for our society."[2] After a four-month imprisonment, she was then tried by the church

---

[1]Kai Erikson, *Wayward Puritans* (New York: John Wiley, 1966).
[2]Ibid., p. 99.

and "delivered over to Satan." It was another ritual trial whose outcome was never in doubt.

BOUNDARY MAINTENANCE

Throughout the civil trial, Mrs. Hutchinson repeatedly requested to know the charges that were placed against her. While all members of the court acted as though the answer was self-evident, no specific charges were ever given. She could only be told that her conduct could "not be suffered" because there existed in the colonies no names for her crimes. However, Erickson concludes that she had to be found guilty so that she could be banished because it was the only way to protect the community's boundaries.

A combination of religious-moral and legal-secular standards were utilized by the Puritans to extract compliance with detailed and pervasive expectations. These two types of standards were interwoven to such a degree that it was almost impossible to differentiate between (secular) infraction and (religious) immorality. A similar overlapping exists today among various religious sects, and a particularly heinous crime—such as child molesting—can simultaneously evoke both types of responses in the population at large; but for the most part, we do not conventionally apply religious-moral evaluations to people who commit secular infractions: cheat on their income tax, receive a speeding ticket, or the like. The far greater overlap existed among the Puritans because of their reliance upon the Bible as the source of law. Thus, by analogy, the biblical injunction to honor they father and mother was extended to include "fathers" of the community as a basis for prosecuting Ann Hutchinson.

The rigid norms of the Puritans allowed little room for people to do their own things. They held to a distinctive way of life that permitted little deviation, and that was the essence of Ann Hutchinson's problem. Because of her, the political-religious leaders believed, the good people of Boston had become contentious. They were challenging the ministers. To maintain a distinctive community with little deviation required that behavior such as Ann Hutchinson's be considered outside of the acceptable boundaries.

Erickson viewed the Puritan's witchcraft hysteria and their persecution of Quakers as attempts to maintain the social boundaries of their communities. When the boundaries were changed, "crime waves" were created. Persons like Ann Hutchinson, whose behavior had formerly been in the acceptable range, were now considered deviant. While Ann Hutchinson's case received a great deal of notoriety, the legal and religious persecution directed at her simultaneously gave notice to dozens of other "rebellious" persons.

To grasp this notion of crime waves, suppose that the "letter" of the law could be illustrated by the unbroken horizontal line in the following diagram. At any given time, most people's behavior deviates somewhat from this ideal. Let their behavior be illustrated by the dots. Finally, consider the broken line (t_1) to present the outer bounds of acceptable behavior at time one.

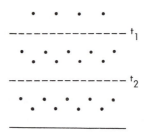

At time one (t₁), most people's behavior, while somewhat different from the letter of the law, is within the accepted limits. Then the boundary changes to t₂. At least temporarily, many people are caught in between the old (t₁) and the new (t₂) boundary. Thus, there is a (usually temporary) crime wave.

To illustrate, consider the effects of changes in people's attitudes and in legal practices on the reporting of forcible rapes to the police. In California, for example, during the early 1970s, there were educational programs which encouraged women to define a sexual experience as constituting a rape, if force was involved, even when the assailant was a friend or acquaintance. Simultaneous efforts to restrict both police and attorneys from inquiring into an alleged rape victim's past sexual history were successful and went into effect late in 1974. Subsequent analysis of police records showed that the reporting of rape, commited by a male acquaintance, previously known to the victim, more than doubled in 1975. Thus, the *official* rate at which certain types of rape occured increased dramatically, though there is no reason to assume that there was much of a change in actual behavior.[3]

To illustrate further, consider marijuana smoking on a typical college campus. The letter of the law probably prohibits any smoking, but many students do occasionally indulge. Within the context of campus norms, their behavior is generally regarded as acceptable. Only the heaviest users, represented by the dots above t₁, are considered deviant. Suppose, however, that student views change somewhat: Marijuana becomes redefined as harmful or dangerous. A more constricted range of acceptable behavior may emerge (t₂) and all those students (that is, dots) who lie between t₁ and t₂ are suddenly deviant. It is a crime wave, even though behaviors have not changed.

The Puritans' persecution of witches, Quakers, and heretics typically resulted in crime waves of this type. The boundaries were changed in order to preserve the distinctiveness, or integrity, of the community. What is regarded as deviant in any community, Erikson concludes, depends upon what is considered to be dangerous, embarrassing, or irritating to people; and this will change with the "shifting moods" of a community. New boundaries can be drawn or old ones maintained through witch hunts, civil trials, courts martial, psychiatric confinements, and so on.

[3]James L. LeBeau, "Statute Revision and the Reporting of Rape," *Sociology and Social Research*, 72 (1988).

In nations, such as the communist states in Eastern Europe, where there is only one political party, it can be difficult to maintain the vitality of national values. The more effectively the party suppresses political opponents, the less open debate there is about these values. They can be renewed, or regenerated, however, by labelling some people as subversive. Therefore, Bergesen concludes, political witch hunts are more common in one-party than in two-party states.[4] Taylor similarly argues that awarding formal honors, such as medals, to those whose behavior exemplifies the values of the elite (and formally dishonoring those who deviate), is especially important for maintaining the legitimacy of the elite in one-party states.[5]

DURKHEIM'S THEORY OF DEVIANCE

Durkheim's discussion of deviance poses as a central question whether crime or deviance should be considered "pathological." His model of society in this case was explicitly physiological and the question was whether crime in society could be seen as analogous to disease in a biological organism. At first glance he believed many people were inclined to regard it as pathological in this sense; but, Durkheim contended, any kind of behavior is normal rather than pathological if 1) it is usually associated with a given type of society, and 2) its rate of occurrence is within certain limits.[6]

The second point above emphasizes a statistical view of normality. Crime, or deviance more generally, is abnormal only if its rate of occurrence deviates from some normal rate, one which is a statistical average for all societies of a given type. This introduces Durkheim's first point; namely, that the forms which deviance takes are intimately related to the social organizations of the societies in which they occur. Thus, behavior can be considered abnormal or pathological if it deviates statistically or if it deviates in form.

Both of Durkheim's points can be illustrated in his classification and analysis of suicide. One type, called *altruistic suicide*, involves an overcommitment to the collective life. As an illustration, consider an adolescent male in a primitive society who is thought by others to be cowardly. This evaluation might lead the youth to believe that he was a public disgrace and an embarrassment to his tribe, and he might respond by deliberately taking his own life. This case provides a good example of an altruistic suicide, and Durkheim argued that suicides of this type were likely to occur, at a specific rate, in societies where individuality is strongly subordinated to collective life. Associated with this deemphasis upon individuality are societies in which the division of labor is minimally differentiated.[7]

[4]Albert Bergesen, *The Sacred and the Subversive* (Storrs, CT: Society for the Scientific Study of Religion, 1984).

[5]Patricia A. Taylor, "The Celebration of Heroes Under Communism," *American Sociological Review*, 52 (1987).

[6]Emile Durkheim, *Rules of Sociological Method* (New York: Free Press, 1950).

[7]Emile Durkheim, *Suicide* (New York: Free Press, 1951).

A certain rate of altruistic suicide was expected to occur as part of the normal course of events in such homogeneous societies. Altruistic suicides would be considered pathological only if their rate of occurrence deviated from the rates typically observed in societies of the same type. However, Durkheim also conceptualized other types of suicide, and their existence to virtually any degree in such primitive societies could be considered pathological. Anomic suicide, for example, occurs in response to rapid social changes when the norms that restrain individual aspirations lose their regulatory force. This results in frustrated ambitions, discontent, and despair for individuals and a high rate of anomic suicide in the society. While there is a normal rate of anomic suicide in modern (that is, highly differentiated) societies, their occurrence in primitive (that is, nondifferentiated) societies would be considered pathological.

Integration and Suicide

Gibbs has argued that the different types of suicide classified by Durkheim all share in common a concern with social integration. For example, *anomic suicides* are a function of low integration while *altruistic suicides* are a function of excessively high integration. Gibbs's initial hypothesis was that suicide rates declined as degrees of integration increased, until the latter reached very high levels; then suicide rates would increase with further increases in integration.[8]

Following Durkheim, Gibbs argued that, in the final analysis, integration involved the strength of individuals' ties to society. Such ties are a function of the stability and durability of social relationships. In a hypothetical society in which everyone remained in the same (or same types of) relationships with others, stability and durability would be very high. In order to maintain such relationships, Gibbs continued, people must conform with socially sanctioned expectations. What makes such conformity difficult is the fact that people simultaneously occupy a number of statuses (occupational, marital, and the like), and the expectations associated with each may conflict.

In order to assess the prevalance of inconsistent statuses, one must examine the actual configurations of statuses in a society. If most bartenders were divorced, for example, it would be inconsistent for a person to be married and a bartender. Finally, the preceding postulates lead to the conclusion that the degree of status integration in a society is indicated by the extent to which people occupy incompatible statuses.

Gibbs and various colleagues have examined status configurations across various countries (Ceylon, Japan, the United States, and elsewhere), and within a single country over long periods of time. While the analyses and the interpretations have been complex and generated some controversies, the findings have rather consistently supported the Durkheim-inspired theorem that rates of suicide decline as the degree of status integration increases.

[8]His first papers on status integration were published in the late 1950s. The most complete statement of the theory was in Jack Gibbs and Walter Martin, *Status Integration and Suicide* (Eugene: University of Oregon Press, 1964). He has continued, through the present, to test aspects of the theory. See the references in Mark C. Stafford and Jack P. Gibbs, "Changes in the Relation Between Marital Integration and Suicide Rates," *Social Forces*, 66 (1988).

CRIME AND PUNISHMENT

Associated with varying degrees of differentiation in societies' divisions of labor, Durkheim distinguished between two kinds of legal systems. The first type, termed repressive, is associated with the mechanical solidarity of an unspecialized society. Because of the absence of specialization, people hold highly similar views of the world and nearly identical values. A collective state of mind, or collective conscience, is very strong and very pervasive. In a society of this type, it is almost impossible for a deviant act not to offend public sensibilities. Any infraction is viewed as an outrage and generally leads to an immediate reaction. Punishment is swift and severe, until "the passions cool," and is intended to deter others from committing similar transgressions.

As the division of labor becomes more differentiated, individuality becomes more pronounced, and the collective conscience shrinks. Both the cognitive and the emotional states of people are then more differentiated from each other, and this is reflected in the "retreat" of the collective conscience. It grows weaker, more indefinite, and smaller. Durkheim pursued another physiological metaphor in describing this gradual decline of collective sentiments: "The organ atrophies because its function is no longer exercised."[9]

The collective conscience shrinks, but it does not disappear. Correspondingly, the repressive law that is associated with it also shrinks, but it does not disappear. For example, even today the people who happened to be around would probably respond immediately to an adult who was molesting a child, and their treatment of the culprit might well be violent. However, such instances are rare. Most infractions do not violate widely shared values. Thus, as previously noted, we are not usually outraged when someone cheats on their income tax, receives a speeding ticket, or the like.

As the collective conscience is shrinking and as the coordination of a more differentiated society becomes more problematic, repressive law is replaced— largely, but not completely—by highly specific penal and civil laws. Durkheim termed this type of law "restitutive" and characterized it by the presence of specialized enforcement groups, by its relative separation from shared values, and by its primary function which is to make amends, or reestablish the integration of a complex society.

The Changing Kibbutz[10]

The nature of social control in Israel's collective farms, or kibbutzim, illustrates many of the features of law described by Durkheim. After spending a year studying a kibbutz in 1950, Schwartz concluded that it had no *distinct* legal system; that is, no specialized group to whom enforcement was delegated. There was relatively little differentiation within the kibbutz; rather, there was widely shared "public opinion"

[9]Emile Durkheim, *Division of Labor in Society* (New York: Free Press, 1947).

[10]The following discussion is based upon, Richard D. Schwartz, "Social Factors in the Development of Legal Control," *Yale Law Journal,* 1954; Allen E. Shapiro and Richard D. Schwartz, "Law in the Kibbutz, A Reappraisal and a Response," *Law and Society Review,* 3, (1976).

and extensive face-to-face interaction among members. Thus, all the conditions Durkheim associated with repressive law seemed to characterize the kibbutz in 1950.

Over the next 25 years there were numerous changes in many of the kibbutzim. Most notable was their growth in size, from a couple of hundred members to collectivities of 1,000 to 1,500 members. Corresponding with this change, there was a declining use of common facilities. A public dining room, for example, became inadequate to accommodate all the members, and many of the newer household units were constructed with kitchenettes for individual family dining. Similarly, agricultural mechanization eliminated the need for large numbers of laborers to work the fields as a mass group.

Due to all of these changes, informal controls should have become less effective. In other words, the ability of the kibbutz public to observe and respond immediately to deviant behavior should have declined. The corresponding increase in size and differentiation should also favor the development of a specialized enforcement group and restitutive law.

It is not clear how many of the changes that would be hypothesized from Durkheim's theory have, in fact, already occurred. Some, at least, are still in process. For example, when a group of teenagers damaged a tractor in an April Fool's prank, they were summoned before the farm manager and a representative of the kibbutz's education committee. At this meeting they admitted their guilt and volunteered their labor to help compensate for the losses caused by their prank. Schwartz notes that the adults who met with the pranksters were not literally a specially designated, permanently operating enforcement or decision-making group. He concludes, however, that such instances probably indicate a transition from the traditional kibbutz pattern toward more specialized legal control in which restitution is a major objective.[11]

THE CONTRIBUTIONS OF DEVIANCE

We can reasonably surmise that people who find themselves ridiculed, jailed, or dishonored for the sake of the collectivity, will feel resentment. However, their punishment, in Erikson's view, promotes solidarity in the remainder of the society and helps to preserve the special characteristics of a community or society. Thus, following Durkheim, Erikson concluded that deviance was beneficial to the collectivity.

The positive consequences of deviance for society were explained by Durkheim as part of his functional theory of social organization. Specifically, he argued that all social facts tend to contribute to the "harmony of society." Criminal or deviant behaviors, if they occurred within certain limits, were regarded as normal social facts. "In the first place crime is normal because a society exempt from it is utterly impossible."[12] In various writings, Durkheim attributed a number of specifically

---

[11]For further discussion of the changes that haved occurred in kibbutzim, largely as a function of their growth in size, see Amia Lieblich, *Kibbutz Makom* (New York: Pantheon, 1981).

[12]Durkheim, *Rules of Sociological Method*, p. 70.

positive consequences to deviance. One was a clarification of social norms. The existence of crime indicates that there is a degree of flexibility among the collective sentiments within a society. In other words, people are not of a like mind on some issues. Deviations can lead to a crystallization of their sentiments and may even help to determine the direction in which public morality will change. Deviance can also make people more aware of the values they share, thereby contributing to social solidarity. Therefore, Durkheim concludes, crime "must no longer be conceived as an evil that cannot be too much suppressed."[13]

It must be recalled, however, that Durkheim was analyzing normality from the standpoint of the society. Hence, what applies to crime does not necessarily apply to the criminal. The person who commits deviant acts may or may not be normal, psychologically. Furthermore, there is no reason to assume that social utility constitutes an important motive for the individual who commits the deviant act.

One major shortcoming in Durkheim's analysis was a failure to specify who might be the beneficiary of deviance. He did not identify any segment or unit more specific than some abstract collectivity. He assumed, of course, that society—as a thing apart—was the beneficiary. However, if society is conceived of as including the deviants, themselves, then this notion can be problematic. It is difficult to view the persons who are punished for being deviant, such as Ann Hutchinson, as somehow benefiting. In an attempt to be more precise about the functions of deviance, several studies have examined discrete groups and organizations. An example is provided in the following analysis of several police departments in Virginia.

Wayward Cops[14]

Within the ranks of police officers, there is typically a strong emphasis upon group solidarity. Mutual protection and loyalty are stressed in a manner which inhibits competitive individualism. This makes it difficult for ambitious young officers to seek recognition from their superiors. If they try to distinguish themselves, their behavior is likely to be viewed, by their colleagues, as a threat to group solidarity.

A certain amount of "brass polishing" is widely practiced and generally permitted by group norms. However, when an individual excessively attempts to impress the senior administrators in the department, the person's behavior is considered deviant, and the person is labelled a "door man." This term is derived from colleagues' perception that the officer is constantly going into the chief's office in order to make a good impression.

A variety of sanctions are sometimes employed by other officers to pull a deviant back within the boundaries that are generally expected. Dirty looks and harsh comments are a mild sanction, letting air out of the tires of the deviant's own car is a stronger sanction, and in extreme instances, colleagues can fail to come to the aid of the officer in a dangerous situation in the street. In most instances, however, "door

---

[13]Ibid., p. 72.

[14]Meyer S. Reed, Jerry Burnette, and Richard R. Troiden, "Wayward Cops," *Social Problems*, 24 (1977).

men" are neither rejected nor punished by their fellow officers. Their actions are tolerated in a benign manner because, even though they are deviant, there are benefits to the group.

For example, in one situation a sergeant was giving preferential treatment to one officer while assigning undesirable chores to others. In another situation two officers cruelly abused some prisoners. In all of these situations, most of the police officers believed that the behaviors in question (that is, favoritism, abuse) constituted a violation of legitimate expectations. They would have liked to bring the wayward cops' behavior to the attention of their superiors; but their emphasis upon group solidarity and loyalty prevented them from "ratting." They resolved their dilemma in such instances by "leaking" the information to a "door man," and sometimes indicating it was the kind of information they were sure the chief would value.

Prompt action usually followed the leaking of information to the "door man." In the situations discussed above, the sergeant's favorite was transferred, and the abusive officers were asked to resign. Thus, even though the "door man's" behavior was deviant, it provided a very useful pipeline, and for this reason "door men" were not usually rejected for their deviance. The investigators conclude: "By maintaining certain individuals in deviant roles, other group members can sustain their moral identities while dealing with contingencies which require greater flexibility than that permitted by group norms."[15]

Because of the positive consequences of deviance, a number of studies, such as that of the wayward cops, have indicated that groups will not typically reject deviants, unless their actions lie too far beyond the boundaries. Thus, Ann Hutchinson's rebelliousness apparently "could not be suffered" in a seventeenth-century colony, but she would have probably enjoyed a leadership role during the campus demonstrations of the late 1960s.

Durkheim's view of the components of society fitting into a "harmonious" whole raises the related question of whether groups simply tend to tolerate deviance in a passive manner, or whether they may actively maintain it, or whether they even promote it. If punishment for a specific type of deviance were suddenly to cease, Durkheim noted, the norms that lie behind it would also grow weak. If, for example, students are not punished for cutting classes, then pretty soon there will be no norm that stresses attendance. Now, the disappearance of any particular norm might not be problematic; that is, it might not be missed.

On the other hand, the norm might be important for the continuation of a social system. The social system—as a thing apart, in Durkheim's view—might "need" the norm. Thus, educational activities might cease if students stopped attending class. If so, then Durkheim's conception of functional integration leads to the expectation that class-cutting will continue, even if some students must somehow be "induced" to cut classes at a rate sufficient to evoke some form of punishment. In general, then, the argument is that 1) social life is organized in such a way that deviant roles are regularly

[15]Ibid. p. 573.

created, and 2) there is some process of negotiation by which some individuals are induced to remain in these roles.

MERTON ON DEVIANCE AND SOCIAL ORGANIZATION

Beginning in the 1930s, Robert K. Merton wrote a number of essays on Durkheim's work which greatly helped to popularize Durkheim's theories of deviance in American sociology.[16] In these essays Merton also carried through on a number of points that Durkheim only partially sketched. One such issue concerned the way in which a social structure could "normally" produce deviant roles and deviant activities that had beneficial consequences.

Political Machines

The big city political "boss," and his "political machine," were a common feature in American cities throughout most of this century. While a number of changes have made this form less prevalent, it continues to persist, to some degree, in many cities. Judged by conventional standards, Merton notes, these machines routinely engage in a variety of deviant behaviors: allocating jobs on the basis of party loyalty rather than qualifications, widespread bribery and graft, and so on. In all these respects, the standard operating procedures of machines violate both laws and moral judgments. Why then, Merton asks, have machines persisted? His answer focuses upon "deficiencies of the official structure."[17]

The American political system is characterized by dispersed and fragmented power, both locally and nationally. This situation results from the Constitution's effort to provide checks and balances, to prevent concentrated power. These very virtues, however, also result in cracks or voids in the system, situations in which no one has authority to act. These unanticipated deficiencies of the system led to an organization, the machine, that was geared to circumvent the problems.

Merton indicates a number of groups that are typically in need of the services a political machine can provide. The "deprived classes" are one such group. Persons in this group may periodically need legal assistance "with no questions asked," help in gaining access to free medical clinics, assistance in dealing with immigration problems, or the like. The machine's precinct captain is always around, Merton notes, "when a feller needs a friend, and, above all, a friend who knows the score." Business groups also rely on the services of the machine in order to obtain special privileges: city contracts, permits, and licenses. There is simply no conventional legal apparatus that serves these business interests as effectively as the machine.

---

[16]A complete bibliography of Merton's writing is included in the final chapter of Lewis A. Coser ed., *The Idea of Social Structure* (New York: Harcourt Brace Jovanovich, 1975).

[17]Robert K. Merton, "Manifest and Latent Functions," in *Social Theory and Social Structure* (New York: Free Press, 1957).

In return for services rendered, the machine expects party loyalty, votes and favors. It will continue to persist as a result of this on-going reciprocity with diverse segments of the society for as long as it provides services that cannot be obtained elsewhere. Thus, Merton concludes, seemingly deviant activities—like political machines—must be understood as a product of the inadequacies of the conventional social structure. In this respect, his analysis further clarifies Durkheim's contentions that deviance is (or can be) functional for, and promoted by, a society or community.

Means and Ends

The way in which deviant behavior is promoted by the social structure was also examined by Merton in conjunction with his further analysis of Durkheim's conception of anomie. (This was initially discussed in Chapter Four.) Of most concern to us in this chapter is Merton's analysis of how varying patterns of deviance result from the differential pressures exerted by a social structure.[18] Following Durkheim's emphasis upon the restraining quality of norms, Merton focused upon the degree of emphasis people placed upon modes of attainment (institutionalized means) relative to aspiration levels (cultural goals). The "danger" in modern society, as he saw it, was that people very much wanted achievements and the satisfactions associated with them; but attaining them according to the rules of the game was not very salient. This produced an innovative mode of adaptation in which people sought success by almost any means they thought would work.

This innovative style is, however, only one of several logical alternatives. By considering different emphases upon means in relation to ends, Merton identified at least four distinctive types of adaptation, as illustrated in the figure below.

	Emphasis on Goals	
	High	Low
High (Emphasis on Means)	Conformity	Ritualism
Low	Innovation	Retreatism

[18]Robert K. Merton, "Social Structure and Anomie," ibid.

The conformist, who similarly emphasizes both means and ends, is, by definition, not deviant. Under conditions of social stability, this mode of adaptation will be most common. Each of the modes, however, entails deviant patterns in response to varying strains within a society.

The innovative type, as already noted, places a great emphasis upon success—wealth, fame, or the like—that is separated from the legitimate institutionalized means—such as apprenticeships or education—by which success is attained. Merton epitomizes this kind of normlessness with the example of a person who cheats at solitaire. When this occurs, "the cult of success has truly flowered."

While an innovative style can be found anywhere in a society, Merton argued that it was most pronounced in the lower classes because the class structure impedes their access to the legitimate means. At the same time, however, cultural goals transcend class lines. It is, therefore, a combination of high ambition and limited opportunity that produces a pressure for deviation that is concretely manifested by participation in organized vice, crime, and so on. Deviance of this type will be extensive in a society that stresses wealth and mobility for everyone when access to legitimate means is unevenly distributed.

Ritualism entails the abandonment of cultural goals along with a continuing commitment to institutionalized means. The zealous bureaucrat in the teller's cage of the bank, who is not "sticking his neck out" because he is "satisfied with what he has" provides a clear example of the ritualist. In Merton's view the socialization patterns of the lower middle class are most likely to produce this mode of adaptation. It is their private escape from the competition for major cultural goals, a competitive arena in which they are less likely to succeed than their upper middle-class rivals. Mass social pathologies, such as the Nazi movement in Germany, may be facilitated by a widespread ritualistic orientation.

Retreatism, involving the rejection of both means and ends, is the least frequent mode of adaptation. It characterizes persons who are in, but not of, the society: addicts, tramps, and other "outcasts." Their repudiation of the society is most likely to occur, Merton conjectured, following repeated efforts that result in failure. Eventually they find it too painful to continue to cling to success goals. In a competitive society there will almost certainly be some who try and fail, and some of them will become retreatists.

As a final type of deviant mode of adaptation, Merton also introduced rebellion. This is a more complex type, involving the simultaneous acceptance and rejection of both means and ends. Rebellion will occur on a large scale when the social structure itself is viewed as the source of frustration; or, in other words, when people perceive an insufficiently close correspondence among merit, effort, and reward.

In sum, it should be recognized that Merton's analysis consistently identified strains in the social structure as the source of deviant behavior. It is the nature of these strains that determines both the type of deviant behavior and its extensiveness. Thus, Merton clearly followed Durkheim's contention that crime, or deviance, must be viewed as a normal part of any society.

INTERPRETING STRUCTURE'S EFFECTS

Durkheim viewed social roles as mandated by the social structure and as rather automatically translating into individual behavior. The actions of people could, therefore, be ascertained through a careful analysis of social structure. To illustrate, a state of anomie in the society was expected to result in a high rate of suicide. The processes which intervene between the structural condition (that is, anomie) and the individual act (that is, suicide) were not considered problematical by Durkheim.

Merton, by contrast, regarded individual decisions as a more significant element. He viewed the social structure as often containing alternatives that directed people in opposing directions: to aspire to wealth or to play it safe, for example. Modes of adaptation—some of which were deviant—were ultimately determined by individual decisions, even though a person's place in the social structure might predispose him or her toward certain alternatives. However, even Merton did not typically examine in detail the processes through which individuals selected or rejected various modes of adapatation.[19]

Durkheim's research on suicide, it must be noted, was a landmark study. It presented the first large-scale assessment of hypotheses that were linked to a global theory of social organization. Its subsequent influence, as a model of social research, is undeniable. However, his neglect of actors' situational meanings has created ambiguities for the sociologists who have followed in his footsteps. Specifically, he began by defining suicide as a death which results from the knowledgeable and deliberate act of an individual. In other words, a person purposefully did something that he or she knew was likely to be fatal.

Because Durkheim paid little attention to the actual processes by which an individual might come to decide to commit suicide, a serious problem of classification arose. Given that a death has occurred, how is it to be classified, with any certainty, as a suicide or as an accident? What meanings do coroners and other officials attribute to a deceased before deciding to call the death a suicide? Without knowing the answers to these questions, the utilization of official rates of suicide in sociological research may be very questionnable. However, Durkheim relied exclusively upon such data, and he was not skeptical of them because he glossed over the processes through which strains in the social structure eventually influence individual behavior.[20]

A criticism of Durkheim's approach by the famous anthropologist, Bronislaw Malinowski, helps to clarify further the issue that is involved here. Malinowski began by questionning Durkheim's dichotomy of law and society: repressive and undifferentiated, restitutive and complex. In all societies, he argued, crime and punishment are pretty much the same; that is, reciprocal obligations keep most people in line. However, in order to highlight his disagreement with Durkheim, Malinowski focused upon undifferentiated societies.

---

[19]For further discussion, see Warren Handel, "Normative Expectations and the Emergence of Meaning as Solutions to Problems," *American Journal of Sociology,* 84 (1979).

[20]He also had a tendency to disregard data that did not fit his hypotheses and to include other data in a very selective manner. For a detailed examination of Durkheim's methodology, see Whitney Pope, *Durkheim's Suicide* (Chicago: University of Chicago Press, 1976).

Durkheim's underlying assumption, according to Malinowski, is that in simple societies the individual is totally dominated by the group; that is, he acquiesces like a passive robot. Malinowski seriously questions this. Does anyone, he asks, either civilized or savage, carry out obligations in this automatic manner? No, is his emphatic answer. There are always complex inducements that are both psychological and social in nature. In addition, systems of law and custom contain contradictory directives that conflict with each other, forcing individuals to make choices and thereby guaranteeing that, from one jurisdictional view or another, some behaviors are certain to be deviant. What will then happen, he insists, depends upon concrete circumstances.[21]

Durkheim's emphasis upon automatic submission, Malinowski concludes, misses the nuances. For example, Durkheim viewed altruistic suicide as occurring in an automatic, nonproblematic sequence, in simple societies. However, Malinowski describes the complex sequence of events that actually led to the suicide of a young Trobriand male. He had violated the community's incest taboo by having sexual relations with his maternal first cousin. The natives express horror at such acts, in the abstract. According to the ideals of native law, such acts cause the world to reverberate and invite disease and death to plague the community. In reality, though, even the people who knew what had transpired were not very outraged or afraid. The Trobrianders had a well-established "system of evasion," consisting of various magical practices that could have been utilized to effectively pacify the outraged gods. Therefore, there need not have been any robotlike adherence to tradition resulting in compulsory suicide to appease a deity.

The situation changed dramatically, however, when a rival for the youth's cousin publicly charged the youth with the crime of incest. Then ideal sentiments became prominent. Feeling intolerable shame, the youth climbed to the top of a sixty-foot palm tree and leaped to an instant death. Thus, Malinowski concludes, the demands of a social structure should not be interpreted as resulting automatically in either deviance or compliance. A complete explanation requires that attention be devoted to the processes in which individuals eventually formulate a course of action that is meaningful to them.

Malinowski was raising an issue that we have encountered before, especially in the earlier discussions of Durkheim (Chapter Four) and of Homans (Chapter Nine). In contemporary sociology, the issue is typically formulated as a level of analysis question. Can we develop an understanding of society by studying individuals? Malinowski, like Homans, argues that we can *only* understand society by studying individuals. Durkheim would, of course, disagree. If he were alive today, I think he would stress differences in levels of analysis. His argument might be very much like that posed by Lieberson, namely, that the most interesting features of society are precisely those that do not operate at an individual level. Therefore, researchers can not correctly infer the distinctive structural qualities of the societal level from studying individuals.[22]

---

[21]Bronislaw Malinowski, *Crime and Custom in Savage Society* (London: Routledge and Kegan Paul, 1926).

[22]See especially pp. 107–110 in Stanley Lieberson, *Making It Count* (Berkeley: University of California Press, 1985).

CONCLUSION

Despite its deficiencies, Durkheim's theory of deviance, law, and society has been enormously influential. It helped to orient sociological thinking away from a view of deviance, or crime, as a mere pathology; and it contributed to a view of deviance, or crime, as a normal (and necessary) part of society which—like any other component of a society—could have beneficial consequences. Perhaps most importantly, Durkheim's writings contributed to a distinctively sociological perspective by emphasizing the relationship between social organization and the form of both crime and punishment. It provides a perspective from which we may reject the possible existence of witches and yet find Ann Hutchinson's trial to be a comprehensible event.

SUGGESTIONS FOR ADDITIONAL READING

ROBERT CASTEL, *The Regulation of Madness,* Berkeley: University of California Press, 1988.
ROBERT A. JONES, *Emile Durkheim,* Beverly Hills: Sage, 1986.
RONALD W. MARIS, *Pathways to Suicide,* Baltimore: Johns Hopkins University Press, 1981.

11
CHANGE
Values and Change
Weber, Marx, Ogburn

There are hundreds of slurs, especially nicknames, that ethnic groups have used to insult and degrade each other in America. In fact, Irving Allen has found, over 1,000 such epithets have been recorded in slang and dialectal English. The specific slurs that are employed vary over time and region, but nicknames tend uniformly to refer to the physical traits (e.g., color, size), personal characteristics (e.g., cheapness, honesty), and distinctive foods (e.g., bagels, tamales) that are attributed to a group. Allen points out that ethnic nicknames usually reflect the hatreds and stereotypes of the people who use them; but they can also influence how a group is going to be perceived. Thus, nicknames can perpetuate invidious stereotypes, as well as reflect them.[1]

The greatest number of nicknames, by far, allude to blacks (i.e., Afro-Americans). The second greatest number allude to whites. Many civil rights activists have been concerned with how these racial slurs fuel prejudice. One can legislate against overt discrimination in housing, schools, public accomodations, and so on. However, the stereotyping and prejudice which racial nicknames express may lead people to try to circumvent anti-discrimination laws. Effective, long-term changes in race relations, they assert, depend upon the elimination of intergroup hatred and prejudice.

The argument against the use of racial nicknames expresses a view of more general social significance, namely, that changes in society depend upon changes in people's values. This same line of reasoning has been expressed in relation to war, regarding wars as resulting from a combination of too great a readiness to spill blood and too little regard for human lives. If there was more sincere respect for life, all life, it could surmount the militaristic tendencies that have characterized most of human history.

---

[1]Irving L. Allen, *The Language of Ethnic Conflict* (New York: Columbia University Press, 1983).

These arguments share the belief that societies are organized about certain widely shared values. Therefore, it is values that will have to change—if discrimination is to end, if future wars are to be prevented, and so on. While emphasizing the centrality of values to social organization, many of these arguments also contend that values tend to exert a covert influence. In other words, people are not very conscious of the values they hold. Correspondingly, the initial step is often to make people aware that they are condone racism, sexism, violence, and so forth. Only then can fundamental social changes occur.

An emphasis upon the salience of values has also been expressed in sociological theories, most notably in the writings of Max Weber. His view, which focused upon the growth of modern capitalism, will be fully discussed in this chapter. However, Weber's position is only one of many that have been presented in the sociological literature. Numerous other theories argue, with supporting evidence, that values are after-the-fact expressions of a social structure. Technology and/or economic conditions are considered the main determinants of both social organizations and values. Therefore, values are not regarded as providing a critical point of leverage from which to enact change. It would be more fruitful to focus upon changing the technological or economic base of the social structure, anticipating that changes in values will occur as a consequence. This position is associated with Marx and Ogburn, among others, and their theories will also be examined in this chapter.

WEBER ON CAPITALISM

In our previous discussion of Weber's theory of bureaucracy (Chapter Seven), it was noted that Weber emphasized the concept of legitimation. For a social order to emerge or persist, people must regard it as appropriate or justified, in conformity with certain standards. In contemporary societies, Weber continued, legalistic standards tend to predominate. That is, there are widely shared notions concerning how rules or regulations ought to be enacted and some general principles of rights and liabilities that they must not violate. However, the question of legitimation applies to all aspects of social life, rather than just rules and regulations. Thus, even the power or the wealth of elite groups in a society must be accepted as legitimate by the less privileged groups if it is to remain stable (that is, unattacked by revolutionary movements). In concrete terms it may be legitimated by Horatio Alger myths that stress how anyone can move from rags to riches; by belief in the superiority of certain blood lines, or the like.

It logically follows from Weber's position that if a society recurrently engages in wars or systematically discriminates against minorities, there must be widely shared values that condone the actions. If we define morality as people acting in accordance with what *they* consider to be right and proper, then Weber considered people to collectively act in a moral way. The shortcoming in this definition is that it disregards the possibility of one society's morality being repugnant to another.

Thus, Nazi war criminals really believed that Jews, gypsies, and others were the source of evil and ought to be exterminated. The Holocaust from their standpoint was legitimate, though the judges at Nuremberg (and millions of others) did not agree.

No matter what others think, most people probably regard their own behavior as legitimate, most of the time. Analytically, the dilemma is which came first? Did people act in accordance with their precepts, or did they "invent" them after-the-fact when their conduct was questioned? What is distinctive about Weber's position is that it argues for a before-the-fact interpretation. As the major example of his position, Weber presented an historical examination of the rise of modern capitalism.[2]

At the core of Weber's definition of capitalism was a rational orientation toward economic profits. A society is capitalistic, therefore, to the degree people deliberately and self-consciously attempt to acquire wealth.[3] For a capitalistic, or any other, orientation to become pervasive, however, legitimation is required. Attaining a profit has to come to be regarded as ethical, and it can not bestow such justification upon itself. Here Weber is simply calling attention to the fact that a capitalistic (like any other) orientation is not intrinsically ethical. To support this position, he describes historical periods in which small groups of people who were capitalistic were looked down upon in the larger society. In fourteenth-century Florence, for example, there was a merchant class conspicuously oriented toward economic profits. The genteel, refined tastes of the landed aristocracy were dominant, however, and the aristocrats snubbed the merchants for their lack of good taste. Shakespeare's caricature of Shylock, in *The Merchant of Venice,* captures the popular contempt in which the capitalists were held. Of course, they had money. This meant it was sometimes necessary to deal with them; for example, to marry off a daughter to the son of a successful merchant. Such marriages were an embarrassment, however, because they were tasteless matters of expedience.

What happened, Weber asks, to change contempt to esteem; to transform the pursuit of profit into a morally justified activity? It was not a change in material or economic conditions, he states, in an explicit rejection of Marx's view. Consider rural Pennsylvania in the eighteenth century, for example. Capitalism reigned, as evidenced by the popular sayings of Benjamin Franklin. ("A penny saved, . . . " "Early to bed and early to rise," and so on.) However, there were few large enterprises in Pennsylvania, only the beginnings of banking, and modern commerce was jeopardized by insufficient amounts of money which threatened to cause trade to revert to barter-in-kind. Four hundred years earlier in Florence, though, there was a great concentration of money and capital. So, if changed material or economic conditions did not account for the legitimation of profits, what did?

---

[2]The following discussion is based upon, Max Weber, *The Protestant Ethic and the Spirit of Capitalism* (New York: Scribners, 1958).

[3]In contemporary analysis there is often confusion regarding the appropriate unit of analysis. Weber was probably addressing the transformation of specific societies. See Immanual Wallerstein, "From Feudalism to Capitalism," *Social Forces,* 55 (1976).

THE PROTESTANT ETHIC

Weber saw the answer as embodied in the Protestant Ethic, most notably in the sixteenth-century teachings of Martin Luther and John Calvin. As a doctrine this product of Protestant reform stood in marked contrast to medieval Catholicism, and its distinctive emphasis provided the legitimation for capitalism. Prior to considering these distinctive characteristics in detail, several features of Weber's argument must be noted. First, for the most part, the Protestant Ethic was not regarded as the "cause" of capitalism, in a conventional sense of the term. Merchants and others were capitalistic in orientation *before* there was a Protestant reformation. Thus, the ethic provided an important legitimation for capitalism, which permitted its development but was not its cause. Second, Weber generally regarded the religious sector of societies as a major source of values and ideas that pervade all aspects of life. It is not literally the religious doctrines themselves that are influential, but their "diluted" form which carries over into everyday life. (This distinction will be further clarified in the following discussion of the Protestant Ethic.) Its change-facilitating effects were considered unusual, however, because Weber regarded religious influences as generally supporting tradition and resisting change. This is moving too far ahead of Weber's thesis, however, so let us now turn to an examination of the Protestant Ethic in detail.

Weber viewed medieval Catholicism as orienting people away from any *systematic* efforts to change the conditions under which they lived. Monks and nuns presented idealized models of the way to retreat from the sordid vagaries of life. It was the hereafter that was important and demanded preparation. In addition, Catholicism viewed the flesh as weak. People were recurrently expected to follow a cycle of sin, repentance, atonement, and release. Thus, even though the medieval Catholic Church took stands on moral issues and provided missionaries and charities, it oriented masses of people away from secular affairs. These affairs were not of paramount importance compared to the "eternal life," and besides, what could a group of weak sinners hope to accomplish?

The Protestant Ethic challenged these notions. First, it rejected the necessity of a continual cycle of sin and repentance. It held out the possibility of systematic mastery. If people were sufficiently determined, they could resist temptation, even in a world where the devil coreigned and temptations abounded. It was not easy, though. To exert such control required prudence and caution *all the time*. Thus, a view of people as weak sinners was replaced by a view of people as captains of their own ship, masters of their own destiny, so long as they were methodical and systematic. (This view was even reflected in the names of some denominations, such as Methodists.)

The turn to secular affairs was also emphasized by the Protestant Ethic's emphasis upon work. Vocations provided a major medium in which systematic mastery was displayed. Work was elevated from the mundane to a "calling." When we refer to a person's calling today, it is largely reserved for the ministry. Sometimes the term is applied to medicine or law, especially if the person made an early and strong commitment to the profession. However, the early Protestant reformers regarded all kinds of work as constituting a person's calling. Being a butcher, a baker, or candlestick maker involved more than just a job. It required zealous commitment in order to indicate, both to one's self and to the community, that one was made of the "right stuff."

Predestination concerns also provided a source of anxiety that motivated people. Unlike medieval Catholicism which stressed an earned salvation through a life of good deeds, Protestantism considered one's afterlife to be predetermined. Wordly events could not ordinarily change fate. To God-fearing people this was, understandably, the source of considerable anxiety. Total immersion in work—that is, in one's calling— was one way to attempt to cope with the ever present fears. In addition, there was a continual search for signs of salvation, any kind of clue that could indicate salvation was preordained. This led to a curious reversal of causes and effects. Would God allow a person to be successful, they reasoned, unless the person's salvation was predetermined? Success might, therefore, be an indication; but to obtain this possible sign, one would have to work very hard. In the context of this belief system, community norms exhorted people to follow their callings as a sacred obligation. Those who did not were regarded with contempt. After all, they showed certain signs of eternal damnation.

Thus far we have talked about success in a calling, but how was success expressed? To understand we must also recognize Protestants' puritanical condemnation of squandering. The diffuse emphasis upon frugality that resulted is again well expressed in the sayings of Benjamin Franklin: "waste neither time nor money," for example. So strictly was squandering defined that people had few modes of allowable consumption. They continuously risked the sin of pretentiousness. As a result, they either saved their wages or reinvested their capital, activities which were highly beneficial to economic growth.

Finally, the Protestant Ethic rejected the notion of medieval Catholicism that I am my brother's keeper. Replacing accountability was the belief that each person will, in the end, face one's Maker alone. Contempt for the unworthy—that is, the unsuccessful—was thereby permitted. At the same time, subtle restraints upon competitiveness were removed. It is not that competition was so much encouraged by the ethic, but that competition was not inhibited to the same extent as in medieval Catholicism. Moreover, given the emphasis upon work and success, Protestants already had plenty to be competitive about.

In sum, the Protestant Ethic was viewed by Weber as resulting in a well-disciplined, highly motivated labor force, and an esteemed group of capitalists, all of whom were seeking signs of salvation by pursuing their God-given callings. Early to bed and early to rise were supposed to make one not only wealthy, but healthy and wise as well. Thus, wealth became a sign of virtue and grace while poverty became the mark of moral failure. To be poor implied that one was also lazy, weak, and generally immoral.

It is not that the pursuit of wealth or economic competition were unthought of during medieval Catholicism. They were, in fact, primary objectives of merchants and other capitalistic groups. Prior to the formulation of the Protestant Ethic, however, they were the values of a relatively isolated minority. For modern capitalism to exist on a broad scale, the pursuit of profit had to be legitimated as an activity and an orientation. It was the Protestant Ethic, Weber concluded, which provided the ethical justification.

In order to further clarify the essential features of this ethic, Weber responded to the question of whether it should more properly be called the Jewish ethic. In many countries it was Jews who, at least stereotypically, seemed to place the greatest emphasis upon profits. Shakespeare's Shylock, for example, was conspicuously Jewish. However, Weber argued, the history of Jews is markedly inconsistent with a central feature of the ethic, namely, the possibility of systematic mastery.[4] That notion is particularly foreign to Jews who have historically been treated like pariahs and faced the dilemma of trying to reconcile this treatment with a self-view as "the chosen people." For Jews, according to Weber, it has resulted in a view of the world as capricious and unpredictable. This attitude cannot be reconciled with the Protestant reformers' belief in the possibility of systematic mastery and control over one's fate. Thus, even if Jews personify some of its aspects, it is most appropriately termed the Protestant Ethic.

Over time, Weber regarded capitalism and the ethic as potentially independent of each other. The pursuit of wealth, for example, has probably been stripped of its former ethical and religious meaning. Once established, any orientation— such as capitalism—can be self-sustaining. It can, for example, be traditionally legitimated. Thus, the relationship between capitalism and the ethic was historically limited to the initial "boost" provided by the ethic to the ethos of capitalism.

Also over time, the Protestant Ethic came to exert the kind of conservative influence that Weber generally attributed to religion. As previously noted, he considered religious values typically to inhibit change. The Protestant Ethic's facilitation of a change to capitalism was, therefore, statistically unusual. However, later efforts at social reform confronted the ethic as a major obstacle when various welfare programs were opposed on moral grounds: Why help the undeserving? To be poor is to be immoral; to need help is to be stigmatized. Whether the issue is rent subsidy, extended unemployment benefits, aid to minorities or to dependent children, many citizens and legislators express their opposition in terms of the Protestant Ethic: If "they" were not lazy and undependable, they would not need help. Thus, by emphasizing a view of rugged individualism and certain success for the perserving, the ethic inhibited appreciation of the structural reasons for inequality, such as institutional discrimination.

CHANGING TRADITIONAL SOCIETIES

Empirical studies of Weber's perspective are very scarce. The specific issue, the relationship between modern capitalism and the Protestant Ethic, almost defies reanalysis because of the kind of relationship Weber envisioned between them. It

---

[4]Max Weber, *The Sociology of Religion* (Boston: Beacon, 1963).

was not causal; capitalism existed first. Moreover, it was not necessarily a continuous relationship; the Protestant Ethic was needed to provide only an initial legitimation. Therefore, further analysis of the specific relationship is virtually precluded because it would require detailed historical data going back to the turn of the sixteenth century. The general relationship between values and social change, however, is more amenable to further analysis and has been the object of several investigations. The typical approach is to analyze changes in a particular society, or category of societies, and then attempt to relate the changes to widespread values. An interesting and illustrative study is reported by Phillip Leis who examined an Ijaw village of about 700 persons in Southern Nigeria.[5]

The Ijaw

The traditional economic activity of the Ijaw was the production and sale of palm oil. Palm oil trees ringed the village, and the men found it relatively easy to gather berries from the ripe branches. An association of men would gather to mash the berries, and each man would then put the oil extracted from his berries into containers. Each year a buyer from the United Africa Company would come to the Ijaw to buy the palm oil.

Palm oil production, in the above manner, was *the* traditional economic activity of the Ijaw. It was the major occupation of virtually all adult males. Furthermore, because of its historic significance, palm oil—and its preparation—was an important part of Ijaw rituals. The initiation ceremony of adolescents, for example, focused upon a young boy's bravery in climbing palm trees and concluded with the coating of his body in palm oil. Thus, to become an adult male was largely equated with the production of palm oil.

By the middle of this century, however, a dramatic change occurred. Almost all of the Ijaw stopped making palm oil for a living and turned to gin; that is, the production and sale of gin. This was not an entirely new activity. The Ijaw had for many years collected and distilled the fruit of palm wine trees; but the alcohol was for their private and ceremonial consumption, rather than their livelihood. Thus, palm oil and palm gin reversed places, the latter changing from pastime to dominant occupation while the former moved in the opposite direction.

Gin making is a much more arduous task than making palm oil. It requires that men go into unpleasant swamps on an established schedule to collect the fruit of palm wine trees. Picking palm oil berries entails a much more relaxed schedule. Then there is the more involved distilling process, performed by Ijaw families, that has no counterpart in the production of palm oil. While gin making is more difficult and unpleasant, the Ijaw's economic return is, overall, very little better than what they would receive from the sale of palm oil. Why then, Leis asks, did the occupational transformation occur? The slight extra return is certainly not commensurate with the extra work, so the answer must lie outside of the economic realm. The answer,

[5]Phillip Leis, "Palm Oil, Illicit Gin, and the Moral Order of the Ijaw," *American Anthropologist,* 66 (1964).

according to Leis, is provided by two fundamental Ijaw beliefs: 1) independence, and 2) hard work.

Because of their belief in independence, the men's association formed to mash the palm oil berries was a recurrent problem. So great was their emphasis upon independence that the association was difficult to organize and a constant source of friction. Gin making required no such association; each family could work alone. Hence, it was more congruent with the Ijaw emphasis upon independence. In addition, as palm oil producers they were dependent on a single buyer (from the United Africa Company). As gin makers, by contrast, they could sell their product to anyone in the marketplace who wished to buy it, at a price determined by supply and demand. Thus, they were no longer dependent upon the bid of a single buyer.

The Ijaw believe that, prior to birth, each individual confronts his Creator and pledges a lifetime of labor. Even the elderly in the village must continue to work hard or risk social condemnation. Therefore, the fact that it was more difficult to produce gin than palm oil made the gin making more congruent with that Ijaw value as well.

The change to gin could not have occurred prior to about 1950. Larger social and economic changes then sweeping across the Delta produced a nearby marketplace. Without it, the Ijaw simply had no alternative to palm oil. There was no place to sell gin; that is, no place providing access to potential buyers. Given the choice, they switched, Leis concludes, to the alternative that was most in accord with their fundamental values.

A case study, such as that of the Ijaw, really does not provide hard proof. It merely suggests that changes *can* occur the way Weber specified; not that they typically *do* occur that way. A case study is also particularly prone to questionable interpretations. For example, perhaps Leis would not go through the rigors of gin making for so little extra money, but perhaps it was economically worth it to the Ijaw.

More readily generalized, albeit less interesting, support for Weber's thesis comes from studies of planned change. These studies typically focus upon attempts to introduce modern technology into traditional societies. Examples include vaccines, birth-control implements, mechanical wells for water, and so on. In a majority of cases, the planned change fails. There is too much resistance to its introduction. The most frequently offered explanation for such failures is their lack of fit with traditional values. For example, birth-control techniques may be regarded as threats to masculinity, a new way to obtain water may be considered offensive to the Gods, and so on. In many of these situations it appears necessary to change values before other kinds of changes can occur.[6] In other words, values really do matter.

As in all the other chapters, the studies discussed here are not intended to provide proof. The perspectives involved are probably too abstract to be proved or disproved.

---

[6]For a survey of 50 planned changes, and their outcomes, see Larry M. Lance and Edward E. McKenna, "Analysis of Cases Pertaining to the Impact of Western Technology," *Human Organization*, 34 (1975).

Moreover, there are a number of studies which support positions quite different from Weber's. However, studies of the Ijaw or of planned changes do illustrate Weber's contention that changes in values occur first, and that is the reason for their inclusion.

WEBER AND MARX COMPARED

In the "Forward" to *The Protestant Ethic and the Spirit of Capitalism,* R. H. Tawney praises the ingenuity of Weber's analysis. However, he also wonders about a change in religious attitudes that proved to be "so convenient" to certain segments. At the very least, he concludes, the Protestant Ethic must have been *molded by* the social order even as it was helping to mold that social order.[7]

Tawney's comments introduce Marx's perspective. It is an important position to consider here because, in part, Weber's thesis was a polemic, specifically intended as a blow to Marx's ghost. In Marx's view, it will be recalled, (Chapter 6) relations to the means of production determined the basic structures of society. Values and ideas were less important, after-the-fact phenomena. Thus, compassion, self-esteem, regard for human dignity, and true consciousness could not emerge until after the basic productive structure was modified. An opposite position is to regard ideas and values as "effective forces," capable of exerting a before-the-fact influence on the social structure. This opposite-to-Marx view is close to the one Weber maintained.[8]

At the same time, however, Weber was critical of all one-sided interpretations, including his own. Weber self-consciously recognized the changes he was analyzing to be too complex for any compact interpretation. The complexity of the issues simply precluded any precise calculation of specific contributions to change. Only loose approximations and rough estimates were possible. Nevertheless, Weber considered a Marxian emphasis upon material conditions to be too prevalent, in general. Therefore, in order to counterbalance this theoretical emphasis, he did offer a rather one-sided spiritualistic interpretation.

It is of historic interest to note that Marx's emphasis upon economic conditions was, in part, a response to what he and Engels regarded as a pervasive tendency in social theory to underestimate its importance. However, they later found themselves without the time, place, or opportunity to attempt to present a more balanced viewpoint.[9] Thus, both Marx and Weber apparently felt a pull toward a centrist position that recognized an interaction among diverse elements; but each took a position off center: Weber leaning toward values and ideas, Marx toward the economic structure.

---

[7]For a fuller presentation of his ideas, see R. H. Tawney, *Religion and the Rise of Capitalism* (New York: New American Library, 1948).

[8]For further analysis of Weber's debate with Marx's ghost, see Chapter 11 in, Irving M. Zeitlin, *Ideology and the Development of Sociological Theory* (Englewood Cliffs: Prentice-Hall, 1987).

[9]Karl Marx and Friedrich Engels, *Selected Correspondence, 1846-1895* (New York: International Publishers, 1942).

This is an opportune time to introduce other studies of values, some conducted from a Marxian perspective. They serve to further clarify Marx's position in contrast to Weber's, and provide interesting illustrations of some of the difficulties encountered when one attempts an either-or interpretation.

VALUES OF THE ELITE

In a capitalistic society, Marx viewed the bourgeoisie (who own or control the means of production) as controlling the processes which disseminate ideology. The mass media are a current example. This control leads the proletariat (who have only their labor to sell) to a false consciousness of their social being. The concrete implications of this view are 1) that the bourgeoisie present a monolithic view, and 2) it is a view that champions their own (economic) self-interest.

One way to operationalize a group that resembles the bourgeoisie is to focus upon the top executives of leading corporations. These can be identified as persons of the rank of vice president and above in firms that have the greatest sales and assets in the nation, corporations such as General Motors and Chase Manhattan Bank. In order to focus upon the key Marxian implications, Seider has analyzed a sample of 500 speeches given by such top corporate executives between 1934 and 1970. They were delivered to civic, political, and economic organizations.[10]

The most common theme expressed in the speeches—specifically, in over one-half of them—was termed a "classical business creed." Its main features are an emphasis upon free enterprise and profits. Free enterprise primarily entails doing business unregulated by government intervention in the marketplace. The emphasis upon, and defense of, profit are clearly illustrated by the following quote from one board chairman: "The profit motive . . . does not need to be camouflaged with shallow pieties about the public service or other noble sounding aims."

The second most common theme, present in about one-third of the top executives' speeches, is "nationalistic." It emphasizes an American way of life that must be protected in a hostile (that is, communistic) world. As might further be expected, the two dominant themes—classical business and nationalism—often occurred, to varying degrees, in the same speech.

The free enterprise, go-for-profits ideology, is viewed by Seider as legitimating the economic position of the executives' firms. Clearly, it is in the interest of giant corporations to persuade the public that regulation is undesirable, not in the best interests of the nation. What industrial sector is served, however, by the nationalistic theme? In other words, if ideologies are to be viewed as self-serving, which industries stand to benefit from nationalistic sentiments? The answer is those who desire to protect foreign markets and/or sell weapons systems. Specifically, this comprises the aerospace, automobile, and steel industries, and Seider finds them ranked first, second,

[10]Maynard S. Seider, "American Big Business Ideology," *American Sociological Review,* 39 (1974).

and third in executives' use of the nationalistic themes. Retail trade, with the least to gain from such nationalistic appeals, contributes the fewest such speeches. (Only 2 percent of the retail executive speeches were nationalistic compared to 59 percent of the aerospace executive speeches. Thus, the differences involved are quite substantial.)

Looking at a variety of other specific issues, Seider shows the speeches of top executives in different industries to be consistently self-serving. As further examples, bank executives' speeches most often described inflation as a danger, while retail trade executives never did; the aerospace industry executives were most likely to favor increased military spending, and so forth.

In sum, on certain issues (such as unregulated business profits), the executives tend to be in general agreement. These are issues of common benefit to all large corporations. This ideological unity is not surprising when it is recalled that several superprominent families and several key conglomerates control numerous corporations. It is tempting to wonder whether ideological unity is an explicit concern of these controlling centers. In any case, it is clear that these top executives have access to public forums, press conferences, and the like, that is unmatched by persons who might present different ideologies.

The wealth that is controlled by major corporations also permits them, ostentatiously, to make charitable contributions which operate like advertising, enabling them to co-opt the general public. Burt presents this view of corporate philanthropy, beginning by asking why some firms appear to be so much more charitable than others. The usual explanations, such as corporations give because it is tax deductible and/or because they recognize a responsibility to their communities, seem unable to explain the *differences* among firms.

From his analysis of tax records, Burt found that when families were the major consumers of firms' output (e.g., food rather than metal products) the firms gave much higher percentages of corporate profit to charities. Their contributions, in other words, were designed to gain the affection or approval of individuals in households in the expectation that it would stimulate demand for the firm's product. Thus, Burt concludes, corporate philanthropy should be seen more as an effort to promote a firm's economic interests than as an expression of civic values.[11]

With Marx's perspective in mind, it is instructive to reexamine Weber's thesis, and consider whether capitalist groups regarded the Protestant Ethic as providing a long-sought legitimation and correspondingly financed the religious reformation in order to ensure its success. To whatever degree that description is accurate, it suggests that Weber overestimated the before-the-fact impact of values.

Now, from Weber's perspective, reconsider Seider's examination of corporate speeches and question whether people's values determine which of them will perform their jobs successfully, and whether successful performance, in turn, leads them to become top executives. If so, then the Marxist interpretation of values as self-serving reflections of an economic structure appears to be overly cynical.

[11]Ronald S. Burt, "Corporate Philanthropy as a Cooptive Relation," *Social Forces*, 62, 1983.

The relative ease with which these illustrative cases may be reinterpreted is a certain sign that the basic issue is very complex. It becomes even more complex when a third position is introduced, namely, Ogburn's view which relates social change to technology. Ogburn's position is closer to Marx's than Weber's in that it relegates values to a reactive role. However, it is a more empirical and less ideological theory than is Marx's.

OGBURN ON TECHNOLOGY AND CULTURE

The nature of social and cultural change provided the overriding problem to William F. Ogburn, the problem which gave coherence to a half-century of productive scholarship. His writing was originally directed in polemical fashion against nineteenth-century, single-factor theories which emphasized a single cause—such as biological endowment, climate, or the like—as accounting for all variation in cultural development. Ogburn's sensitivity to rapid twentieth-century changes led him to reject these theories as too gross. During some brief periods of time, he noted, there are very rapid social changes without any corresponding changes in the relatively fixed biological or climate factors. Therefore, from a methodological position, he reasoned that a constant could not explain a variable.[12]

This initial awareness of the complexities of change appeared to have cautioned Ogburn from presenting an overly simplified analysis of his own. Throughout his writing is an appreciation of the complexities. However, he did feel justified in emphasizing the role of "material culture"; that is, of artifacts, technology, and their related processes. The material culture was juxtaposed to the nonmaterial culture which involved social institutions, values, and norms. His basic thesis was that changes in material culture *tend* to occur first. A delay, or "culture lag," then typically ensues prior to the adjustment (or readjustment) of the nonmaterial culture to new material conditions.

In later detailing his intellectual debts in formulating the theory of the cultural lag, Ogburn expressed an appreciation of Kark Marx.[13] His materialistic interpretation of history provided a base, but Ogburn insisted that his own cultural-lag theory was different both from Marx's and from related theories of economic determinism in two basic ways. First, Ogburn was not committed to the idea of material changes occurring first. In fact he explicitly presented contradictory illustrations. He simply argued that empirical observation suggests the statistical tendency for nonmaterial culture to change more slowly and in response to material conditions, especially in the contemporary Western world. A second, and more important, difference lies in the form of Ogburn's theory.

[12]William F. Ogburn, "Culture and Sociology," *Social Forces,* 16 (1937).

[13]William F. Ogburn, "Cultural Lag as Theory," *Sociology and Social Research,* 16 (1957). His major work, *Social Change,* was originally published in 1922 (B. W. Huebsch) and reprinted in 1950 (Viking Press).

The sheer existence of invention or material innovation is not sufficient grounds for inferring the applicability of the cultural-lag concept, he argued. It must first be shown that two variables (associated with material and nonmaterial culture) were in adjustment during time one: for example, illiteracy and simple agricultural subsistence. Next it is necessary to show that one of the variables has changed more than the other: For example, illiteracy remains relatively unchanged while industrialization is renovating the means of subsistence. Finally, it must be shown that the differential change has produced "a less satisfactory adjustment" between the variables than was formerly the case. It is only when an initial adjustment is mitigated by differential rates of change that the notion of culture lag applies. Thus, Ogburn's theory focused explicitly upon the *form* of change. It was a materialistic explanation of the causes of change implicitly and only because of the sequence of change most typically observed by Ogburn.

One of Ogburn's approaches to the thesis was historical or evolutionary. He noted that over 100,000 years ago, during interglacial periods, people first fashioned a technology by deliberately chipping stone implements for drilling, hammering, scraping, and the like. This was followed in the last glacial period by the development of bone-fashioned implements such as chisels and blades which were used in conjunction with the previously developed stone tools. Still later, he noted, the use of copper, bronze, and iron in addition to stone and bone. Ogburn saw that the basic point was an accumulation, "the stream of material culture grows bigger."[14] He recognized that some material culture is "lost" as environments change or as new techniques permit the construction of alternatives with greater utility. The overall trend is cumulative, however, because knowledge of how to make an implement is perpetuated in the nonmaterial culture, even if the artifact is no longer produced.

The number or rate of new implements depends upon invention; but, Ogburn insisted, the rate of new inventions is not primarily dependent upon the mental ability of inventors. He conceded that the inventors will always tend to be above average in ability in comparison to the population at large. However, they need not be superior in ability to inventors at an earlier period and yet there are typically more, and more elaborate, inventions in the later period. This apparent paradox is resolved by recognizing the importance of a cultural base. Specifically, Ogburn argued, inventions require a culturally transmitted background of prior inventions. There could be no cart, for example, without the previous invention of the wheel; no modern printing press without thousands of prior cultural achievements.

A cultural base, therefore, both limits and directs the nature of invention. Ogburn claims that this assertion is supported by the great frequency with which independent inventors have made virtually simultaneous discoveries, including the steamboat and sewing machine, the theory of infection of microorganisms, and so on. After surveying an even larger array of discoveries in various scientific

[14]Ogburn, *Social Change*, p. 73.

fields, Merton has concluded that multiple discoveries are actually the dominant pattern.[15]

Simultaneous discoveries were important to Ogburn as an argument against "Great Man" theories of history. In his time, and even now, many people see human history as shaped primarily by the efforts of a few great people. For example, the settlement of America by Europeans, according to Ogburn, is overly credited to Columbus and Queen Isabella. The importance of a multitude of inventions and discoveries which resulted in sails, large boats, accurate compasses, and the like is correspondingly under-appreciated.[16] Because many of the necessary technologies were simultaneously discovered, Ogburn concludes, one ought to emphasize not a few individuals, but the collectively developed cultural base that drives history by producing new technologies.

New customs, in Ogburn's view, are also dependent upon technology because people's behavior is a response to inventions. An interesting illustration of how technology alters social practices is provided by CB radio prostitution. By eavesdropping on CB radio broadcasts and by unobtrusive observations at interstate highway truck stops, a study in Oklahoma found that many prostitutes used CB radios to arrange liaisons with long-distance haulers. (These truckers present a large corps of lonely and bored men who are on the road all night.) The women openly solicited over the airwaves: "Come on, one of you horny truck drivers out there. Would you like to see a Beaver tonight?"[17] A driver would respond and the two would arrange, while in route, to meet at a truck stop or rest area. If they could agree on price and police surveillance did not seem oppressive, the prostitute would park her car and enter the truck.

CB radios involve a number of changes in the traditional practice prostitution. There is, of course, the obvious displacement of prostitutes from street corners to highway rest areas. The role of the pimp as mediator has also been reduced. While many of the prostitutes still rely on pimps for protection, and some of the pimps sell drugs on the side, the prostitute can easily negotiate directly with a potential john by herself. Thus, the technological developments that resulted in long-distance trucking and CB radios have led to new forms of prostitution.

Over time, as the number of inventions accumulate, there is a rapid growth in the cultural base. Therefore, the rate of new inventions increases at an exponential rate. These accelerated innovations in the material culture create an increasing strain

[15]Robert K. Merton, "Singletons and Multiples in Science," in Norman W. Storer (Ed), *The Sociology of Science* (Chicago: University of Chicago Press, 1973). The degree to which Ogburn and Merton are correct may depend upon whether credit for a discovery is attributed to a person only if it was a major point in at least one journal article published by the alleged discoverer. See Don Patinkin, "Multiple Discoveries and the Central Message," *American Journal of Sociology*, 89, 1983.

[16]William F. Ogburn, "Inventions, Population and History," in Otis D. Duncan (Ed), *William F. Ogburn on Culture and Social Change* (Chicago: University of Chicago, 1964).

[17]Joan Luxenburg and Lloyd Klein, "CB Radio Prostitution," in Sol Chaneles (Ed), *Gender Issues, Sex Offenses, and Criminal Justice* (New York: Haworth Press, 1984).

in the nonmaterial culture which is trying to accommodate to these changes. In effect then, there is also a tendency for cultural lags to accumulate. They become dramatically eliminated, according to Ogburn, by wars, revolutions, and other instruments of rapid social change.

As a contemporary example of Ogburn's perspective, consider the varied changes that have recently been occurring in women's roles. His theory of cultural lags would apply if we make several assumptions. First, many children spaced closely together is consistent with wives-mothers spending their days caring for children. Thus, the absence of birth-control techniques (material culture) is associated with traditional definitions of women's roles (nonmaterial culture). The next assumption is that changes in the nonmaterial culture occurred. This involved, not only more (and more efficacious) birth-control techniques, but labor-saving household appliances and innovations in child-care apparatus: disposable diapers, premixed formula, and the like. As a result of those changes in the material culture, women have fewer children, and each child also requires less time. Values in the nonmaterial culture, which view the woman's place as limited to the home, are now out of line with the nonmaterial culture. Technological advances make these values more and more out of line, but the traditional values are tenacious. It finally takes a feminist social movement to reduce the cultural lag.

The above description of changes in women's roles is obviously very simplified. Numerous other changes also impinged upon it. However, the above description is a heuristic example of Ogburn's typical mode of analysis. For our purposes its most sailent feature is that values are viewed as reactive, as changing in response to material conditions. It must also be noted, however, that Ogburn allowed for reversals in this sequence; that is, he considered it possible for changes in the nonmaterial culture to occur first. Thus, he would admit the possibility of traditional role definitions being the initial source of change and leading to congruent innovations in the material culture. In this case, modern role definitions lead to more effective contraceptive techniques, disposable diapers, and so on. Ogburn simply argued that this latter sequence was statistically less likely to occur.

One of the more subtle insights in Ogburn's work was his conception of an on-going, but not necessarily equal, reciprocity among social institutions. He proposed that the parts of a total society were interrelated in a way that resembled the components of an engine more than the links of a chain. A modification of one component would therefore be likely to affect others, though not to the same extent because the different parts of society are not equally interrelated. In contemporary societies, for example, medicine is more closely related to science than to religion. Thus, a change in science would have a greater effect upon medicine than would a change in religion. This specific situation would, of course, be reversed in societies where the stronger relationship is between medicine and religion.

Following largely from the works of social anthropologists, such as Radcliffe-Brown and Malinowski, sociologists have stressed a view of culture (and social organization) as composed of interdependent elements. In this view as it developed, there is a tendency not to differentiate degrees of interdependence. Correspondingly, the possibility suggested by Ogburn that some sectors of a society exert unequalled influence upon social organization was largely ignored for a number of years. In fact, it was forty years after the original publication of Ogburn's classic book on social change that Gouldner and Peterson explicitly re-examined his ideas about unequal influence.

Technology and Social Organization

In order to examine what dimensions of society are the most influential, the research inspired by the ideas of Ogburn and others has had to compare large samples of societies. The first study, by Gouldner and Peterson, focused upon seventy-one preindustrial societies. The follow-up study examined over 300 societies, including both preindustrial and modern societies; but, the major findings of both studies were highly consistent with each other.[18]

Both studies devised measures of the material and nonmaterial culture. The former was termed technology or technoenvironmental and it primarily involved the varying capacities of societies to weave, mine, work with metals, and so on. The nonmaterial culture of the sampled societies was measured in a variety of ways including favoritism for either the male or female lineage in matters of inheritance and descent, the development of codified laws and elaborate ceremonies, and so on.

Overall, the various aspects of material and nonmaterial culture tended to be interrelated; for example, if items of value were inherited down the female lineage in a particular society, then, rules of residence usually required a groom to move near to the bride's family. However, the highest relationships among components of societies tended to involve technology as one of the variables, and technology appeared to explain more variation in the overall social organization than anything else. Thus, the level of technological development seems, from these analyses, to influence overall structure and values of societies more than anything else.

While agreeing in their emphases, both sets of investigators were concerned that their results would be interpreted in too simplistic a way. To have proven that technology is, in relative terms, the most influential dimension, Gouldner and Peterson stated, is not the same thing as claiming that technology, by itself, determines everything. Heise and others similarly concluded that the nonmaterial culture was more dependent upon the material culture than vice versa; but, they emphasized, much is still left unexplained. While aspects of social organization seem generally to be more influenced by technology than anything else, there are other forces operating, and there are some features of social organization that are apparently unaffected by technology.

[18]The first study was Alvin W. Gouldner and Richard A. Peterson, *Technology and the Moral Order* (Indianapolis: Boss-Merrill, 1962). The replication was reported by David Heise, Gerhard Lenski and John Wardwell, "Futher Notes on Technology and the Moral Order," *Social Forces,* 55, 1976.

CONCLUSION

The cross-cultural surveys we have examined suggest that the values espoused in societies are generally more influenced by levels of technology than those values, in turn, influence technology. Does this finding suggest that values do not matter? No, for two reasons: First, there are "circumstantial" instances where values appear to be predominant—the change from palm oil to gin among the Ijaw may be an example; second, even in situations where technology predominates, values may also be of some importance. In examining various historical events, Ogburn presents several examples which may be illustrative of how values operate, even if in a secondary way.

The Civil War, for example, from Ogburn's perspective, was due mostly to technological differences between the North and South. The industrial technology emerging in the North led to favoring protective tariffs. Such trade restrictions would permit Northern manufacturing to develop when it might otherwise be overwhelmed by competition from more industrialized nations, especially England. In the South, by contrast, cotton was king. It was processed by the cotton gin which required an abundance of cheap (that is, slave) labor. The Southern economy was highly dependent upon cotton exports, to British mills in particular. Thus, the South favored free trade with England, fearing that protective tariffs would lead to reciprocal British restrictions.

In the final analysis, Ogburn viewed the Civil War as possessing a technological conflict at its roots. Different values in the North and South were shaped by these technological differences. The need for cheap labor generated by the cotton gin, for example, led to legitimations of slavery. While value differences may have helped to mobilize armies and civilian support, the war was best seen as a conflict of opposing technologies, rather than opposing values.

Ogburn's position, it should be noted, is reasonably compatible with Marx's. Technology, for Ogburn, includes the means of production as emphasized by Marx. In addition, Ogburn recognized the importance of economic interests—such as desires for protective tariffs or free trade—and often considered them to be important catalysts. Further, both regarded values and institutions as typically reactive, or after the fact. However, Ogburn placed more emphasis than Marx upon the consequences of material artifacts (for example, guns, radios), was less sensitive to differential relationships to technology (that is, social classes), and was willing to concede the possibility of value primacy in some instances.

The results of the studies we have reviewed will probably be interpreted pessimistically by many people who are commited to change because they suggest that values are often not the cause of various social ills. In all probability, wars are not primarily due to low regard for human lives; discrimination is not primarily due to prejudicial sentiments; and so on. However this does not mean that changes in values are irrelevant, and most of us will continue to find values more accessible to change efforts than technological structures which seem more distant and remote from us as individuals. Moreover, there is the more optimistic note, bolstered by numerous empirical examples, of situations in which value changes work miracles, or at least, near-miracles.

SUGGESTIONS FOR ADDITIONAL READING

WILLIAM V. D'ANTONIO and JOAN ALDOUS, *Families and Religions.* Beverly Hills: Sage, 1983.
IVAN SZELENYI, *Socialist Entrepreneurs.* Madison: University of Wisconsin, 1988.
MICHAEL USEEM, *The Inner Circle.* New York: Oxford, 1984.

III

THE NATURE AND FORM OF SOCIOLOGICAL THEORY

INTRODUCTION TO PART THREE

Scholarly, including scientific, disciplines resemble cultures in a number of important respects. Cultures evolve and change as a function of innovations whose acceptance depends upon their congruence with traditions and values within the culture. Similarly, the content of scholarly disciplines evolves and changes as a function of innovations (such as new ideas or computer systems). However, while traditions and values set the stage upon which cultural innovations are accepted or rejected, theories serve this function in most scientific disciplines. In other words, the contents of disciplines and the directions in which they change are established largely by the nature of a discipline's theory.

Particular characteristics of any culture at any given time often seem to be arbitrary and capricious. Similarly, the special topics and distinctive modes of inquiry that are associated with disciplines often appear to be due to who happened to do what, when. For example, the fact that a new technology happens to be developed by a biologist, rather than a physicist, may have long-term implications for subsequent developments within both fields. However, all happenstance is not equally likely to have an enduring impact. In the long run, it is the compatibility of discoveries with the previously developed theoretical tenets of a discipline that largely determines which will persist and become more or less integral to the discipline. Thus, the most important bases for differentiating among disciplines are embodied in theories which stipulate the kinds of questions that are most crucial to consider and the kinds of answers that are most desirable.

For the most part, theories define the core subject matters of disciplines and the major modes of treating those core subjects. The core of each discipline tends to be distinctive; that is, rather easily distinguished from other disciplines. However, cores tend to be small, relative to peripheries, and the peripheral areas of disciplines frequently overlap greatly. It is extremely difficult, for example, to identify the precise boundaries that differentiate between sociology and psychology or between biology and chemistry. As a result hybrid disciplines emerge, such as social psychology and biochemistry; but irresolvable "borderline disputes" typically continue. The intellectual tension this sometimes creates can be productive in its consequences, though. Just as important discoveries can lead to a redefinition of what a discipline encompasses, so too can changes in a discipline's boundaries lead to dramatic new ways of viewing phenomena.

In sum, in order to understand a discipline, both its core and its periphery, it is necessary to examine the major theoretical positions which influence its course of development. The main difference between these theories and those previously discussed in this book is their point of reference. In the preceding chapters we examined theories about social interaction, social organization, and change. The two chapters in this concluding section, by contrast, present theories about theories; that is, some general notions about the form and content of sociological theory. Chapter Twelve focuses upon diverse aspects of a single problem, namely, the degree to which sociological theory can isolate a distinctive set of issues and explanations. Chapter Thirteen addresses the nature of theory in a social *science*, focusing upon the relationship between theory and measurement, the proper range of sociological theory, and the possibility and desirability of theoretical neutrality.

12

Uniquely Sociological Theory
Spencer, Durkheim, Homans

During the last decades of the nineteenth century, theories of evolution were center stage in virtually every scientific discipline. With only minor modifications to fit specific realms of inquiry, essentially the same concepts and theories of change were applied in sociology, psychology, biology, and so on. Herbert Spencer was a key figure in the diffusion of an evolutionary approach across diverse fields of study. The basic principles of organization and change, he contended, are everywhere the same.

Durkheim's "rules" of sociology were offered, in part, as a response to Spencer's thesis. Durkheim argued that sociology's subject matter was distinct and that, conceptually, it required a special mode of analysis. In particular, Durkheim felt that it was essential to eliminate psychological and biological considerations from sociological explanations. There was simply no reason for the same principles to be operative in different realms, and the social realm was considered separate and irreducible.

In recent years some sociologists, in response to Durkheim's influence, have argued that sociological explanations have been overly separated from the psychological and biological principles upon which they must rest. It is necessary, in their view, to bring people, or the "beast" within people, back into sociological analyses. (However, this does not necessarily entail returning to an evolutionary perspective, as well.)

This chapter will examine the major arguments about the purity, or uniqueness, of sociological theory. Historically, it has been a very contentious debate but also a very important one for determining the thrust of the discipline.

SPENCER'S PRINCIPLES

According to Spencer, all conceptions tend to pass through a series of stages as they move from the more particular to the more universal. With each suceeding step, some of the specific aspects of a phenomenon cease to be distinguishable as they become fused into more abstract notions. Some examples may help to clarify this general rule of Spencer's. Thus, consider the relationship between a concept and its indicators. Most concepts, because of their abstractness, are not directly observable; but their manifestations are, and there tend to be many such indicators of any given concept. As a concrete example, consider the concept of anxiety and its manifestations, such as a higher pulse rate, nail biting, floor pacing, and the like. Each of these manifestations, or indicators, may temporarily command our attention. However, as we formulate the more abstract conception of anxiety, the particular indicators (like nail biting) become less salient, and eventually, imperceptible. Spencer illustrated this process by describing how aborigines attributed anthropomorphic qualities to such diverse objects as idols or mountains. Over time the specific and multiple objects were merged into more general conceptions of deities, and eventually, to the notion of a single God. The trend is always the same: from the multiple and specific to the universal.[1]

This conceptualization trend, in Spencer's view, applied to all forms, whether inorganic, mental, or social. By observation and inference a scientist—in any field—must work toward the most universal, or terminal, conceptualization. It is a difficult process though, because the specific aspects which were apparent at one time become almost imperceptible at a later time. Their particular existence is blurred as the universal conception of which they are a part becomes dominant. Thus, it is difficult for us to trace the clothing we wear back to the caterpillar's cocoon; then back to the nitrogen absorbed by the caterpillar from plants; on back to the gases in the air and the minerals in the soil, and so on. In order to arrive at a "final" explanation, the entire "natural history" of the conceptualization must be examined in this manner.

The inferential skills required of the scientist to carry out this task are obviously demanding. As an invaluable aid, however, Spencer believed that he had deduced the principles of change and that they were everywhere (that is, in every field) the same.

Instability of the Homogenous

The first major principle Spencer applied to all phenomena was, "the instability of the homogeneous."[2] By homogeneity he meant essentially an absence of differentiation within any entity, whether it was a cell, an organism or a society. His general rule was that homoegeneity would not persist because of external forces that differentially affect the undifferentiated entity, resulting in greater heterogeneity. To illustrate, consider an undifferentiated lower form of life, such as a portion of protoplasm. Whether it is on the leaf of a plant or at the bottom of a pool, there are external forces that surround it: light, heat, oxygen, the movement of water, and so forth. The various sides or parts of the undifferentiated mass are unevenly exposed to the surrounding forces. It is normal for any life form to be modified by its

---

[1] Herbert Spencer, *Essays*, vol. 2 (New York; Prentice-Hall, 1892).

[2] Herbert Spencer, *First Principles* (New York: Prentice-Hall, 1900).

environment, but because its parts are differentially affected, the change is not uniform.

Undifferentiated masses of people, Spencer continued, show the same proclivity as other masses. The directors of a company, for example, may initially start out as a homogeneous group with each possessing comparable authority. However, each also represents an outside constituency that exerts (external) pressure. This will eventually lead to inequalities. The influence of one member becomes greater than another, and a process of differentiation is set in motion within the group. As a logical extension of this thesis, Spencer contended that every society would have social classes. The initial homogeneity of any society must ultimately be destroyed by an externally induced "struggle for supremacy" that results in more pronounced forms of stratification.

Heterogeneity and Multiple Effects

A second principle, operating conjointly with the instability of the homogeneous is "the multiplication of effects." The initially uniform force which leads to differential changes becomes a multiform force, exerting multiple consequences. A small dose of virus, for example, will initially cause accelerated pulse, headache, and other symptoms not characteristic of a distinct illness. In the second stage it leads to itching, sore throat, and other symptoms that are less general, but still not diagnosable. In the third stage, however, it leads to symptoms of pneumonia, pleurisy, or the like. The effects themselves, in other words, become increasingly differentiated from each other.

The principle of multiple effects similarly leads societies toward an ever increasing heterogeneity. Suppose, Spencer suggests, that one member of a tribe becomes particularly adept at making weapons. His companions may try to induce him to make theirs too. With increasing practice, he becomes still more skilled while, from lack of practice, they become less skilled; hence, differentiation increases.

This is only the first of the effects, though. If others are to continue to induce him to make their weapons, they must offer something in return, Thus, trade or barter begins. However, the weapon maker will not always be willing to accept the same commodities in return. How many fish nets can he use? So, the others begin to make a variety of items for trade. In turn, they will differ in their ability to make fish nets, floor mats, or animal skins. Naturally, Spencer concludes, the weapon maker will take from each of the others that which they make best so specialization is again increased. Thus, the original cause has multiple effects, all of which lead to greater heterogeneity.

After the homogeneous becomes heterogeneous, and then still more heterogeneous, another of Spencer's principles states that there will be a segregation of the differentiated parts. Early in the autumn, for example, a strong wind will sometimes blow the brightly colored decaying leaves from the trees. The green ones remain firmly attached while the orange and yellow leaves collect together in piles. A uniform force, the wind, separated the living from the decaying leaves and placed each among its own kind. Correspondingly, Spencer concludes, the human races tend to differentiate themselves, and education, occupation, and the like also operate to establish stratum. People are moved toward others like themselves by feelings of "sympathy" which lead them to congregate together.

Spencer's Influence

By the 1930s Spencer's evolutionary theory was considered largely irrelevant by sociologists and other social scientists. (There was a resurgence of interest in the 1960s, but in substantially modified versions of his theories.) Talcott Parsons, for example, offered the pronouncement, "Spencer is dead."[3] He was, of course, referring to the man's impact. (Spencer had been dead since 1903.) Part of the sudden demise in Spencer's once great influence was due to the ease with which racist ideologies were able to utilize his principle of segregation. It seemed to suggest that racial integration was a violation of natural law and hence not desirable.

In addition, Durkheim (and others) criticized Spencer for failing to appreciate the distinctiveness of society, and thereby of sociology. Durkheim was correct, but his critique of Spencer was not balanced. In particular, he overlooked Spencer's long-range contribution to the study of society as *sui generis*; that is, as a separate and fundamental reality. For example, it was Spencer who introduced the term *superorganic* in order to differentiate between cultural and physical, or biological, qualities. This concept was later emphasized by Kroeber in an enduring theoretical distinction between the symbolic aspects of objects or actions and their organic features.[4]

Durkheim's own writings also indicate Spencer's influence. The organic-superorganic distinction, phrased in different terms, was an important part of Durkheim's theoretical position. In addition, Durkheim's work followed Spencer's in several distinctive ways. Both placed similar emphases on change as entailing a movement from simple to complex forms, the influence of population growth upon social organization, and the interrelationship between social structure and social function. Durkheim's writing, like Spencer's, was also replete with organic, or biological, metaphors and analogies. Yet, Durkheim was generally critical of Spencer's contribution because he regarded it as reductionistic; that is, as failing sufficiently to appreciate the essentially superorganic quality of social life.

DURKHEIM'S RULES

Durkheim insisted that society be viewed as a separate, external phenomenon. "Sui generis," it was a fundamental reality of its own kind that could not be reduced to concrete individuals or to organic substances. He conceded that the active elements of any society were individuals, but he insisted that the whole was both more than, and qualitatively different from, the sum of its parts.

[3]Talcott Parsons, *The Structure of Social Action* (New York: McGraw-Hill, 1937).

[4]A. L. Kroeber, "The Superorganic," *American Anthropologist,* 1917. See also the introduction by Robert L. Canniero, ed., in *Herbert Spencer* (Chicago: University of Chicago Press, 1967).

Durkheim maintained that society is the result of collective experiences which lead to collective representations; that is, ways of viewing the world which are widely shared within a society, but are distinctive to that society. For example, an abstraction like time cannot be conceived by individual minds except in relation to the units into which it is divided in the collective representations. Thus, time is meaningful to individuals in some societies only if it is thought of in terms of minutes or hours. In other societies, only the number of moons that pass is a meaningful conception. Regardless of how they are specifically conceived of, however, all such representations are coercive in the sense that they place constraints upon the way everyone thinks and feels.

Social Facts

The ways of thinking and acting which are relatively universal in a society constitute *social facts*. They persist from generation to generation and are transmitted either verbally or in writing. These relatively permanent expressions (that is, social facts) are illustrated by written laws, popular proverbs, standards of taste, and the like. As they are imparted, Durkheim realized that each person also "individualizes" the institutionalized ways of thinking and acting. There is a range of latitude of compliance so that each individual creates "his own morality, religion and mode of life . . . But, sooner or later . . . one encounters the limit that cannot be crossed."[5]

One reason for this uncrossable boundary is that the very ways in which people think—the alternatives which occur to them—are strongly molded by the collective representations from the time thought first begins. Further, even in those extreme cases where individuals band together in opposition to institutionalized forms, the new social facts they create by their interaction are still a synthesis of their separate thoughts. Thus, the result remains outside of each individual and "the result surpasses the individual as the whole the part."[6]

Durkheim supported his antireductionist argument with numerous analogies. To be a consistent reductionist, he argued, would require equating the human mind to living cells. It would deny the autonomy of mental processes. Further, life itself would have to be reduced to protoplasm since it contains nothing more. The whole, in each case, could not exist without the parts, Durkheim conceded; but in each case, the parts do not determine the whole. It is the relationships among the parts—whether cells, protoplasm, or individuals—that form the whole. Therefore, no part (for example, individuals) can be equated with the whole (for example, society).

Associated with his conception of society as a reality apart from individual consciousness, Durkheim presented a distinctive methodology. It entailed an ambitious paradigm for the "objective" study of social facts. Because no part is a perfect representation of the whole, subjective introspection was denied as the means by which a sociologist could ever understand society. While any individual's thoughts

---

[5]Emile Durkheim, *The Rules of Sociological Method* (Chicago: University of Chicago, 1938). See especially the preface to the second edition.

[6]Emile Durkheim, *Sociology and Philosophy* (New York: Free Press, 1953), p. 26.

and feelings are the results of decades of prior collective experiences, they are nevertheless incomplete and imperfect representations.

The focus of sociological research must be upon social facts rather than individual consciousness. However, because of individual variations in conformity to institutionalized patterns, Durkheim realized that it was sometimes difficult to isolate such social facts. He offered two interdependent defining characteristics: generality and external restraint. To be a social fact, a way of thinking or acting must be widely shared or pervasive. This indicates that the pattern or form lies outside of any individual and that it is, therefore, coercive. Sooner or later one reaches the boundary. Further, Durkheim reasoned, how could these ways of acting and thinking—which are parts of the external social reality—become a part of us "except by imposing themselves upon us?"

The institutionalized forms of thought and action have a supra-individual constitution of their very own, a distinct form or composition. The sociologist is therefore, like the physicist, exploring an "unknown realm" that is indicated by, but not synonymous with, individual expressions. For example, rates of birth, or marriage, or suicide are the collective results of individuals' actions. By taking averages, though, the distinctive qualities of each individual's contributions are "neutralized." Thus, the resultant average expresses the state of "the group mind" and it, unlike its individual components, is a social fact.

Then the sociologist is directed by Durkheim to interrelate these averages, in other words, to search for correlations among social facts. Because they are external to and greater than any individual, it logically follows that a social fact can only be explained by another social fact. An individual's despair, for example, may explain why that individual commits suicide. However, the social fact is a rate of suicide characterizing a social aggregate, and it must be explained by other social facts—such as economic downswings or rapid industrialization—rather than by an individual's motives or moods.

Explanation, for Durkheim, involved demonstrating causality by showing that one social fact varied consistently with another; for example, rates of suicide and the rapidity of social change. These relationships, he proposed, disclose the internal workings of the "mysterious social realm." After they are obtained, however, the relationships must be explained in functional terms; that is, according to their consequences in relation to some social end. Durkheim added this last requirement because of his view that social facts would ordinarily be "harmoniously" integrated with each other. (See Chapters Four and Ten.)

Some sociologists complain that Durkheim's method of interrelating social facts tends to leave out an emergent link that would complete the explanation and make it more meaningful. The notion of a *group mind* (which Durkheim presented, but did not fully describe), might resolve this problem. However, some theorists fear that emphasizing such a notion would create other problems that would be worse.[7]

---

[7]For further discussion see Peter A. Remender, "Social Facts and Symbolic Interaction," *The Wisconsin Sociologist,* Fall, 1973.

Social Facts and Internalization

In order to further clarify the nature of social facts, Durkheim compared them with individual habits. Both are alike, he stated, in that "they dominate us" and "impose practices upon us." However, social facts exert their influence from outside the individual while habits rule from within. Only habits belong to individuals. Social facts are part of a separate (social) realm.

This conception of the externality of social facts appears to be at variance with Durkheim's view of the collective conscience as composed of beliefs and ideas that are held in common. The notion of shared beliefs suggests that such beliefs are, in fact, parts of individuals even if their origin is external to individuals.

The confusion created by this seeming contradiction is due to the fact that Durkheim was trying to account for two different phenomena. First, he clearly observed that many values and ways of acting persisted from generation to generation, either within an entire society or within some distinct segment of a society. People are born and die, but patterns persist. Thus, he reasoned, these patterns appear to have a life of their own. Because they are not subject to the same rules of human mortality, they must lie outside of individuals. However, this conception of social facts raises the question of how it is that social facts influence people, Durkheim's second concern. While they can be viewed as "things," social facts are not tangible like fences or locks. Therefore, if they remain external, how can they act as coercive restraints?

The answer to this dilemma lies in the concept of internalization. If people incorporate social facts into their personal belief systems, then such facts can exert influence, just like any other personal standard. However, the internalized belief within any individual need not be equated with the social norm or value itself. The latter can persist as an external fact apart from individualized internalizations.

In the course of Durkheim's career, according to Parsons, he came to place more emphasis upon the role of internalization. In this regard a comparison of Durkheim and Freud is illuminating. Durkheim began with a conception of society apart from, and outside of, individual personalities. Gradually, Parsons notes, he recognized that the standards of society were incorporated into individuals. By contrast, Freud began with a conception of individual personality as a separate and autonomous phenomenon. Only later did he come to view it as entailing the interpenetration of society. Thus, despite fundamentally different points of origin, they converged.[8]

While Durkheim was prepared to accept the internalization of social facts into individual psyches, this did not mean that individual psyches, as such, were a proper subject matter for sociological study. Durkheim regarded each person as individualizing that which was common to all and, therefore, as an imperfect representation of the collectivity. Social facts, which were the proper subject matter, could be inferred only from group averages or collective rates.

Durkheim categorically rejected the possibility of personal motives ever serving as the explanation for a social fact. This disdain for motives stemmed from his general

---

[8]Talcott Parsons, "Durkheim's Contribution to the Theory of Integration of Social Systems," in *Essays on Sociology and Philosophy,* edited by Kurt H. Wolff (New York: Harper and Row, 1964).

insistence that the social and the psychological realms be differentiated from each other. In addition, Durkheim seemed to doubt the veracity of motives, especially if they were self-reported. He questioned whether people "really" knew why they acted as they did. According to Durkheim, people recognized social facts only dimly or not at all, but these social facts were the cause of all widespread patterns of behavior. For example, he noted that there may be as many stated reasons for commiting suicide as there are suicides. However, none of them necessarily reflects the social facts that account for the actual rate.

SOCIETY, PEOPLE, AND BEASTS

In separating social facts from individual thought or behavior, Durkheim staked a claim for an autonomous science of society. Given this separation, sociology could not be regarded as a "corollary" of psychology. Moreover, Durkheim's strict antireductionist position excluded the possibility that psychological or physiological principles could be invoked in sociological explanations.

Later generations of sociologists followed Durkheim's directives because they believed he was correct; that is, that he had outlined a fruitful paradigm—one that would produce insightful explanations of social phenomena. In addition, Durkheim's position also legitimated the relatively new science of society, putting it on an equal footing with other, more established, disciplines. This had to be a comforting thought around which early sociologists could easily rally. Thus, in part, it was a sign of the discipline's maturity when sociologists began to question aloud the strict boundaries Durkheim had proposed. There were always some skeptics, of course; but their voices began to grow louder in the 1960s and 1970s. One of the most influential statements of this kind was presented by George Casper Homans, in his presidential address to the American Sociological Association, entitled, "Bringing Men Back In."[9] The meaning of this title, in relation to Durkheim's position, should be apparent.

Homans on People

Homans's argument begins where the antireductionsts leave off, namely, with norms and roles. They are, he states, the minimum units of *distinctive* sociological analysis. However, Homans continues, how are norms and roles to be explained? Why do they exist and why do people play roles and conform to norms? It is, he answers, because of rewards and punishments. They are what people respond to, what keeps people in line, what determines the form and content of interaction.

To propose that people will select among the alternatives they perceive by choosing the one that seems most rewarding is not, Homans notes, a statement about

[9]George C. Homans, "Bringing Men Back In," *American Sociological Review,* 29 (1964).

society. Rather, it is a statement "about the behavior of individual men."[10] There is, therefore, no distinctively sociological theory. Explanation, Homans concludes, is provided by psychological propositions. Thus, we are all psychologists in disguise.

In order to illustrate his contention, Homans selected several examples of apparently sociological explanations and showed how they could be (and should be) reinterpreted. One such example was Smelser's analysis of changes in the British cotton industry between 1770 and 1840.[11] Smelser began this study with a general theory of social equilibrium in which technological innovations were analyzed in a larger societal context that emphasized the previously existing level of technology, labor force availability, and the like. However, Homans states, these sociological abstractions do not explain what happened in the British textile industry. What happened was that *men* perceived an opportunity to make profits if they utilized new, labor-saving machinery, and because the availability of such profits constituted a desirable outcome which they considered attainable, they introduced the new technology.

The actual explanation, Homans proposes, has little to do with the equilibrium of society. It is, by contrast, based upon principles of learning theory in psychology. It may be just "a little unfair," Homans concludes, to imply that Smelser's sociological (non-) explanation stemmed from his failure to recognize that "there were people around."[12] However, it is time to end our "intellectual hypocrisy" and "double-talk" and explicitly bring sociology into line with psychology.

Blau and Schwartz also point out that the increased reliance of sociological research upon sample surveys has encouraged an emphasis upon psychological processes. The data obtained from such surveys include individuals' attitudes, attributes and self-reported behaviors. The analyses of these data typically involve searching for inter-connections among these individual level variables. For example, it may be noted that people of high socioeconomic status (an attribute) tend to favor the Republican Party (an attitude). To explain such relationships almost necessarily requires that sociologists search for the psychological processes that connect the attributes and attitudes of individuals.[13]

Ten years after Homans's essays, Pierre L. van den Berghe decided to take a good idea one step further. If sociological theory would be enriched by "bringing men back in," then it would be further enriched by also admitting their biological predispositions. And so with a bow to his mentor, George Homans, van den Berghe proposed. "Bringing Beasts Back In."[14]

---

[10]Ibid., p. 814.

[11]Neil Smelser, *Social Change in the Industrial Revolution* (Chicago: University of Chicago Press, 1959).

[12]Homans, "Bringing Men Back In," p. 817.

[13]Peter M. Blau and Joseph E. Schwartz, *Crosscutting Social Circles* (Orlando: Academic Press, 1984).

[14]Pierre L. van den Berghe, "Bringing Beasts Back In," *American Sociological Review*, 39, (

van den Berghe on Beasts

The behavior of virtually every animal species, van den Berghe notes, is determined by biological predispositions, though it is modifiable by environmental conditions. Why assume there is a sharp discontinuity between human and nonhuman species in this regard? While humans may be unique in many respects, why not assume these species-unique qualities to be the result of an interaction between biogenetical and sociocultural forces? These are, of course, rhetorical questions. In order to show how explanation would be enhanced by broadening sociology's perspective, he specifically focuses upon human aggression.

Van den Berghe specifically begins from the premise that humans are the most aggressive species; that is, that they assault and kill *each other* more than do other species. (This definition of aggression excludes killing members of other species for food .) The most important general reason that aggression occurs within any species is competition for resources. That competition is generally regulated either by territoriality—which assigns members exclusive access to the resources of a particular place—and/or by social hierarchies which rank members' order of access to resources. However, while territoriality and hierarchy regulate conflict, the physical and social orders they establish require constant defense against encroachment. Humans are the most aggressive species, van den Berghe contends, because their social hierarchies (that is, stratification systems) and their sense of territoriality are the most developed of any species.

All three of the major variables in this scheme—hierarchy, territorialty, and aggression—are regarded as having a biogenetic basis. Thus, while there is cross-cultural variation in the form of stratification, in the conditions which evoke violent responses, and the like, these features invariably characterize human communities because they are parts of the genetic endowment of the species. The great magnitude of these variations is a tribute to the modifying influence of culture. However, in van den Berghe's view, our cultural capability has tended to make our biological adjustments even more maladaptive. Specifically, biological predispositions have interacted with cultural conditioning, and their combined effect has been "pathologies," such as an elaboration of hierarchy resulting in obsessive status concerns and effective weapons that multiply the destructive effects of innate aggressiveness.

For sociology, van den Berghe's message is clear: The superorganic quality of social life cannot be ignored, but neither can the biological. It is necessary to develop theories which are sensitive to the causal consequences of the interaction between social and biological forces. Few sociologists have been persuaded, though. To most, sociobiology (searching for the genetic foundations of social behavior) entails not only a reduction, but a subordination, of sociocultural concerns.[15]

---

[15]For further discussion, see James Silverberg, "Sociobiology, the New Synthesis? An Anthropologist's Perspective," in George W. Barlow and James Silverberg (Ed), *Sociobiology: Beyond Nature/Nurture?* (Boulder: Westview, 1980).

WHAT IS THE QUESTION?

Homans's (psychological) and van den Berghe's (genetic) arguments pivot about the issue of what is important for sociology to explain. If humans are innately the most aggressive species, should that aggressive predisposition be considered sociologically significant? Alternatively, should sociologists be more interested in the structural and cultural conditions under which expressions of aggression vary?

In the latter case, biological influences are not denied, It is, in fact, absurd to deny that people have genetically determined species-specific attributes: upright movement, opposable thumbs, capacities for abstract thought, and so on. Moreover, these features of our biological endowment make a difference. Without the distinctive human hand, for example, people could not make pottery, shoot bows and arrows, or write with a pencil. Lacking these developments, human societies would be very different.

Similarly, people have a psychological makeup that is also undeniable. When they are frustrated, for example, most people will eventually strike out in anger, either at the source of their frustration or at a convenient scapegoat. These psychological predispositions also make a difference. In most societies there are few people saintly enough to act kindly toward a person whom they feel has deliberately hurt them.

Thus, even the most extreme sociological perspective cannot reject the existence of psychological or genetic predispositions. They can, however, be considered either unimportant or irrelevant to "appropriately" formulated sociological questions. Importance and relevance are, of course, separable considerations. However, they tend to be very highly related, in fact. It is difficult to admit that some factor exerts an important influence without simultaneously regarding it as relevant. It is far easier to disregard that which seems not to matter much anyway.

Sociologists following Durkheim have been able to disregard genetic factors in particular because the basic questions they have formulated are ones to which genetic factors make little, or no, difference. For example, if the question is what accounts for differing birth rates among societies, genetic factors are virtually eliminated from consideration. A constant (genetic endowments) can not explain a variable (different rates). It is true that procreation ultimately rests on a biological sex drive, but rates of birth vary mostly as a result of sexual norms, marital arrangements, and the efficacy of contraceptive devices. If the question were why is a given couple childless, then biological considerations could not as easily be ignored. That is a very different question, though.

The problem with van den Berghe's thesis is that it cannot account for variations, such as birth rates, which from Durkheim's perspective are the focal points of sociological analysis. To further illustrate, in Chapter Two we discussed Margaret Mead's field work in New Guinea from which she described extensive intersocietal differences in people's aggressiveness. These differences defy genetic explanation. Both the prevalence and the form of aggression seem to be socially patterned. Perhaps because of our species-specific endowment, every society will have to contend with the potential aggressiveness of its "members." Such genetic factors may account for the near universality of certain institutions. However, the sociological problem, as formulated from a Durkheimian position, is to explain the form of these institutions and their relationship to other institutions. Thus, genetic factors provide the parameters of the human condition without explaining how or why societies differ from each other.

The above conclusion parallels the classic debate of 60 years ago between Malinowski and Radcliffe-Brown. Arguing against Durkheim's position, Malinowski contended that biologically determined drives set the limits on the variability of a culture or society. Every social organization must make provisions for these drives, assuring the existence of some "adapting" institution.[16] The core of their disagreement was expressed in a debate about magic and religion. Malinowski observed that Trobriand Islanders' open-sea fishing was accompanied by a great deal of ritual. As the boats moved further from the shore, Trobriand fishermen increasingly utilized charms and amulets. When they fished at the inner lagoons, however, there was no comparable use of magic. The two types of fishing differed, Malinowski contended, in the degrees of danger and uncertainty that were involved. Open-sea ventures were more precarious and the likelihood of success was more problematic. Given the people's ignorance of the efficacy of magic, Malinowski viewed the Trobrianders as resorting to supernatural practices in response to their feelings of danger and uncertainty. Note that this interpretation is perfectly consistent with Malinowski's general view of social institutions as a functional response to individual needs.

Radcliffe-Brown, as might be anticipated, preferred a different explanation. Moving back a step, he insisted that it was society that defines the uncertainties in life and dictates the appropriate response; whether religious supplication, magical invocation, or the like. In effect, society would not be possible unless people learned what to feel, and when and how to express their feelings. Births and deaths, for example, are significant events for a *society,* entailing the entrance and exit of its "members." This would be true for society, regardless of individual sentiments pertaining to births and deaths. In order for individuals to be linked together, however, they must be taught to have the appropriate feelings. This is viewed by Radcliffe-Brown as the "essential function and ultimate reason" for the existence of magic or religion. These rites, he states, "exist and persist because they are part of the mechanism by which an orderly society maintains itself in existence, serving as they do to establish certain fundamental social values."[17]

Even those drives whose origins may be genetic are totally shaped within a society, he argued. People are taught what feelings are appropriate and when and how to express them. These learned and shared patterns, which are distinctive in each society, are the mechanisms by which a social order is maintained. The focus must

---

[16]Bronislaw Malinowski, *Sex and Repression in Savage Society* (New York: Harcourt Brace Jovanovich, 1927).

[17]A. R. Radcliffe-Brown, "Taboo," in *Structure and Function in Primitive Society* (New York: Free Press, 1955), p. 152.

be upon explanations of the (genetically autonomous) social patterns that provide the basic structure of a society. Thus, both Radcliffe-Brown and Durkheim rejected the idea that individual needs had an autonomy capable of determining the nature of social institutions.

It is easier, conceptually, to relegate genetic than rather psychological factors to a peripheral position in sociology. Every social pattern, every rate, is dependent ultimately upon the behavior of individuals. Is it possible, or reasonable, to exclude psychological principles from the explanatory chain as Durkheim suggests? For example, if a change in sex norms (indicated by a group average, hence a social fact) can be shown to affect birth rates (also a social fact), can the relationship be meaningfully interpreted without considering the intervening processes by which individuals respond and adjust? Homans's point is more specific, namely, that a relationship among social facts presupposes a relationship among psychological variables. Stated conversely, there will be no social uniformities unless there are psychological uniformities.

From Homans's position, it logically follows that sociological theories must incorporate, or build upon, psychological theories. It is the latter that specify the mechanisms or processes that explain why a relationship between social facts is attained. Thus, sociology cannot stray very far from its psychological underpinning, and Durkheim's disdain for psychology (as an integral part of sociology) must be viewed as misguided.

Homans's perspective has been most conspicuously pursued by social psychologists, within both psychology and sociology. Especially in controlled laboratory experiments, they have attempted to interrelate personality and social interaction, to identify the psychological bases of social behavior. (Examples of such studies are presented in the discussion of Homans in Chapter Eight.) During the 1960s, a psychologist named Kenneth Gergen made some notable contributions to this type of social psychology. In the 1970s, however, he had some misgivings about the enterprise. Some of his concerns far transcend the issues before us, but some of them are very instructive with regard to the consequences of following Homans's rather than Durkheim's position.

Gergen's Lament[18]

It was the ability of the natural sciences to develop general principles that led social scientists to apply similar methods to the study of human behavior. However, Gergen notes, there may be some marked differences in the fundamental nature of these two realms. In particular, the events or actions to be explained may be more stable in the world of nature. The velocity of falling bodies, for example, can be demonstrated in any laboratory, now or in 100 years. If not for the repeatability of such phenomena, what we term natural science would actually be natural *history*.

---

[18]The following discussion is based upon Kenneth J. Gergen, "Social Psychology as History," *Journal of Personality and Social Psychology*, 26 (1973), and Kenneth J. Gergen, *Toward Transformation in Social Knowledge* (New York: Springer-Verlag, 1982).

The experimenters who have examined personality in relation to social interaction have assumed that there would be comparably enduring patterns, but their research results have often suggested an absence of such stability. To illustrate, Gergen reviewed a number of studies conducted during the 1960s that utilized personality characteristics to predict political activism (joining in marches, demonstrations, and the like). It is their inconsistent findings that stand out. From the early stages of the Vietnam War through its ultimate conclusion, the personal characteristics associated with political activism changed. There was a consistent increase in the amount of political activism (a social fact); but no consistency to the qualities that accounted for individual differences. (This finding is reminiscent of Durkheim's admonition that motives for suicide could be as varied as the number of suicides, and hence, were not to be trusted.)

As a remedy for problems of this type, Gergen proposes that social psychologists place more emphasis upon "psychological dispositions" that are enduring. To test their persistence, relationships must be examined cross-culturally and/or across different historical periods. (This was, of course, Durkheim's strategy as well, but Gergen advocates a more impressionistic and qualitative analysis than Durkheim followed.) Useful theories will then emerge, Gergen claims, if the psychological characteristics of individuals are systematically related to larger historical and institutional contexts. "Psychology alone," he concludes, "provides a distorted understanding of our present condition."[19]

Following Gergen's reasoning, it does not at all follow that sociological theory is erected upon psychological principles; in fact, quite the reverse is suggested. However, it is probably not fruitful to argue for the primacy of either one and Durkheim, it should be recalled, did not. Rather, he urged a vision of sociological theory which, like its subject matter (that is, society), was "a thing apart".

CONCLUSION

At the very least, Durkheim's "rules" sensitize sociologists to be careful about their levels of analysis. There will inevitably be interstitial areas where questions about the individual and the aggregate merge into social psychology. However, these units of analysis do not overlap entirely, and those relationships which are found at the aggregate level may have no counterpart at the individual level, and vice versa.

The classic example of such differences across units of analysis is illustrated by the "ecological fallacy." One of the first demonstrations of this fallacy was presented by Robinson in an analysis of census reports. Looking first at geographical areas, he reported a negative relationship between the percentage of residents who were foreign born and the proportion who were illiterate. Those areas with larger numbers of foreign born in 1940 had lower rates of illiteracy. These social facts were characteristic at the aggregate level of analysis. However, when Robinson proceeded to

---

[19]Ibid., p. 319.

examine the same variables at the individual level, he obtained a positive relationship; that is, persons who were foreign born were *more* likely to be illiterate.[20]

If a sociologist were to have attempted a reductionistic explanation for the aggregate-level relationship, it would almost certainly have entailed erroneous inferences. Geographical areas that had large numbers of foreign-born persons in 1940 were located disproportionately in the Northeast and they had lower rates of illiteracy than in the South, for example. This relationship was not due to a tendency for foreign-born persons to be literate; in fact, the reverse was true. Therefore, aggregate level patterns—social facts—need not rest upon congruent individual-level patterns. This is not meant to imply that relationships which hold for aggregates will necessarily not hold for individuals, or vice versa. It is sometimes possible to infer correctly across these levels.[21] Because we do not know the conditions under which it is safe to infer across levels, however, it is prudent to be timid in making such inferences.

SUGGESTIONS FOR ADDITIONAL READING

JAMES S. COLEMAN, *Individual Interests and Collective Action*, Cambridge: Cambridge University Press, 1986.
S. N. EISENSTADT and H. J. HELLE (Eds), *Macro-Sociological Theory*, Vol. 1, Beverly Hills: Sage, 1985.
DAVID H. GILMORE, *Aggression and Community*, New Haven: Yale University Press, 1987.

[20]W. S. Robinson, "Ecological Correlations and the Behavior of Individuals," *American Sociological Review*, 15 (1950).

[21]Walter S. Gove and Michael Hughes, "Reexamining the Ecological Fallacy," *Social Forces*, 58, 1980.

13

Theory in a Neutral Science
Weber, Merton, and Others

Scientific sociology is erected on the premise that the social world is orderly; that social life—like the natural realm—is patterned, and hence, amenable to generalization and prediction. Since the preceding assumption of scientific sociology was stated over 125 years ago by the French positivists, it has not often been rejected. However, there have been substantial disagreements among theorists and methodologists concerning how to go about identifying social patterns; that is, how to develop a science of society. Almost all of the specific issues have important implications for the nature of sociological theory: its form, its range, and the ease with which its basic concepts must be measurable.

In this chapter we begin with an examination of the positivists and the view of modern sociology that they espoused. We will note that the specific issues that subsequently arose typically entailed disagreements over the degree to which sociology can be viewed as precisely emulating the natural sciences. This chapter concludes with an examination of the value-free position and the question of whether a "neutral" sociology is either possible or desirable.

POSITIVISM (COMTE)

The man most frequently cited as the "father" of modern sociology is the French scholar, Auguste Comte. Beginning around 1830, he presented a positivistic philosophy which outlined the form and nature of sociology as a contemporary science. In order to understand Comte's view, positivism is the key term. As he employed it, positivism had two distinct meanings: precise, certain and true, on the one hand; beneficial or useful, on the other hand.

Comte described the emergence of specific scientific disciplines as following a cumulative pattern of building upon each other. He described this evolutionary process as beginning with astronomy, followed by various physical and biological sciences, and culminating with sociology. Each of these sciences showed a portion of the universe—that related to their own area of specialization—to be governed by natural laws. Each science also contributed to the development of a systematic methodology by which these laws could be observed or inferred. By the time modern sociology emerged, it was clear that all phenomena, including social phenomena, were subjected to "invariable natural laws."[1] Thus, because of its relatively late arrival on the scientific scene, sociology did not have to contend with uncertain philosophies. (The intellectual battles had already been won.)

For Comte, the certain and precise knowledge that sociology was expected to yield would not merely satisfy people's idle curiosity. It would be put to immediate and important use in establishing a new social order. Comte viewed France, and Europe more generally, as betwixt and between, in a shambles. Industrialization had not yet generated stable patterns to replace feudalism, and it was difficult to foresee how the chaos would end. The emergence of a precise science of society was therefore very welcome. The new science, sociology, would be used to establish a new social order based upon reason and people's concern for each other. Thus, sociology was positivistic, both in the certainty of its formulations and in its usefulness to humanity. This latter theme in Comte's work was associated with the actual formation of secular religious groups, an activity which led to Comte's disrepute in French academic circles.[2]

A highly similar positivistic view of sociology was introduced to American sociology by Lester F. Ward. His view of sociology, like Comte's, emphasized an evolutionary development of scientific disciplines in which sociology was perched on top of the "subordinate sciences." Ward also echoed Comte's assumptions that precise social laws could be discovered and that they must be usefully applied to the betterment of humanity.[3]

For many of the pioneering sociologists, the analogies between the natural and social orders were so pronounced that they mandated sociology's adoption of the assumptions and methods of the already-established natural sciences. However, everyone did not fully agree with this contention, then or now. Weber, for example, regarded the meaning of behavior as constituting an intrinsic and profound difference between the natural and the social sciences. To illustrate, a biologist can explain the behavior of a molecule without concern for the point of view of the molecule. Its patterns of behavior can be described by an aloof observer. By contrast, according to Weber, adequate explanation of human behavior requires that the meaning attributed to the behavior by the actor be taken into account. An explanation which describes

---

[1] Auguste Comte, *The Positive Philosophy* vol. 2, trans. by Harriet Martineau (New York: Prentice-Hall, 1854).

[2] For further discussion, see George Simpson, *Auguste Comte* (New York: Crowell, 1969).

[3] Lester F. Ward, *Outline of Sociology* (New York: Macmillan, 1898).

overt behavior without regard to its subjective meanings is necessarily inadequate. Thus, Weber argued that while a generalizing science of society was possible, he did not regard its form as identical to that of the natural sciences.[4] It will be instructive at this point to examine in greater detail what Weber meant by scientific generalizations and how they relate to the disclosure of patterns.

WEBER ON CONCEPTS AND PATTERNS

To be scientific is highly valued. The social sciences make claim to the status in their very name; but the name alone does not make it so, as illustrated by library science, a discipline that is rarely considered to be a science, in fact. However, there is disagreement over the precise qualities that distinguish between scientific and nonscientific disciplines because those features which seem to be characteristic of sciences are also found, in varying degrees, among nonsciences.[5] For example, an organized body of knowledge is one such characteristic, but it describes history as well as biology; qualification is another characteristic, but it is employed in recipes for baking cakes as well as in physics.

In order to differentiate between sciences and nonsciences it is helpful to begin by looking at objectives. Specifically, sciences are committed to prediction, and their capacity to predict is an important criterion by which they are judged. (There are, of course, certain methodological considerations as well, but they are not germane.) To predict any behavior, event, or the like, the phenomenon in question must be examined in such a way that patterns can either be directly observed or else inferred from other observations. For example, the Russian Revolution of 1917 was a unique, and therefore unpatterned, event. It obviously cannot reoccur and so cannot be predicted. However, that Russian Revolution may share some features in common with the French Revolution of 1789, the American Revolution of 1776, and so on. If it is possible to identify features common to each of the specific revolutions, it may be possible to disclose a pattern according to which future revolutions could be predicted.

As illustrated in the above example, the identification of patterns frequently requires that specific events, behaviors, or "things" be examined as manifestations of more general and abstract phenomena. This requires the formulation of (general) concepts. Throughout preceding chapters we have discussed many examples of this process in sociology. For example, each prison is a unique organization in some concrete respects; but there are similarities among most prisons, and between prisons and mental hospitals, prisons and military bases, and so on. Concepts such as *bureaucracy* or *total institution* are based upon these similarities, but in turn, these concepts also help to make the similarities more apparent. Thus, there is a strong

---

[4]See especially Weber's discussion of the differences between scientific sociology and history in Max Weber, *The Theory of Social and Economic Organization* (New York: Oxford, 1947).

[5]For a discussion of the ideologies which help to set the boundaries between science and nonscience, and the material advantages associated with the distinction, see Thomas F. Gieryn, "Boundary—Work and the Demarcation of Science from Nonscience," *American Sociological Review*, 48, 1983.

connection between the identification of pervasive patterns and the development of general concepts.

Concepts, and the patterns associated with them, both involve some modification of concrete cases. Once a concept is superimposed over an event or behavior, it alters the way the phenomenon is perceived. For example, it becomes difficult to identify the nuances which may distinguish a prison when that prison is being viewed as a manifestation of a more abstract and inclusive category, such as a total institution. At the same time, the concept of total institution sensitizes one to look for certain characteristics in any particular prison that might otherwise be overlooked. As Weber noted, when the specific is regarded as a manifestation of the general, it simultaneously clarifies and distorts the specific phenomenon.

The "reality" of scientific generalizations and the patterns they help to identify have historically provided the subject matter for a great deal of scrutiny. An extremely witty and penetrating argument was put forward at the turn of this century by the English writer, Gilbert K. Chesterton. His main point was that the patterns described by all of the sciences are more fantastic, and less real, than fairy tales.[6]

One of Chesterton's main criticisms was directed at the inclination of scientists to observe an association between events and assume there *must* be a lawlike relationship between them. However, Chesterton insisted, anything the mind can imagine is possible. Apples may typically fall to the ground rather than fly through the air, but that does not mean that apples must fall, as Newton claimed. If a witch advises, "Blow the horn and the ogre's castle will fall," she is too wise to assume, like scientists, that there is any necessary connection between the two events, even though she may have seen many castles fall after horns were blown.

Given a world in which anything can happen, Chesterton contended that magic is as good an explanation for why things happen as any scientific law. If a body of water runs down hill it is because it is bewitched; if a blossom bears fruit it is because it is growing on a magic tree. Because there are no unalterable laws, we might as well consider everything that happens to be a miracle.

Chesterton obviously took a very extreme position. Few of us are prepared to argue that each event in life in an unpatterned miracle, to reject the idea of scientific laws in favor of the maxims of fairyland. And yet, it is useful to consider Chesterton's argument now and again because it reminds us that the entire enterprise of scientific sociology rests upon an assumption, namely, that the social order is orderly and that its patterns are discernible.

Sociology has, of course, proceeded on this assumption, and it has entailed an explicit emulation of the natural sciences. The major contentions are over whether this emulation should be complete or whether, at some point, social sciences (including sociology) must forge a different path because of differences in their subject matter. Two of the specific issues involved have immediate implications for sociological theory; specifically, they include the proper form of theory and the ease with which its concepts must be measurable (that is, operationalized).

[6]Gilbert K. Chesterton, *Orthodoxy* (New York: Dodd, Mead, 1908).

FORMAL THEORY AND OPERATIONALISM

Throughout most of this book we have treated the notion of theory very loosely. It has sometimes been roughly equated with a general view of some phenomenon (e.g., bureaucracy). In many other instances we have equated theory with what may more properly be termed a *perspective,* an *orienting strategy,* or a *paradigm.*[7] (Functionalism is a good example.) These perspectives, in many people's opinion, should be called *metatheories* rather than theories because they emphasize what a theory should look like. That is, they note the concepts and the interrelations among concepts that a theory should include when a theory is being developed. Perhaps the most important difference between a metatheory and a theory is in its form, or internal structure.

In a science, the preferred form of theory is called *formal.* A formal theory contains a set of logically interrelated statements. These statements present empirically testable assertions about the properties of some general phenomenon. Several aspects of this definition warrant further attention. Specifically, the testable statements are essentially hypotheses, that is, expectations (reasonable guesses) about the relationship between variables. A variable is a concept that is capable of exhibiting a range of values. A group, for example, is a general concept, but not a variable because it includes no characteristic capable of occurring in varying amounts or degrees. The size of a group, by contrast, is both a concept and a variable because it can assume different values. The size of a group could be related to another variable, such as its degree of prestige. The relationship between size and prestige could be empirically tested and combined with other, logically interrelated statements of relationships to form a general theory. Statements of definition ("a group is . . . ") may be necessary, but strictly speaking, they are not part of a formal theory.

The above examples were deliberately selected to illustrate an important difference between variables, namely, the ease with which they can be measured, or the degree to which the concept implies measurement procedures. The size of a group and the prestige of a group obviously differ in this regard. Group size is more directly quantifiable than prestige, and propositions which contain such variables can more easily be empirically tested.

Everyone agrees that any discipline with scientific pretensions ought to construct testable theories. This ultimately requires the formulation of measurable variables. Those concepts which seem to defy measurement are correspondingly of less value. So far, so good; but dissensus soon appears over where to "draw the line" and whether a line should be drawn at all. Differences arise over the issue of whether unmeasured (or unmeasurable) concepts are completely worthless. There is also the related issue of whether a variable, as measured, encompasses the totality of a concept. Should the concept of occupational prestige, for example, be equated

---

[7]For further discussion, see George Ritzer, *Sociology: A Multiple Paradigm Science* (Boston: Allyn & Bacon, 1980).

with any particular scale that measures the standing of occupations? These issues in sociology have historically been contested about the notion of operationalism.

Operationalism

A strict operationalist position was perhaps most influentially espoused in sociology by George Lundberg. He argued that, in the natural sciences, operational measures define subject matter. Thus, "space *is* that which is measured by a ruler; time *is* that which is measured by a clock."[8] Lundberg was correspondingly impatient with those who insisted upon detailed examination of a phenomenon, in the abstract, prior to measurement. Furthermore he rejected the argument that the social sciences were intrinsically different from the natural sciences, especially in terms of demands for operationalization.

Lundberg illustrated his contention that operationalization was equally feasible (and necessary) in the social sciences by examining the seemingly "messy" notion of values. What are values, he began; how do we know what a person values? The answer is we infer values from people's behavior. If through their actions people try to obtain more of something (like wealth or prestige), it is because they value it. Thus, "values are empirically observable."[9] Note, Lundberg did not argue that values are *indicated* by people's behavior any more than he argued that clocks indicated time. Values themselves are observable in people's behavior, according to Lundberg, and it is this view that has produced the most extensive criticism.

Disagreement with the operationalist viewpoint stresses how concepts are "translated" into operational indicators. According to Lazarsfeld, such translations involve four steps. They are:[10]

1) Imagery—the investigator begins with a vague concept. Mere words are not quite adequate to define the intuitive notions that are involved; hence, the term imagery.

2) Concept specification—the initial image is divided into components, or dimensions, which are more thoroughly defined, but still unmeasured.

3) Selection of indicators—measures are devised for each dimension. Each selected indicator is understood to stand only in a probabilistic relationship to the concept. (For example, accelerated pulse, coughing, or nail biting could each be viewed as a probabilistic indicator of anxiety.)

4) Formulation of indices—from the observed relationships among indicators, some are selected and combined into an operational measure of the initial concept. (Thus, if accelerated pulse and nail biting were found to be highly interrelated, they might be the basis of a combined index of anxiety.)

[8]George Lundberg, "The Thoughtways of Contemporary Sociology," *American Sociological Review*, 1 (1936), p. 711.

[9]George Lundberg, *Can Science Save Us?* (New York: D. McKay, 1947), p. 27.

[10]Paul F. Lazarsfeld, "Concept Formation and Measurement in the Behavioral Sciences," in *Concepts, Theory, and Explanation in the Behavioral Sciences*, edited by Gordon J. DiRenzo (New York: Random House, 1966). For further discussion of Lazarsfeld's approach and his influence, see Robert K. Merton, James S. Coleman and Peter H. Rossi (Eds), *Qualitative and Quantitative Social Research* (New York: Free Press, 1979).

Lazarsfeld's entire process is illustrated in the diagram below.

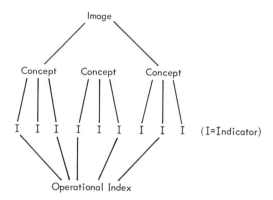

The most important feature of Lazarsfeld's scheme is that the operational index, or measure, is not equated with either the initial imagery or the derived concept. In sharp contrast to Lundberg's strict operationalism, Lazarsfeld states that even the best index is only a manifestation of the underlying concept and that there will always tend to be an image residue; that is, some aspects of the concept that are not adequately reflected in any operationalization. Most sociologists, circa 1990, tend to agree with Lazarsfeld's view and emphasize a probable relationship between concepts and operationalizations, rather than their literal equation. Strict operationalism, such as that advocated by Lundberg, simply entails costs that are not offset elsewhere by any advantages. Specifically, if concepts are equated with indicators, it is more difficult to construct theories with greater levels of generality and to bridge substantive problems by deriving corollaries from general theories. In short, some of the advantages of formal theory are lost with a strict operational approach.

On the other hand, operationalists such as Lundberg made an important point, especially if they are viewed in the context of sociological theory of fifty years ago. It was dominated by Parsons whose theory was extremely abstract and general, but extremely "loose" in a formal sense. Parsons was virtually unconcerned with operationalizing concepts, for example, and many sociologists wondered whether concepts as abstract as his could, in fact, ever be measured.

THE MIDDLE RANGE

Parsons's theory, which was the dominant model of theory in sociology, was as global as he could make it. He attempted to synthesize highly diverse perspectives into an all-inclusive theory of action. Specifically, Parsons saw lines of theoretical convergence among, "anthropological studies of culture, the theory of learning, the psychoanalytic theory of personality, economic theory, and the study of modern social structure"; and he thought they could be combined into a single coherent theory that would account for the motivations, orientations, and cultural goals, "of an individual actor or of a collectivity of actors."[11] It is difficult to imagine a more ambitious objective. Needless to say, any such effort would have to be formulated in extremely abstract terms.

The level of generality, combined with Parsons's clumsy writing style, drove many sociologists to the brink of despair. C. Wright Mills even "translated" portions of Parsons's writing into "straightforward English." Mills contended that he could translate the 555 pages of one of Parsons's books into about 150 pages, just by clearly presenting the basic ideas.[12] However, Mills recognized that some insights would be lost in such a translation, and he thought that "grand theory"—such as Parsons's—did contain numerous insights. In addition, Mills looked with trepidation at the then main alternative, the mathematical and methodologically oriented sociologists (including the strict operationalists) whose work he considered trivial. For them, he stated, the sheer availability of a relevant research method determines which issues or problems they choose to study.

Robert Merton similarly responded to the extreme alternatives. He viewed efforts to develop grand theory as great in challenge but small in promise; in other words, laudable, but not likely to be successful. At the same time, like Mills, he had little regard for the "minor hypotheses" which were routinely tested by the formal methodologists of the day. Their contributions may have been elegant in form, but they lacked significance. *The* problem, to Merton, was how to build the continuity that characterized the growth of theory in the physical sciences into sociology. Neither grand theory nor "abstracted empiricism" seemed to offer much promise.[13]

Merton, like Mills, advocated an approach that would combine the best features of the two extreme alternatives and still be realistic. He termed the kind of theory he sought, "middle range," and his vision in this regard greatly influenced subsequent developments in sociological theory. The concepts that would ideally be involved in middle-range theory would, unlike grand theory, be concrete enough to permit the construction of operational indicators. This would permit the contentions of middle-range theory to be subject to empirical assessment. However, unlike abstracted empiricism, the research would include operational indicators that could be related to concepts of general sociological significance. Thus, research and theory would interface, resulting in the long-term and interconnected growth of both.

Merton was particularly sensitive to the ways in which theory and research mutually influenced each other in science and to the fact that comparable interaction between them was not occurring in sociology. In the classical deductive model, hypotheses for investigation are derived from theory. Little of this was happening

---

[11]Talcott Parsons and others, *Toward a General Theory of Action* (New York: Harper and Row, 1962) p. 4. (Originally published in 1951.)

[12]C. Wright Mills, *The Sociological Imagination* (New York: Oxford, 1959).

[13]Robert A. Merton, "The Position of Sociological Theory," *American Sociological Review*, 13 (1948). See also, *On the Shoulders of Giants* (New York: Free Press, 1965).

in sociology because the philosophical discourses of grand theory did not contain empirical implications and hence did not encourage the derivation of hypotheses. However, Merton also noted that this classical sequence is often reversed in practice. In other words, unanticipated and perplexing research findings serve as a spur to the development of theories, but this "serendipity" occurs only when the unexpected findings are strategic, in the sense that they have important implications. The possibility of theoretical implications is virtually precluded when empirical research involves strictly operationalized, but theoretically meaningless, variables.[14]

The growth of scientific sociology, Merton concluded, depends upon sociologists' emphasis upon middle-range theories. In prescribing this strategy, Merton explicitly assumed that sociology could, and should, emulate the already-established natural sciences. Despite obvious differences in the nature of its subject matter, sociology could, and should, walk the same path.

How Theories Grow

Merton and others thought that a more intense interplay between theory and research would provide the seedbed in which theory would grow. Generally left unspecified, however, were answers to the question of *how* theories grow. More recently, Wagner and Berger have pointed to three such ways in which theory can grow:[15]

1) *By elaboration*—as a result of research which examines an established theory, a new theory is developed that is more comprehensive or more precise than the older one. For example, tests of the functional theory of stratification (see Chapter Six) indicated that the rewards of a position were more dependent upon the scarcity of qualified personnel than upon the position's functional contribution.

2) *By proliferation*—theories which were developed to apply in one realm or problem area are applied, in research, to different domains. For example, in Chapter Five we noted how a population ecology perspective that was originally applied only to individuals was more recently utilized to explain the rates with which new organizations were founded.

3) *By competition*—a new theory is presented which promises to explain some phenomena better than an established theory. The competing claims would ideally be examined by research which compares the accuracy of the predictions derived from each theory. For example, Homans (as discussed in Chapter Nine) has claimed that behavioral principles provide better explanations for change than do concepts linked to social structure.

When Merton first presented his essays on the ideal interplay between theory and research in the 1940s, they were in largely separate realms within sociology. The kinds of growth explicated by Wagner and Berger could not occur. Fortunately,

---

[14]See the essays by Merton on the bearings of theory for research, and vice versa, in *Social Theory and Social Structure* (New York: Free Press, 1956).

[15]David G. Wagner and Joseph Berger, "Do Sociological Theories Grow?" *American Journal of Sociology*, 90, 1985.

however, the kinds of developments Merton called for seemed to have occurred (though one could always wish for more). One indication of the ensuing pattern is provided by a study reported by Wells and Picou. They examined a sample of over 700 articles in the *American Sociological Review* that were published between the middle of the 1930s and the end of the 1970s.[16]

From the earliest to the latest time period in their study, they found that approximately twice as many of the articles were theory based. Further, and more relevant, they noted an even larger increase in the number of articles that tested theoretically derived hypotheses. In the final fifteen years of their study period, over one-half of all the sampled articles relied upon theory to develop hypotheses which were then tested.

NEUTRALITY

The growth of formal theory in sociology has been most vigorously pursued by sociologists trying to emulate the natural science model. As we have seen, the appropriateness of a natural science model depends upon a number of assumptions. In addition, there is the potential problem created by the fact that sociologists may have feelings about the things that they study such as religion, politics, family, and so on. Biologists and physicists typically differ in this regard. Can sociologists still maintain the same degree of detached indifference?

Those sociologists, like the strict operationalists, who emphatically endorsed the natural science model felt that the answer was unproblematical. Those who doubted were dismissed as confused. Lundberg, for example, conceded that sociologists, as citizens, had feelings about the things that they studied. As citizens they are entitled, perhaps even obligated, to pursue their preferences in the public arena. However, Lundberg states, their preferences and their research are associated with different roles. Thus, they do not have to affect each other, and they should not. The chemists' scientific analysis of certain gases is not influenced by the same chemist-as-citizen's desire to see these gases banned from use even in wartime.

The only danger to sociology, Lundberg concludes, is self-inflicted; that is, if sociologists permit their values to corrupt their scientific work. They can rise above such immoral actions by recognizing that the scientific process in which they are engaged is, itself, nonmoral and non-evaluative. If they will behave like unconcerned scientists, they will ultimately develop laws that will contribute to the alleviation of social problems. However, they must not try to short-circuit the process by bringing their values to bear on their research.[17]

[16]Richard H. Wells and Steven J. Picou, *American Sociology* (Washington, D.C.: University Press of America, 1981).

[17]"There is nothing in scientific work, as such, which dictates to what ends the products of science shall be used." Lundberg, *Can Science Save Us?*, p. 26.

In an ideal world, Lundberg's assertions might be persuasive. In the real world, however, I am not so sure. Does it absolve the scientist of all moral responsibility? Consider the dilemma faced by Steven Taylor, a sociologist conducting research in an institution for mentally retarded adults. In return for letting him observe there, institutional officials made him promise to maintain confidentiality and not to interfere with institutional activities in any way. This is a standard research bargain. Unfortunately, though, he soon discovered that attendants—who were his major informants—were deliberately abusing the residents, making them swallow burning cigarettes, smear feces on themselves, and so on. "What should you do," Taylor asks, "when . . . the people with whom you have worked hard to establish rapport, harm other people?"[18] While he was deliberating whether to blow the whistle, it turned out that as a result of a patient's complaint the state police had placed an undercover agent in the institution, and his report led to the arrest of twenty-four attendants.

Almost two years later Taylor also led a group of reporters through the institution; but what if the state police had not acted when they did? Do the objectives of the research permit the sociologist simply to ignore people's suffering? Taylor does not think so. Lundberg's apparent assertions to the contrary probably need to be interpreted, at least in part, as expressions of his disapproval of the "pop sociologists" of his day; those pseudo-scholars who commit fraud by espousing values in the name of science. In this regard, Lundberg's formulation was quite like Weber's: both a directive and a rebuke to those in the profession who were regarded as deviant.

Weber's position

Weber noted one important difference between sociology and the natural sciences. In the latter, observation of overt behavior (of molecules or atoms) can be sufficient to develop theoretical explanations. However, the sociologist must also examine the meanings that people attribute to their behavior. In this respect the study of people is different from the study of molecules or cells, and social meanings often entail values. Further, Weber asserted that the values people share often have profound effects upon social organization, the sociologists' subject matter. (See Chapter Eleven.) Nevertheless, Weber was convinced that sociologists could be objective in their analyses of values, and that it was their obligation to be objective. Many of Weber's views in this matter were directed at the social scientists of his day in their dual capacities as researchers and disseminators of knowledge in the classroom. It is helpful, therefore, briefly to examine the conditions that were prevalent in German universities during Weber's career (roughly 1890–1920).

In the German universities, some senior faculty members (including Weber) had "chairs" which offered them stable salaries. Others worked as short-term lecturers and were paid according to student enrollments in their courses. Therefore, it literally paid an instructor to have as strong a student appeal as possible. In Weber's view,

---

[18]Steven J. Taylor, "Observing Abuse," *Qualitative Sociology*, 10, 1987, p. 293.

many of them became popular by pandering to the provincial nationalistic fervor that characterized German youth prior to World War I. Weber, himself, was regarded as an inspiring and dynamic teacher whose courses were always in great demand, and on occasion he too would discuss public affairs from a value perspective. However, he carefully labelled his values as such and objected strongly to the tendency, of less secure professors in particular, to deal extensively in moral issues in order to attract a student following.

While Weber's illness-shrouded career was primarily academic, he was also extensively involved in public affairs. He participated in a number of diverse investigations involving, for example, the living conditions of farm workers and the regulation of the German stock exchange. Perhaps most notable was his service on the commission that drafted the Weimar Constitution. While he was performing these public service activities, directed at specific objectives, Weber continued to strive to keep them separate from his scholarly role at the university. Thus, for Weber, value neutrality was a way of life.[19]

In a university speech, Weber articulated his position by stating that science is "free from presuppositions," and he proceeded with examples to clarify what this meant. It means, he said, that physics can show how to control matter, but not whether it makes sense to control it; that medical science can prolong life, but cannot decide whether it is worthwhile to live and so on. In all of these instances, only nonscientific values can offer an answer to the question of what is worthwhile. Thus, values enter the picture where science leaves off. However, values as such are not part of the scientist's proper role, and they have no place in the classroom (disguised as science).[20]

At this point in his lecture, Weber spoke out against some students who had recently surrounded the desk of a professor and disrupted the class because they disapproved of his pacifist position. After condemning their behavior, he condemned his colleague as well for inappropriately bringing politics into the classroom. For a scientist to introduce value judgements, he said, was "irresponsible" and "outrageous." Then he reminded his audience of the vast difference between taking a political stand and an impartial analysis of political parties. Only the latter belongs in the lecture hall.

THE VALUE-FREE MYTH?

Until perhaps the 1960s, Weber's value-free position was widely shared in sociology. Few people doubted the possibility or the desirability of detached neutrality. In the turbulence of the 1960s, however, many sociologists (and their professional association) found it impossible to remain neutral and questioned whether that really ought to be their position. Further doubt arose as long-standing theories were

[19]For further discussion of the man, his times, and his writings, see Reinhard Bendix, *Max Weber: An Intellectual Portrait* (New York: Doubleday, 1962).

[20]Hans H. Gerth and C. Wright Mills, *From Max Weber: Essays in Sociology* (New York: Oxford, 1958).

analyzed and shown to have had political and economic implications all along. It appeared, to some critics, that sociologists had been value-free more in name than in practice.

The attack on the assumed value-free nature of sociology began with critiques of functionalism, the dominant theory group in sociology at the turn of the 1960s. Associated with the perspectives of Durkheim, Parsons, and others, all the functional theories shared an interest in how social institutions, social roles, or patterns of interaction contribute to the perpetuation of a stable social organization. Social changes which could potentially disrupt stability were correspondingly viewed by the functionalists as threats to a society. As a result, most functional theories tended to have a conservative bias. They provided support for the "establishment," critics claimed, while pretending to be neutral.

As a representative illustration, consider the functional analysis of the coronation in Britain by Shils and Young. "There is a recurrent need in men," they begin, "to reaffirm the rightness of the moral rules by which they live . . . ."[21] However, consensus is also viewed as problematic, and the people's recognition of the Queen is seen as reinforcing that consensus. The Queen's oath, the Archbishop's presentation of the Holy Bible, and other aspects of the coronation are all seen by Shils and Young as reaffirmations of collective values. Each step relegates the Queen's private morality to a place beneath that of public standards. The coronation, they conclude, provides the entire society with an "intensive contact" with collective morality. Thus, it is "a great act of national communion."

All the specific inferences and assumptions made by Shils and Young are open to further questioning; but they do not provide the critical issue here. What should be noted is that this approach is supportive of the coronation. It might easily be interpreted as a plea for the continuation of the coronation. However, consider how different a sociological analysis might be if it started out by rejecting the assumption of moral consensus in Britain! Such an analysis would recognize that many persons in that country were opposed to the Royal Family and all its attendant trappings, such as the coronation. After all, the millions of pounds allocated annually for the support of this institution might be better spent, and the royalty can be viewed as vestiges of a stratification system in which the privileges of ascribed ranks were extensive. From initial assumptions such as these, the coronation might be viewed as serving the interests of some segments of British society as the expense of others. The functional analysis of Shils and Young, from this nonconsensus perspective, has a conservative stance. It is procoronation, and we can therefore deduce that it is supportive of those segments of the society that are served by the continuation of the institution.[22]

A second reason for the typically conservative bias of functionalism has been the tendency of its proponents to share the classically conservative fear of change.

---

[21]Edward Shils and Michael Young, "The Meaning of the Coronation," *Sociological Review*, 1 (1953), p. 67.

[22]For further discussion of the political aspects involved in the definition of functions, see Howard Becker, *Outsiders* (New York: Free Press, 1963).

Assuming society to be functionally integrated leads to an emphasis upon the continuing repercussions of even seemingly minor changes. Thus, for example, Parsons saw tracing the repercussions of change as the crucial question in his theory of social change, and he intimately tied the existence of manifold reverberations to the very conception of society as a social system.

Gouldner's analysis of Malinowski's theoretical contribution to British colonial policies is an example of how uneasiness toward change has made functional theories more susceptible to a conservative bias. Malinowski's romantic view of native practices, combined with a warning that any change would have unpredictable consequences, was highly compatible with the colonial goal of maintaining European dominance. It meant that native societies would be protected much like endangered species, and this clearly meant no political autonomy and no "modernization." While some functionalists, Gouldner concludes, "conceived it as their societal task to educate colonial administrators, none thought it their duty to tutor native revolutionaries."[23]

Sociology emerged, Gouldner notes, near the turn of the eighteenth century when traditional beliefs were knocked asunder. They were not replaced by a new and meaningful social order, and this led to widespread alienation. People were left feeling unattached to the existing social order and either perceived no alternatives or were afraid of whatever alternatives they could see. Thus, they tolerated the status quo, not because they loved it, but because they were afraid of conflict in the event of change. Objectivity, Gouldner concludes, is the "ideology" of the alienated, the safest course for people who are not involved or committed, who wish to hide from the ideological implications of their theories.

In sum, the critiques of Gouldner and others question the possibility of value-neutral theory. Weber, Lundberg, and others simply did not view theory in sufficiently broad perspective to recognize its virtually unavoidable implications for some segment of a society. If neutrality is not possible, then its desirability becomes a problematic issue. On the one hand, sociologists could continue to strive for neutrality as an objective in a more self-conscious way than they have in the past. On the other hand, if neutrality is not ultimately attainable, why not take sides explicitly? Then, at least, ideological implications can be considered and debated rather than exert an insidious influence.

CONCLUSION

All of the issues considered in this chapter concern the processes by which sociology can become the science envisioned by its positivistic founders. Then and now, the natural sciences represent *the* models of scientific disciplines. Therefore, to be-

---

[23] Alvin W. Gouldner, *The Coming Crises of Western Sociology* (New York: Basic Books, 1970), p. 132. Gouldner's argument is not that sociology should be on either side. Rather, sociologists must be aware of these political influences in order to "protect" sociology. Alvin W. Gouldner, *For Sociology: Renewal and Critique in Sociology Today* (New York: Basic Books, 1973).

come a scientific discipline, it has generally been assumed that sociology would have to emulate the natural sciences. If their model were to be copied in exact detail, theory in sociology would be formal theory and its basic concepts would include operational measures. As we have noted, the question which divides sociologists—even those who share scientific aspirations—is whether a literal emulation is either possible or necessary. Do the special features of the subject matter of sociology make a difference in this regard?

The issue raised in the preceding chapter, namely, the reducibility of sociological theory and explanation, is also interconnected with these questions about scientific form. This connection arises because the best examples of formal theory with operational terms involve analyses which are generally considered to be reductionistic. This quality was previously illustrated in the earlier discussion of the exchange perspective (Homans and others, in Chapter Eight). In focusing upon individuals' behavioral exchanges, it will be recalled, it was possible to present a number of formal propositions with operational terms.

It has also been possible to extend this perspective and apply it in a similarly formal manner to more abstract sociological issues if operational definitions continue to focus upon individual behavior. For example, culture has been conceptually defined by the presence of homogeneous values which have been operationally measured by similarities in people's responses to reinforcers. Thus, a common culture is indicated when people similarly respond to such potential reinforcers as food, money, sex, status, and the like.[24] However, the "reduction" of higher level abstractions (such as culture) to individual actions raises the conceptual problems discussed in the preceding chapter.

It is possible to do scientific sociological analyses, and construct formal theories, without reducing the unit of analysis. Many such nonreductionistic studies have, in fact, been conducted; but their incidence has historically been higher among studies that have employed individual-level measurement. As a result, discussions of scientific sociology often implicitly raise the spectre of reductionism. This is an unfortunate association, however, because it confounds issues that are best considered separately.

SUGGESTIONS FOR ADDITIONAL READING

JERALD HAGE and BARBARA F. MEEKER, Social Causality, Winchester, MA: Unwin Hyman, Inc., 1988.
PETER LASSMAN (Ed), Politics and Social Theory, New York: Routledge, 1988.
GEORGE RITZER, Toward an Integrated Sociological Paradigm, Boston: Allyn & Bacon, 1981.

[24]Robert L. Hamblin, R. Brooke Jacobsen, and Jerry L. L. Miller, A Mathematical Theory of Social Change (New York: John Wiley, 1973).

Index